MAP Paglesham, Essex   ~~Inside~~
ACKNOWLEDGEMENTS   (ii)
FAMILY TREES   *HARRIS*   (v)
              BROWNING/PETTITT   (v)
              WISEMAN   (vi)
ZILLAH'S FAMILY, 1947   (vi)

1   ZILLAH'S VILLAGE   1
     Paglesham – Zillah's Family – Records

2   INTRODUCTION   3
     Village Changes – Zachary Pettitt – James F T Wiseman – Fred Wiseman
     Senior – Shuttlewood's Boatyard – Government

3   HARRIS FAMILY IN PAGLESHAM   6
     Rector – Wedding Visit – Delays – Bernard Harris – Testimonials – Wedding –
     Hornsey – Children

4   FRED WISEMAN's DEATH   11
     Jubilee Year – Fred Wiseman – The Will – Arthur Wiseman

5   PET's NEW FAMILY   14
     Headline News – Zillah Harris's Childhood – Country Holidays

6   EDWARDIAN PAGLESHAM   19
     Population Changes – Coronation – Pettitt Wedding – JFTW's Death –
     Ethel Ada – Oyster Depression –Rectors – Sybil Brand - Shops – Schooldays

7   RETURN TO PAGLESHAM   27
     A New decade – Return to Paglesham – Sea Change

8   THE GREAT WAR : 1914 - 1915   30
     The Country Calls – Waiting for Action – Overseas Postings – Home Routine –
     Casualties

9   GALLIPOLI   36
     To War – First Blood – There and Back Again

10   PAGLESHAM – 1915   40
     Zeppelin LZ38 – Territorials – Reg Cook – Bernard's Return – Walking –
     Dissention – Christmas 1915

11   GREAT WAR : 1916 – 1919   49
     Evacuation – Breaks in Routine – Zachary Pettitt's Death – Christening – Family
     Tragedy – Athelstan Rifleman – Athelstan Radio Operator

12   BETWEEN THE WARS   58
     *Removal – Mrs Pettitt and Hector – Change of Rector – Postwar Blues – Fred
     and Arthur Retire – Farming – Lunts Farm – Dogs, Cats and Nature – Athelstan
     in Australia – Village Changes – Out and About – Drought – Romance, Alan
     Boardman – Year of Royal Changes – Cupola House – Impending War*

13   WORLD WAR 2   75
     *Evacuation – Winter 1940 – All Change – Close to Home – Zillah's War Work –
     Home Guard – Restrictions – Rations – War-time Memories – Air Raid Shelters –
     Raids and Bomb Damage – Uncle Fred – Better News – Most Bombed Village –
     School – Rochford Hospital – Doodlebugs and Rockets – Womens' Institute &
     Kalorama – Church Hall and East Hall - Peace*

14   POST-WAR   99
     *Paglesham Village Produce Association – Change at East End – Church
     Changes – Flooding – Boats – Queen's Coronation – Time Away –
     Mechanisation and Farming Change – Women's Institute – A Generation
     Passes – A New Start - Plough and Sail and Punch Bowl - Athelstan –
     Organists – Church End – East End – History – Threats Defeated – Oysters –
     Elm Trees – School Centenary – Waterside Farm – Neighbours – Fundraising –
     Zillah Harris*

15   POSTSCRIPT   129
     *The Chase – Redcroft - Cupola House – Fairs and Exhibitions – Farming –
     HMS Beagle – Organisations – St Peter's Church*

APPENDIX 1 - BERNARD HARRIS'S FAMILY   134
     Devon – Broad Gauge – London Life – Attraction – Somerset Wedding

APPENDIX 2 - BERNARD'S VOYAGES   137
     Off to Sea – Postcards – Titanic – Further Voyages

BIBLIOGRAPHY   142
NAMES INDEX   143
GENERAL INDEX   145
MAP Paglesham Village   148

World's End Cottage, St Peter's Church
and Church Hall, Paglesham, c1905.

Zillah's Village

A Family's Record
of War and Peace in
Rural Essex

Zillah Harris 1896 – 1979

Mark and Rosemary Roberts

TO
All keepers of diaries and letters,
especially the Wiseman family and their descendants.

***

ACKNOWLEDGEMENTS

Our thanks are due to all those who have helped us with our research over fifty years, particularly the many villagers who talked freely to Rosemary. We are as always particularly grateful to Margaret Pinkerton, who currently holds the Wiseman archive and the joint Wiseman/Harris postcard collection, for allowing us free access to a superb resource. We would like also to thank more recent contributors, David and Susan Wiseman, Tony Pettitt and Paulette Nicholls, whose forebears appear in *Zillah's Village*. Others who have assisted in different ways are Allison Bond, Peter Thorogood, Barbara King and the Hornsey Historical Society.

***

By the same authors:

Rosemary Roberts,

Paglesham	1972
The Children of Paglesham	1990
A Century of Paglesham Life (With Angela Puzey)	1993

Mark Roberts

Mini Roundabouts in England and Wales	1972
Ed. *Rochford Historian*	1992 - 1999
Ed. *Smugglers' Moon* by LE Jerram Burrows	1993
Ed. *Rochford Great War Memories*	1995
Ed. *'What was it like in the Olden Days, Grandma?'*	1998

Mark and Rosemary Roberts

Under the Flight Path	1995
Paglesham Natives	2006

***

ISBN 978 0 9516370 4 3

***

Published by M A & R Roberts
Springvale, Beach Road, St Osyth, Essex CO16 8SB

Originated by Entrac, Harwich
Printed by Formara Limited, Southend-on-Sea

***

The Authors would be pleased to hear from anyone
with further information on Paglesham's past.

Family Trees

HARRIS

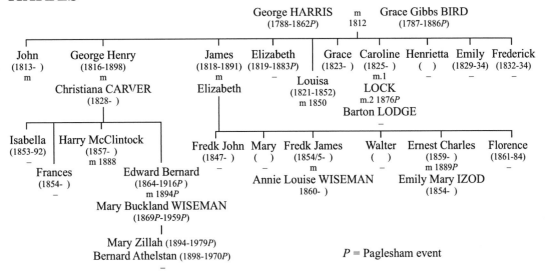

George HARRIS   m   Grace Gibbs BIRD
(1788-1862*P*)   1812   (1787-1886*P*)

| John (1813-) m | George Henry (1816-1898) m Christiana CARVER (1828-) | James (1818-1891) m Elizabeth | Elizabeth (1819-1883*P*) | Grace (1823-) | Caroline (1825-) m.1 LOCK m.2 1876*P* Barton LODGE | Henrietta ( ) | Emily (1829-34) | Frederick (1832-34) |

Louisa (1821-1852) m 1850

Isabella (1853-92) | Harry McClintock (1857-) m 1888

Frances (1854-)

Edward Bernard (1864-1916*P*) m 1894*P* Mary Buckland WISEMAN (1869*P*-1959*P*)

Mary Zillah (1894-1979*P*)
Bernard Athelstan (1898-1970*P*)

Fredk John (1847-) | Mary ( ) | Fredk James (1854/5-) m Annie Louise WISEMAN 1860-) | Walter ( ) | Ernest Charles (1859-) m 1889*P* Emily Mary IZOD (1854-) | Florence (1861-84)

P = Paglesham event

PETTITT/HUTLEY

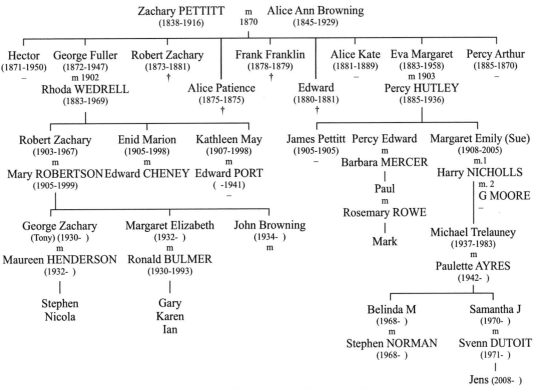

Zachary PETTITT   m   Alice Ann Browning
(1838-1916)   1870   (1845-1929)

| Hector (1871-1950) | George Fuller (1872-1947) m 1902 Rhoda WEDRELL (1883-1969) | Robert Zachary (1873-1881) † | Frank Franklin (1878-1879) † | Alice Kate (1881-1889) | Eva Margaret (1883-1958) m 1903 Percy HUTLEY (1885-1936) | Percy Arthur (1885-1870) |

Alice Patience (1875-1875) †

Edward (1880-1881) †

| Robert Zachary (1903-1967) m Mary ROBERTSON (1905-1999) | Enid Marion (1905-1998) m Edward CHENEY | Kathleen May (1907-1998) m Edward PORT (-1941) |

James Pettitt (1905-1905)

Percy Edward m Barbara MERCER
Paul
m Rosemary ROWE
Mark

Margaret Emily (Sue) (1908-2005) m.1 Harry NICHOLLS m. 2 G MOORE

| George Zachary (Tony) (1930-) m Maureen HENDERSON (1932-) | Margaret Elizabeth (1932-) m Ronald BULMER (1930-1993) | John Browning (1934-) m |

Stephen
Nicola

Gary
Karen
Ian

Michael Trelauney (1937-1983) m Paulette AYRES (1942-)

Belinda M (1968-) m Stephen NORMAN (1968-)

Samantha J (1970-) m Svenn DUTOIT (1971-)

Jens (2008-)

† = *Commemorated in West window of Paglesham Church*

Fred and Rose WISEMAN

Frederick John   m   Rosaline PIZZEY
(1829-1897)   1859   (1840-1910)

| Fredk William (1860-1941) – | Edgar (1863-70) | Edith (1865-71) | | Mary Buckland (Pet) (1869-1959) m 1894 Edward Bernard HARRIS (1864-1916) | Frank Buckland (1874-1936) m 1910 Edith Hope DANNATT (1884-1981) | Percy Edgar (1877-1940) m 1911 Mamie BROOKS – |

Arthur (1862-1937) m 1862 Alice (Tottie) LEECH

Alice Maud (Minnie) (1867-1955) –

Mary Zillah (1896-1979) Athelstan (1898-1968) –

Joan (1911-1977) m 1 John WESTON m 2 George KNOWLES

Vivienne (1916-1982)

Eric (1895-1957) m 1 Irene SHERWIN m 2 Ethel THORY

Marjorie (1898-1962) –

Ralph (1905-) m 1934 Dorothy REED

David m 1 Jenny MANUEL m 2 Susan ROSSITER

Peter m Doreen FITZGERALD

Jillian

Judith Margaret m David PINKERTON

Theresa Jane m 1 Richard PERKHART m 2 Nick KOPP m 3 William HARRISON m 4 John BROADHEAD

Hannah
Lyndsey
Stephanie

Sally Ann m David deHAAS
|
Rebecca
Laura

Richard m Melonie DODIMEAD –

Nicola m Will KENDRICK
|
Anya Jessie

Melanie . Charlie CLOWES
|
Mia Rose
Poppy May

Alan John M m Susan Maria ENGLISH
|
Katie Maria
Matthew John S

Joanna Catherine –

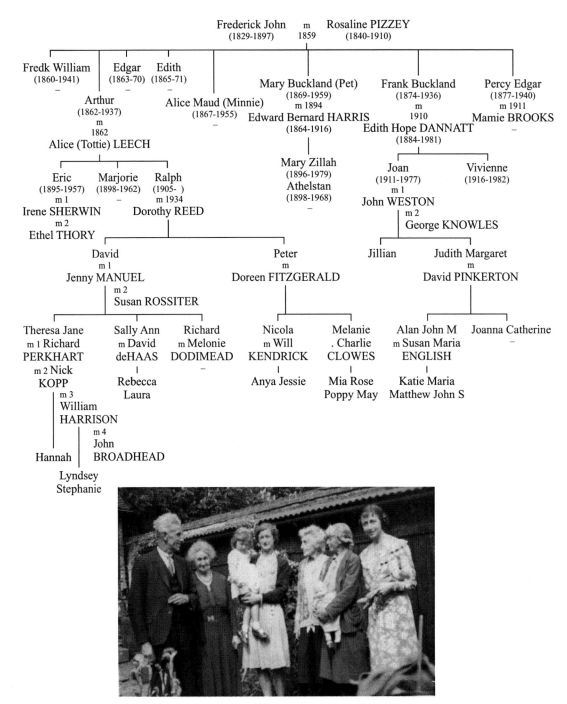

Family group in Chaseway garden, 1947.
(Left to right) Athelstan, Pet, Margaret and mother, Joan Weston (daughter of Frank Wiseman),
Minnie, Hope Wiseman (widow of Frank), Zillah.

1 ZILLAH'S VILLAGE

This is the story of Zillah Harris and the village where she lived most of her life. Her mother, a Wiseman, came from Paglesham, and her great-uncle Harris was Rector there for thirty years. It follows the family's lives and the main characters and events in the village from her parents' first meeting until her death in 1979, with a postscript covering the last thirty years.

The two World Wars dominate her life and her diaries give fascinating descriptions of activities in Paglesham during those periods as well as showing the changes, particularly in the way of life, before, between and after them.

Rosemary was born and brought up in the village – her arrival noted in Zillah's diary – and, with Mark and their children, lived there again for 28 years. There is therefore a personal element to the authors' descriptions in later years.

Zillah's village, Paglesham, has survived the twentieth century remarkably unscathed to all outward appearances, but social changes, mechanisation of farming, natural events and modern mobility have changed the lives of its people. It is unique in the Rochford area today by having had no major development. It is possible to visualise Zillah's village as it was when she was born. There are no new roads; no estates added; its church, chapel and Mission Room are still the centres of worship and village events and there is still a feeling of remoteness despite its proximity to large urban populations. Rochford is still its local shopping centre, although the old market town and its bigger neighbour, Southend-on-Sea, have grown almost unrecognisably even in the last thirty years since Zillah's death.

Paglesham is a cul-de-sac, or rather two as the road from Ballards Gore splits left to Church End or right to East End. Zillah and her mother were regular churchgoers, walking over a mile to the ancient church for services most of their lives, but the family members all lived at East End, which had developed for the oyster industry.

When Zillah's parents met in 1889, Paglesham was famous for its oysters and there were three big Paglesham oyster merchants operating in the river: Zillah's grandfather Fred Wiseman senior, his cousin James F T Wiseman and Zachary Pettitt. Church End was dominated by farming, East End by oysters. The six farmers employed 61 labourers; the oyster merchants employed 54 oyster dredgers. These would all have lived and worked in the village, giving a sense of activity in the fields and at the waterside With a total population of 490 and 80 or so children at the village school, the two Ends would have been busy all the time.

Today, the majority of residents are retired or commute to their work, the fields are usually deserted, the river is used by non-residents for leisure and few people can be seen walking or cycling round the houses. This is not to say that the village has died – far from it; there are more organisations and as many events as before, while the two pubs busily cater for the needs of locals and many visitors.

ZILLAH'S FAMILY

There were Wisemans in Paglesham at the beginning of the 1600s. Zillah's great-great-grandfather James was born there in 1754 and built up a large oyster business. Two generations later it was his grandsons, James (JFTW) and Fred, already mentioned.[1]

Although Zillah Harris was born in Hornsey, north London, she lived in Paglesham from 1911, when she was 15 years old, for the rest of her life. She had often visited her Wiseman relatives there as a child and was the last descendant of the Wiseman family to live in the village. Zillah came to Paglesham with her mother, Pet, and brother Athelstan when her father went to sea.

Pet had been born Mary Buckland Wiseman in Paglesham, and others of her generation were still living in the village when she returned. Her eldest two brothers, Fred and Arthur, were earning their livings from oysters, the source of all their family's previous prosperity. Her sister, Minnie, lived with her brother, Fred, both unmarried, in the family home after their mother's death in 1910.

The Harris family originated in Devon, but her father and grandfather Harris were living in Hornsey when she was born.[2] However her great-uncle was Rev James Harris, Rector of Paglesham, who was the reason her parents came to meet.

RECORDS

The Wiseman family was remarkable for keeping its records – ledgers, diaries, letters and photographs. The earlier Wiseman family seemed unaffected and impervious to national and international events, despite keeping records through the Napoleonic and Crimean wars, having family in Australia and with HMS Beagle, the ship made famous by Darwin, in Paglesham's river for 25 years. The Harrises, in contrast, could not be unaffected by the two world wars; indeed they were closely involved in each, recording certain events for our future interest.

This book is effectively a sequel to '*Paglesham Natives*' which followed the life of the village and the Wiseman and Browning/Pettitt families up to about 1900 through those records.

The Harrises continued to extend the archive with letters, postcards and diaries. We now take the story from Zillah's parents through much of the twentieth century using the Harris records. It starts in a very different world from that of the present day, gradually evolving through the decline in the oyster industry, social change in the Great War, the effects on jobs of mechanisation after the Second World War, and increased levels of education and mobility.

Rosemary adds her own memories and records to the story, both during Zillah Harris's lifetime and after her death. She knew the Harris family well, while Zillah made numerous entries in her diaries about Rosemary and her parents. '*Miss Harris*,' as she was always known, helped the authors with historical talks and exhibitions in the 1960s and with Rosemary's first book on Paglesham in 1972, but it was not until she died in 1979 that the remarkable extent of her family records became apparent. This book is a tribute to Zillah and her family.

---

[1] The Wiseman family is included in Paglesham Natives'. [2] See Appendix 1 to this book.

2 INTRODUCTION

VILLAGE CHANGES

The last dozen years of Queen Victoria's reign saw many changes in Paglesham, particularly for the oyster merchants' families. At the beginning, little had changed for many years – farming was still in recession, the oyster trade was still ticking over, if not at its peak, the same families lived in the village.

The population at the time of the 1891 census was 490, with 207 at Church End and 270 at East End. The other 13 lived at Grapnells on Wallasea Island, then part of the parish.

Over a third of the population were children under 14, with 117 aged five and over. The school leaving age was thirteen, although children were only in full-time education until the age of ten. The school had to be extended in 1894 to take rising numbers although numbers had fallen to 97 by 1899. The school leaving age was raised to 14 in 1902.

In 1899 the three oyster merchants were still the major influences in Paglesham, but things were changing.

ZACHARY PETTITT

Zachary Pettitt successfully combined being an oyster merchant with farming. Coming from Aldham in north Essex, he had married Alice Ann, the daughter of George Fuller Browning, in 1870. The Brownings had been in the Paglesham oyster business for generations, and at one time were known to the Customs men as smugglers. Indeed Cupola House, which they built in 1803 on Lunts Farm, was reputed to have been paid for with smuggling money. The cupola had views all round and would have been ideal for keeping an eye on the Revenue men and signalling the *'all clear'* to the smugglers. Zachary Pettitt took over his father-in-law's oyster business and became very successful. He and Alice Ann lived at Cupola House until, as the family grew, they built a larger house and farm, Loftman's, Canewdon, in 1880. This was just across the parish boundary from West Hall in Paglesham, which he also farmed and where his brother Robert lived in 1894.

Cupola House, 1973

Zachary Pettitt had been a major player in the restoration of the church in 1883, as a churchwarden, a major contributor to the costs and donor of two stained glass windows. The east window is in memory of his father-in-law, George Fuller Browning who died on 7 June 1878. The west window is in memory of four of his children who sadly had died, all under the age of nine. Later, a fifth child, out of his nine, also died young.

West Hall, oldest part at rear.

3

Mission Room, 1993

In 1893 Zachary gave the Mission Room to the village. This still stands in the corner of a field close to the houses in East End. The corrugated iron building was of the sort that could be ordered from a catalogue, 36 feet long by 20 feet wide, with a porch facing the road. It was given for the use of the village, particularly for holding services in the winter to save the long walk across the roads and fields to the church. It was also used in its early days as a reading room and for entertainments,[3] and helped to foster the social changes of the twentieth century. It is still used for its original purposes.

JAMES F T WISEMAN

James F T Wiseman (JFTW) had also prospered as an oyster merchant who farmed extensively. He had developed the modest Marine Cottage into the imposing gentleman's

The Chase, from Sale Catalogue, 1903

residence, The Chase. He owned all the fields around East End and had farmed in the next parish, Stambridge.

JFTW's wife, Annie, died in 1889, and with his eyesight failing as a result of diabetes, he finally decided that he should leave Paglesham, which he had loved. In July 1891 there was a sale of his books and paintings at the Corn Exchange, Chelmsford. His collection was impressive with, according to the catalogue, paintings by Van Dyck, Lely and a Constable *Mistley Quay*, sets of prints by Hogarth and others, and 5000 books including several histories of Essex. A large cellar of upward of 170 dozen bottles of vintage wines, ports, sherries, clarets and burgundies was also sold.

JFTW's property in Paglesham was rented to Mr Arthur Nicholls, who lived at The Chase and continued the oyster business. He and his wife, Jane, had a daughter, Bessie, and a son who became a Colonel in the Great War.

FRED WISEMAN Senior

The departure of his cousin, JFTW, left Fred and his family as the only remaining Wisemans in Paglesham, at Buckland House. Frederick John Wiseman married Rosaline Pizzey in 1859 and between 1860 and 1877 they had eight children. Frederick William and Arthur

---

[3] *'A Century of Paglesham Life'* celebrated a hundred years of activities in the Mission Room.

eventually took over their father's business. Edgar and Edith tragically died of scarlet fever a year to the day after each other in 1870 and 1871. The next to be born were Alice Maud (Minnie) and Mary Buckland (Pet), Zillah's mother. After a five year gap came Frank Buckland and finally Percy Edgar in 1877.

Fred and Rosaline, more often known as Rose, had a stormy marriage. Fred was a male chauvinist, a fairly typical employer who felt that the working classes should be

Buckland House, 1995

kept in their places and that education was dangerous to the stability of the country. Rose, in the diaries which she kept between 1887 and 1889, indicates strongly how moody and critical he could be, both of her and the children. She clearly stood up to him and eventually took the courageous step of finding a house in the growing Southend, leaving him in October 1888. Her diary records *'Left my unhappy home. A most fearful day.'* Fred's says, *'Jezebel left'!*

When she left, the elder two boys, Fred aged 28 and Arthur 26, were already working for their father, while Minnie and Pet looked after the family home. The youngest boys, at 11 and 13, were at school in Southend, near their mother, calling on her frequently as did the girls. Early in 1889, Arthur became engaged to 'Tottie' - Alice Leech from Chelmsford - and in the autumn, Pet met Bernard Harris, her future husband, for the first time.

SHUTTLEWOOD'S BOATYARD

Two other events were of significance to Paglesham in the 1890s. One was a change at the boatyard in 1895, with the Shuttlewood brothers, James and Henry, taking over from William Hall. The Halls and Kemps before them had been building traditional smacks, barges and smaller boats since the eighteenth Century. The Shuttlewoods continued the tradition into the post-second world war period, although working boats became fewer as time went on.

The *'Waterside Premises'* were sold in 1903 (they had belonged to JFTW). Their description gives an idea of the scale of the operations. *'The Boatbuilder's Workshop, 82 feet long by 24 feet wide, with Launching Ways, Windlass and Mooring Chains, Paint Shop, Smithy with 2 Steam Kilns, Boiler and Tank, Store House, Saw Pit, Timber Yard, Small Grass Pightle* [field], *Wharf and Yard, The whole having a frontage of about 150 feet to the seawall of the River Roach.'* They therefore had the means of storing timber, converting it into planks, steaming timbers to shape, forging the metalwork required, building a vessel under cover and fitting out, painting and launching her.

GOVERNMENT

County Councils were first created in 1889, and Parish Councils in 1894. Instructions were sent out to the Rector for the formation of a Parish Council, requiring nominations etc. However the people of Paglesham felt that a Parish Council was unnecessary, so no nominations were made and Rev Lea returned the forms unused. Five years later there was no change of attitude, the Rev Lea reporting to the County in March 1899, *'I duly called the*

Parish Meeting by Public Notice – only one parishioner attended & no nominations were sent in, hence there could be no election – no one attended either of the Parish Councils during the past year for the simple reason that there was nothing to be done'.

This remarkable state of affairs continued until 1915 when a Parish Council was tried but soon abandoned. Another after the Second World War lasted until 1958, and it was only in 1964 that the present Parish Council was formed.

3 HARRIS FAMILY IN PAGLESHAM

RECTOR

Bernard Harris's uncle, Rev James Harris, had been Rector of St Peter's church, Paglesham, since 1860 and was 71 years old in 1889. His family came from Devon and he had been born

The Rectory

in Barnstaple. When Rev Harris was installed, there was no suitable Rectory as the parish had been looked after by a curate. He therefore built a huge, typically Victorian rectory with fashionable gothic windows near the junction of the roads to the two Ends.

Various members of the family appear briefly in the Paglesham records. His parents came to live with him, but his father, George, died in 1862, soon after they arrived. His mother, Grace Gibbs Harris, however, lived for a further 24 years until

her death in 1886 at the age of 99. They are buried in the graveyard. The Rector had a handsome monument placed on the north wall of the chancel in their memory, *'erected by their loving children and grandchildren'*. His sister Elizabeth had been the village schoolmistress; she appears as such in the 1881 census. Two of the Rector's grandchildren, Violet and Vera, were baptised at Paglesham in 1887 and 1889. They were the children of Frederick James Harris, the Rector's second son, and Annie Louise Ley Wiseman, one of JFTW's children.

Rev James Harris was Rector of Paglesham for almost 30 years from 1860 to 1890. Apart from building the Rectory, he had overseen the major restoration of the church in 1883 with his two churchwardens, Zachary Pettitt and JFTW. The church had been in an almost ruinous condition when he arrived, but it had taken him over twenty years to get it done. The roof was completely rebuilt, losing the pair of dormer windows it once had, and most of the window stonework was replaced. He took his last wedding in July 1889, his last baptism in September, and his last funeral on 29 March 1890 just before he retired. He died on 26 April 1891. His successor, Rev Thomas Lea, was inducted on 30 June 1890.

Another of Rev Harris's sons, Ernest Charles Harris, aged 35, married in Paglesham Church on 4 September 1889. The weather was hot and the day before, Pet Wiseman and her sister Minnie had just returned exhausted from rowing on the river and walking back up the dusty unmade lane from the waterside when their father told them to hurry up and come down to meet the Rector's son Fred and his cousin. The girls were dishevelled and dirty and Minnie refused. Pet had heard sounds and had looked out of the window and seen the two men. She wrote, *'Fred Harris was one and a stranger, very tall & thin & dark, wore spectacles. Such a strong determined face which should possess an equally strong will of his own.'* Despite concerns for her appearance Pet went down and was introduced to Fred and his cousin, Dr Bernard Harris. He and Pet Wiseman seem to have been immediately attracted to each other.

Harris-Izod Wedding Group at the Rectory, 1889.
Rector, seated; Bernard Harris behind, bearded.

Pet went to Ernest's wedding to Emily Izod, the daughter of a *'Surgeon,'* and it was Bernard who took the group photograph using the delay mechanism, which gave him time to appear in the back row.

Events moved fast at first. Bernard and Pet met again on the following day, and he also took another photograph of both Pet and Minnie. Bernard wrote on it, *'Pet in the dress in which I first saw her.'* For him it was *'love at first sight'*. A page of his diary has two quotations, *' 'To see her is to love her*

 And love but her for ever.'
     Burns. 'Bonny Kesley"
and
' 'who ever loved that loved not at first sight'
          Marlowe, quoted by Shakespeare in 'Hero & Leander'.'

Dr Edward Bernard Harris, c1890.

Two days later, only four days after first seeing her, Bernard proposed to Pet on Saturday 7 September. He wrote, *'Je t'aime, Si tu savais comme je t'aime'*. This was rather too sudden for Pet's mother, Rose, who wrote in her diary, *'I told him I could not give the final answer, but he was to wait three months'*. Pet was not quite 20 years old.

He tried again on 1 January 1890, and wrote in his diary, *'Molly, darling, accepted me'*. He always called her Molly as he disliked the family's nickname of Pet. Pet's father was asked separately and requested a week to consider the proposal. Bernard noted wryly in his diary, *'He had no objection to me personally, as a son-in-law, but wishes I had a practice of my own. (Equally with him, so do I.)'* Had Bernard asked Fred in September, or had he felt that her Mother was a safer person to start with? We do not know. Whatever Fred's answer was, Bernard and Pet had to wait almost five years before they were married on 4 November 1894. Pet was by then a week short of her 25th birthday; Bernard was 30.

BERNARD HARRIS

Bernard had trained at Guy's hospital. His testimonial, written and signed by *'F W Parry M.D., F.R.S 'Physician to Guy's Hospital'* on 17 March 1887 reads, *'I have much pleasure in stating that from the manner in which Mr E. B. Harris has availed himself of the opportunities afforded to him to have acquired a very satisfactory knowledge of his profession.'* Dr Harris certainly *'availed himself of opportunities'* later, suggesting a man with an open and enquiring mind.

Later in 1887 he joined the steamship *Denbighshire,* presumably as the ship's doctor. Two letters survive which tell us of his outward passage from London, passing Cape Finisterre on 26 October 1887, his sister Frances's birthday. One of the letters he wrote to her with a sketch of the Cape at the top of the page, and another scene below.

> *'My dearest old darling sister,*
>
> *The best way to write you a letter I conceive to be just to jot down what we have seen each day and what we have done (though that does not amount to much!) and I have added one or two sketches! (save the word) my first attempt at such amusement...'*

He continued in similar vein as the ship passed Gibraltar (*'What a cheek our holding a strip of land 3 miles long by ¾ mile broad at the end of the Spanish territory'),* Gozo and Malta before reaching Port Said on 5 November. He said they were due to spend six hours there before going through the Suez Canal on their way to Japan. The second letter was to his father duplicating that to Frances, including two of the sketches. He added that he expected to spend Christmas in Yokohama.

This experience at the age of 23, with his letter-writing and his illustrations, were to be highly significant another 23 years later.

TESTIMONIALS

In 1888 Bernard worked at the Finsbury Dispensary. Another testimonial, dated 8 January 1889, gives a greater insight into Bernard's character, *'We have much pleasure in bearing testimony to the many excellent qualities of Mr Bernard Harris. Whilst acting as Resident Medical Officer at the Finsbury Dispensary during a period of five months, he proved himself a very well-trained Medical Practitioner. He fulfilled his duties with tact, energy and interest, and showed a kind consideration for the poor patients.'* It was signed by two Physicians, the Surgeon and the Hon Secretary.

This was nine months before his first proposal for Pet's hand. The delay in getting married enabled him finally to achieve his father-in-law's wish that he had his own practice. Bernard appears in the Kelly's Directory for 1891 as *'Physician & Surgeon'* at No 1, Holy Innocents Road, Hornsey (now Rokesly Avenue), so the further delay must have been hard for them both.

Bernard and Pet's marriage took place at St Peter's, Paglesham, on Sunday, 4 November 1894 at 8.45am. It was a quiet one, as Pet's parents were separated. There had been a *Farewell At Home* with dancing a week before in the Court House in Rochford, hosted by Pet's mother, Rose, but she did not attend the wedding ceremony. A French friend from Pet's schooldays at Cassiobury Terrace, Southend, had suggested a honeymoon in Paris, and they stayed at the Grand Hotel St James in the Rue St Honore. While there they visited, presumably because of Bernard's curiosity, various places with a medical connection, most oddly the morgue, as well as the usual sights. Rose wrote advising them '*It is amusing about the beds but it is the same in Ostende. Of course you occupy the two but ours were large enough for two people to occupy at the same time.*' Rose was distressed at losing her daughter. Had she delayed the wedding?[4]

Mary Wiseman in dress for 'Farewell' dance, 1894.

Pet created a notebook diary including samples of the materials of her clothes and included sketches, drawn by Bernard, of the many wedding presents they received.

HORNSEY

They returned to live at No 1 Holy Innocents Road, on the corner of Tottenham Lane. Though hardly rural, the area was still fairly rustic then, with old cottages beside them in Tottenham Lane and open spaces nearby, but it was rapidly being developed. No 1 was a new double-fronted house with two storeys and an attic. Pet had to get used to a very different life and

always thought of Paglesham as home. Bernard had already become involved with Holy Innocents' Church, a few doors up the hill from No 1, and had been elected People's Church Warden in 1893 and was Vicar's Warden in 1896 and 1897, so the church was a link for Pet.

Bernard's family had moved to '*St Dunstan's, foot of Muswell Hill*', soon after Bernard had established his practice. This was actually a substantial house near Alexandra Palace, and less than a mile from Holy Innocents Road, so Pet was able to get to know Bernard's family. His parents were George Henry[5] and Christiana Harris, and his older sister Frances lived with them.

CHILDREN

Life changed further for Pet in 1896 with the arrival three weeks early of Mary Zillah on St Valentine's Day, 14 February. Bernard recorded the details in Pet's notebook and became a devoted father. Zillah (the family seemed to have used the second names, as had Bernard) was christened on 18 April at Holy Innocents' Church. Pet's brother Fred

Zillah Harris as infant, c1899.

---

[4] A longer account is given in *'Paglesham Natives'*.
[5] Details of George Henry Harris's family are given in Appendix 1.

Wiseman, one of the two running the oyster business, was Godfather and the Godmothers were her sister, Minnie Wiseman, and Frances Harris, Bernard's sister. Pet soon took Zillah back to Paglesham, no doubt to show her off to all the people who knew her.

In Hornsey, Zillah had her first birthday at the beginning of 1897. Pet listed her presents in her book, starting with, '*From Mummy and Daddy – £1.1 to put in the bank, the Art Bible to be her family Bible.*' Granny Wiseman gave her '*a cream silk dress*', Granny Harris '*a china cup and saucer and 2/6*' while Grandpa George Harris put a guinea in the bank for her. One Godmother, '*Aunt Frances – a coral necklace (a Hundred years old), and a musical box*'; the other, '*Aunt Minnie – a pair of blue silk shoes, socks and silver bangle for her now.*'

Bernard's family were quite close and Pet came to know them well. They would have met and been visited by them quite often, judging by the close knit family relationships which developed. However, Bernard's father, George Henry Harris, died in April 1898, which was a sad blow so soon after the new family had begun nearby.

When Bernard Athelstan Harris arrived on 21 September that year, Pet had a difficult time and she wrote the last entry in her diary,

> '*Despite all that has been done to alleviate the pains of labour, child bearing is for a woman what going in to action is for a soldier. Many a soldier escapes scatheless from the hottest fight. Every woman who goes down to the gates of death in order to bring back the gift of a new life, suffers the pains of the wounded and faces the chances of death*'.

There were no more children.

Athelstan, as he was known, was a well-loved child, probably always his father's favourite (it was Bernard's correspondence to him at school, later, which survives) rather than his mother's. Pet told an Australian cousin, Madge Doak of her new baby. Madge at some point replied, '*he does not come up to Zillah in your heart, but then she is a girl and the first born.*' Athelstan's painful birth may also have been part of the reason.

The family went to Holy Innocents' church, and Pet also liked to go to St Peter's when they returned to Paglesham. She was friendly with the Paglesham Rector, Rev Lea, and made a gift to the church after the birth of Athelstan.

4 FRED WISEMAN'S DEATH

JUBILEE YEAR

1897 was a memorable year in more ways than one. The Queen's Diamond Jubilee was celebrated in Paglesham in typical patriotic style – a service in church, a Procession, Dinner in the Church Hall barn for 250 adults and 200 children, Sports and a Concert.

> *'A band will play during the day. Much interest is taken in the holiday, which is fixed for Friday 24ᵗʰ June,'* it was announced.

Although Fred wrote in his diary, *'Very Hot. Thunder and Storm,'* Paglesham missed the severity of it that affected much of Essex, with large hailstones devastating large areas of crops.

They were not so lucky on *'Black Monday'* when the coast suffered a tidal invasion along much of its length. Fred wrote,

> Monday 25ᵗʰ November. *'Went to the waterside, an <u>appalling</u> high tide, over flooded greater part of the land about here & the Islands. A break at Purleigh Shawl.'*

A strong wind the previous day had caused widespread damage, but the coast had had the worst time. The wind had gone round to the north-west, the tide had rushed in and sea walls broke in many places. Wallasea Island was flooded and a third of Foulness. Southend, Leigh, Canvey Island and Burnham-on-Crouch were also flooded.

Heavy rain and floods were devastating for oystermen as they could disturb the oyster beds and then smother the oysters with mud. Farmers were already in the third decade of a depression and these events posed yet more problems for them. Zachary Pettitt was able to keep men employed from his oyster revenues, for which his men were very grateful.

FRED WISEMAN

Of direct consequence to the Wiseman family was Fred's death on the 31 December 1897, aged 68. He was widely regarded in the area as a *'staunch Conservative ... and a prominent Freemason.'* He was known elsewhere, having managed the Herne Bay Oyster Fisheries and surveyed oyster layings as far away as the Isle of Wight, Cornwall and Scotland, and he had contacts in London.

Many friends and family attended the funeral on 5 January 1898 and the coffin was borne by his dredger-men. He was buried near the other members of the family on the north side of Paglesham church.

One report of his death said,

> *Under cover of his big burliness, his rugged exterior, but withal fine and handsome appearance, there lay a woman's heart, soft and tender, open at all times to the need of those*

Frederick John Wiseman, 1829 - 1897.

situated less fortunate than himself. Outwardly stern, inwardly gentle, loving, and beloved by his children, his grandchildren, and his friends, the memory of Fred Wiseman will be kept green for many a year.'

It is difficult to reconcile this eulogy with the views of Rose, who knew a different side of him.

A little while after his death, a newspaper revealed an interesting find. *'In his home there is a room that he used as a smoking room, and which he allowed nobody to enter. This apartment has just been cleared out and, in a box stowed away in a cupboard, bank notes to the value of £3000 were discovered.'*

THE WILL

Zachary Pettitt and his own son, Arthur, were the executors of Fred's will. In it he left Rose, who had been at his deathbed, an annuity of £52 payable quarterly; *'The reason I make no further provision for her is that she is provided for under her father's Will.'*

The will also reflected his obsession with ensuring that the oyster business did not get fragmented, as his father's will had done. That will entailed the ownership of half the oyster layings to each of his two sons, and to their heirs. When Fred's brother Charles, who shared the layings, died in Australia in 1873, his layings were inherited by his several children, and they had to have separate, costly, transactions to sell them back to Fred. To avoid this happening again, he bequeathed these to Fred junior and Arthur.

Fred senior's inherited layings, although they had been enfranchised *'by me for their benefit'*, were still destined to be split between all the children. Fred therefore had written into his Will that within three months of taking their interest in them, they should *'sell or enter into a binding interest to sell'* them to his sons Fred and Arthur. If they did not do so, Fred dictated that they would not get any inheritance at all!

The *'oyster layings... and the stock brood and spat on the same and all the boats tackle implements utensils and things used therewith'* had to be offered to them jointly at a valuation excluding goodwill, and with a ten per cent discount, and had to be accepted within a calendar month. They did accept.

This had severe implications for young Fred and Arthur. While they all appear to have been happy with this arrangement, Fred and Arthur were not left with the cash to buy them! As a consequence, Minnie and Percy appear to have provided them with the mortgage to enable them to comply with the provisions of the will.

Buckland House was offered to his sons, by seniority, and young Fred took his option and continued to live there, with his sister Minnie. All the remaining assets were to be split equally between the six surviving children.

ARTHUR WISEMAN

Arthur had married Alice Leech, known as Tottie, on 4 August 1892, having been engaged for three years. They were married at the Wesleyan Chapel in Chelmsford. Arthur's brother Fred had been best man while Minnie, Pet and Tottie's sister, Mary, were bridesmaids. *'Their dresses were of stone grey, trimmed with white silk, with white hats. The bride wore a dress of peach-coloured cloth, which her hat matched. ... The wedding presents were numerous'.* Arthur's father, Fred, merely put in his diary, *'Went to the Waterside. Arthur married at Chelmsford.'*

It is not clear where they lived in Paglesham while he continued to work the oyster layings with his bachelor brother Fred. Arthur was closely involved with church work all his life. He played the organ and was choirmaster, Sunday School teacher and lay reader, and was Rector's warden for many years during and after Rev Lea's time (1890 – 1905).

Although Fred and Arthur continued to work the layings, their inheritance of capital was limited. When Arthur built Redcroft for his growing family, that property was also mortgaged to his brother and sister. Eric had been born in 1895, Marjorie in 1897 and Ralph arrived in 1905.

Arthur had bought five acres of Decoy Field, just beyond the Pettitt land opposite Cupola House, in 1896. His father's death and the inheritance problems must have delayed his plans

Redcroft, 1995.

as Redcroft was not completed until 1899 and was fully mortgaged to Minnie and Percy. Despite this he managed to build a substantial gentleman's property with two large reception rooms, an office, kitchen, larder, pantry and scullery, four main bedrooms, one with a dressing room, a bathroom and separate WC and two servants' bedrooms with back stairs. Soft water was collected in a cistern but the cellar was regularly flooded. In the days of steam ploughing, the engine boilers were filled from Redcroft's cellar. With a well in the garden and pump by the back door, an outside WC and a coal room, the house was well appointed. There were, however, no substantial outbuildings, one of the few 'economies' which might have been expected in the circumstances. They did, however, install a tennis court on the south side, so that they could exchange invitations to tennis parties with the other 'big houses' in the village.

Arthur was also clearly interested in his garden and trees in particular, as he lined the semi-circular drive with a wide variety of trees, with other species elsewhere. In the crescent between the two gates he planted hazels and fruit trees. With over an acre of garden, there was plenty of space for vegetables, and there was an orchard and a paddock.

5   PET'S NEW FAMILY

Life in Hornsey was not without incident. A press-cutting of 1898 reads,

> *'DR BERNARD HARRIS, of Holy Innocents Road, Hornsey, was crossing the Tottenham-lane on Monday evening when he was knocked down and run over by a pony attached to a light-cart, the driver of which made off.   Sergeant Blake of the Hornsey police was called, and the injured man was taken into the Chemist shop of Mr Gay, where he was seen by Dr. Down, who found that Mr. Harris's eye was cut and his ribs injured. After receiving attention he was removed to his home.'*

No 1 Holy Innocents' Road, Hornset, 2009.

An *'E Harris, 29 Forte Street, Barnstable, North Devon'* was in her eightieth year when, on 29 December 1898, she wrote to Emma Laver, a Wiseman relation, about a trip to Wales and then to London, which adds to the picture.

> *'I meant to go to Hornsey, also to St Dunstan's Cottage, Muswell Hill where Frances and her mother live but the weather was too bad and I not well.   Pet is most comfortable in a house of her own and she has the sweetest tempered fine boy I ever saw and the little girl is very nice. Bernard can get to his mothers in 5 minutes on his bicycle and Frances rides and goes over to Hornsey, and Pet and the children can walk the distance.   I was sorry to hear of Bernard's accident, it must have been a severe one.   I hope he soon recovered.'*

Another undated cutting gives a further glimpse of their life.

> *'ROBBING A HORNSEY DOCTOR – Lewis H Jones, 43, of no fixed abode, was charged with stealing from 1 Holy Innocents-road, Hornsey, a surgical instrument of the value of 10s, the property of Dr E Bernard Harris.   On the 4th inst. prisoner called and asked for the doctor, and was invited inside.   When Dr Harris arrived he asked for a packet of lavender which he had left on the previous day.   He was put out, and after he had departed an instrument was missed from the consulting room ...'*

Jones pleaded guilty and was *'Sent to prison for two months, with hard labour, his peddler's certificate to be cancelled.'*

ZILLAH HARRIS'S CHILDHOOD

Zillah was brought up with both her parents' Christian and writing traditions. She wrote in September 1900, when only four years old,

> *'My dear God and Jesus,*
> *I hope you are quite well.   Please make everyone good, especially Mr Stephenson and*

Athelstan and Tatam and all wicked people. Did you hurt yourself on the cross, but now you are happy in heaven with God and please make me a good girl and Mummy and Daddy and everybody. I must end now with love and kisses from your loving little subject, Zillah – x x x x x X The Big Kiss for God.'

In November 1900, Bernard and Pet took a break in Clovelly, without the children. Bernard wrote a postcard on the 5th to Zillah who, with Athelstan, was staying with her Granny and Aunt Frances at St Dunstan's.

'Your dear Mummy & Auntie Mimi [Minnie] are having a quiet day in Bideford. I have seen Dr May here! ... I am riding a lady's machine! Without any chain – a 'Quadrant'. Goodbye dear little children. Be good. Love to Gran-gran & Auntie. Your loving Daddy & Mummy.'

This is the earliest postcard which has been preserved, the first of several hundred sent over the years, which with letters enable us to follow their lives. In lieu of telephones, postcards kept them in rapid touch. They could be relied upon to get to their destinations on the following day.

COUNTRY HOLIDAYS

Soon after Fred's death, Rose Wiseman moved with her youngest son, Percy, from Southend to Earl's Cottage, Woodham Walter. Several times in the spring, starting in 1903 when she was seven years old, Zillah went to stay with 'Granny Wise' at Earl's Cottage. It was an idyllic place for a child and where she learnt much about country life. She sometimes picked wild flowers and posted them into a box to her mother, knowing how her mother missed the countryside. She mentioned going to Maldon to pick bluebells. Zillah wrote letters and postcards home. She loved the countryside but at first she missed her mother very much... *'I have left off crying but I want you very much, perhaps I shall cry in bed.'* But when a little older she wrote *'I do not want to go home. I don't like London and I don't like school!'*

Earls Cottage, Woodham Walter.

Rosaline (Rose) Wiseman, 1890s.

On another occasion in 1905, Zillah described how she and Auntie *'went to drive the ducks home, they do waddle from side to side and stumble over the step into the yard.'* On one holiday her cousin, Eric, and his father, Arthur, from Redcroft, were also staying with 'Granny Wise'. *'Eric and I do have fun. Last night we got a stick in Uncle's [Percy's] bedroom and dressed it up in his clothes with a hat and all. It did look fine, then we put things in his bed, and hung up his night shirt at the top of the bed.'* Auntie Minnie also lived there.

They also went to West Mersea in 1903, a place which became another favourite despite Bernard's comment on a card to Pet's mother that September, *'The place has grown wonderfully. Pet says it is spoilt, a lot of small red brickers.'*

Athelstan and Zillah Harris, c1903.

Letter from Zillah, 1906.

In July 1904 Zillah wrote from West Mersea, to her father, still at work,

'It is so hot here Boysie [as she called her brother] *is as brown as a berry. I am writing this on Mummy's knee so I have written it very badly. We are waiting for the tide to come up on the beach so that we can paddle.'*

Athelstan also sent a card to his father, telling him, *'...Mother went to Bradwell yesterday in a sailing boat & 2 men. She said it was rough, 'a swell'...'*

They seem to have a car by then, as Bernard visits them and on his way back sends a card from Maldon.

'At H. Leech's. Arrived here safely via Peldon, Wigborough, Darcy & Goldhanger, through Heybridge. 1½ hours. Splendid road. Now moving on to W Walter. Seen Mrs L & Baby. Love...Bernard'

In 1905, Athelstan stayed with his Granny Harris at St Dunstan's Cottage in Hornsey, so he could continue going to school when Pet and Zillah went back to West Mersea. Zillah sent Athelstan a postcard of the Roman ruins at West Mersea. She wrote:

'Dear Boysie,

Mummy is in bed for some rest. We went for a long walk along the beach last night and are going to get some sea pinks today. Mummy hopes you are a good boy and I hope you are good at school have you been detained since we had been away. Love from Zillah.'

School registers show that Athelstan must have been at school in the Hornsey area, (Zillah also), but by 1911 he was attending Ongar Grammar School.

In July that year, Bernard and Pet went by themselves to Belgium, sending postcards on various days to his mother, Zillah and Athelstan, all at St Dunstan's. They visited Bruges, Brussels and Angers, returning home via Ostend.

Zillah was very close to her mother, and often says how she is missing her, when she visits her Granny by herself. *'Do write to me soon. My eyes do keep watering you know what for it is because I want you down here or with me somewhere. With love from your loving, loving little daughter Zillah.'*

There must have been great excitement when they bought their motor car. Photographs of 1 Holy Innocents Road showed that they added a small garage to the left side of the house. Zillah wrote on 23 April 1906, '*I hope you got home safely in the motor-car.*' She continues, telling us of her interest in flowers and of her economy,

Bernard and Zillah in car outside Holy Innocents Road, c1906.

> '*Please, Mummy, don't forget to write to Miss Phillips and tell her I shall not be able to have a violin lesson on Friday. I hope you will get on with the Spring cleaning.....We have walked 8 miles today and got the flowers I hope you will enjoy this morning, I hope you will like the King-cups, cowslips, bluebells and primroses. ... I have only spent 3 half pence on some gelatines.*'

At the end of July 1907, her parents went down to Exeter, where Bernard was at a medical conference, while Zillah stayed at home, apparently looked after by Aunt Frances. On the 30th Pet wrote a card to her,

30 July 1907. 'This building [Exeter Museum] *is where some of the 'medical' work takes place ... the whole place is alive with Doctors ... Just been to the Medical Exhibition & this afternoon go to a Garden Party. Daddy kept very busy at work all day at present, but hopes to get off tomorrow. Mrs Hunnaford* [a Devon Harris relation] *& I went for a drive yesterday.'*

The next day a postcard of Tintagel was posted in Boscastle merely saying, '*Mummy & Daddy send love. It is grand weather. Daddy.*' This must have been an exhausting and exciting drive in the cars and on the roads of the day. It was over 120 miles for the trip from Exeter to the coast and back.

Three weeks later Zillah was at Redcroft, and Athelstan at Burnham-on-Crouch. Zillah enjoyed playing with Eric and Marjorie in the small pit from which sand had been dug to build the house. She wrote later, '*We did enjoy ourselves at Paglesham, and it was very hard to leave.*' Athelstan, aged 9, wrote two cards from Burnham. He reported to Aunt Minnie at Redcroft, in a matter-of-fact way,

19 July 1907. 'Dear Auntie, ... We did not go to Church. One of the Captains fell down dead on deck, the funeral was Sunday. BAH'

And later to Zillah, also at Redcroft,

28 July. '... I cannot come home tomorrow as it is the regatta and I am going on the water. I have been for a lovely ride to Maldon in the trap ... your loving Brother, B.A.H.'

Only ten days later, Zillah was writing from Bideford in Devon,

7 September. 'We have found our way to the postcard shop. So I hope you will not be in want of postcards ...'

8 September. 'The Miss V's [another Devonshire Harris] *are very sweet as you said. .. We are going to Westward Ho tomorrow before starting for Clovelly ...'*

She was taken to Devon by her Aunt Frances. They stayed first at 20 High Street, and then on the quayside at 55 The Quay, returning via Barnstaple on the 27th and writing from Exeter,
3rd October. 'We are coming home tomorrow & I am going to stay the night at Auntie's. I do wish I was back at Clovelly ... I shall not come home like a coffee-berry' [A note added] *'Let Athelstan take this card to StD ...we shall arr between 9 & 10. FH'*

In April 1908, Zillah again stayed on Mersea Island with her mother and her cousin Annie, telling her father '*... I don't want to come home on Tuesday because I like it here so ....'*

In August 1909, Zillah and Athelstan stayed at a new place, Hoe Mill Farm, Woodham Walter, beside the Blackwater Navigation and not far from their Granny at Earls Hall, where cousins Eric and Marjorie from Redcroft were staying. Zillah wrote,
11 August. 'I am just in my element – 7 cats. 4 grown cats & 3 kittens, such dears. There are also baby chickens. A sheep has just been got out of the river. Love from ZH'
The next day Athelstan sent a card from Maldon to his father, who was at the White Hart Hotel, West Mersea,
12 August. 'I have just been up the canal on a coal barge towed, and invited to go again on Friday and have also been fishing – NO LUCK B.A.H.'

'Quiz', 1907.

Bernard himself was out sailing with Fred and Arthur in the smack *Quiz,* built for their father in 1872. His drawing and painting skills resulted in some watercolour sketches of the two brothers in humorous postures below decks! He had been to Mersea before going on to Felixstowe on the 20th and then to Frinton, from where he was going on to Brightlingsea. He sailed back to Paglesham from there on the 14 August, sending a card to his wife.

'Many thanks for yours received this morn at Mersea. I am glad you were not in the smash – the roads are very tricky for a motor, so narrow and curving. We arrived here safely at 6 o'clock this evening. No rain at all. Love B.'

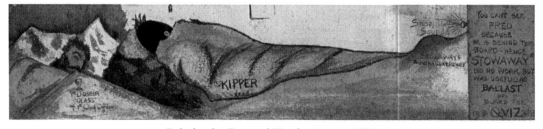

Painting by Bernard Harris, August 1909
Arthur and Frank Wiseman (and Fred) on *Quiz.*

6 EDWARDIAN PAGLESHAM

The 1901 Census was taken on 31 March, less than three months after Queen Victoria's death in January 1901. The population of Paglesham was continuing its gradual decline, standing at 456 compared with 514 twenty years earlier despite a similar number of households. There were only two thirds the number of households (20) with six or more family members in them.

The oyster industry involved 42 men in 1881, peaking in 1891 at 61, when it employed 49. The agricultural depression which had been going on for over 20 years is reflected in the reduced number of agricultural workers —54 in 1901 as against 77 in 1881. In 1901 far more were given status such as 'Shepherd', 'Horseman', or 'Hay Binder'. A note in the church Service Book on 23 February 1902 gives another insight. *'Many families have left the village in the last two years & the majority have been church people & communicants.'*

CORONATION

Queen Victoria died on 22 January 1901. Rev Lea noted in the church Service Book on
26 February 1902. 'This day was appointed for the Coronation of King Edward VII, but in consequence of the sudden & dangerous illness (& the critical operation) [for appendicitis] of the King, the services ordered & the festivities for which preparation had been made were postponed indefinitely, & a special service of intercession for the recovery & safety of the King was held.'

The Coronation was delayed until 9th August the same year. Paglesham celebrated it ten days earlier on 30 July, in a style similar to that of the old Queen's Jubilee, with a general holiday, bunting and a dinner for the whole population in the Church Hall barn. *'Eight long tables groaned beneath the weight of good things provided.'* The celebrations had again started with a service and there were roundabouts and sideshows in a field nearby.

PETTITT WEDDING

There was great excitement at Loftman's as the plans unfolded for the wedding of Zachary and Alice Ann Pettitt's only daughter, Eva.

Eva Margaret Pettitt married Percy John Hutley in Paglesham Church on 15 October 1903, with Rev Lea officiating at a choral service. A society page clip says,
'[Percy is] *the second son of Mr & Mrs James Hutley of Shoebury House. ...* [Eva] *wore white crepe-de-chine, trimmed with chiffon, her mother's veil and orange blossoms. The bridesmaids , (sister of the bridegroom) and Miss Margaret Mumford —wore pale crepe-de-chine, and large black picture hats. Mr Ralph Hutley was best man to his*

Percy Hutley and Eva Pettitt, 1903.

19

brother. After a reception held at Loftman's, ... Mr & Mrs Percy Hutley left for Devonshire.'

The couple came back to live at Cupola House where Percy had been living before his marriage. A brick wall was built along the road to hide the side garden, with curved walls to recessed double doors for vehicles and urns on the piers.

Percy's grandfather, William Hutley came from Powers Hall, Witham. His son James had farmed at Downham from 1868, at Thorpe Hall, Southchurch (1887) and North Shoebury House from 1891.

J F T WISEMAN'S DEATH

If the Hutley wedding in 1903 started a new era, the death of James Foster Turner Wiseman ended another. JFTW was born in 1835, the second son and youngest child of James and Ruth Wiseman, and grandson of James and Susannah Wiseman, the founders of the main branch of Paglesham Wisemans. He had inherited his father's oyster business in 1851 and became a very successful oyster merchant and farmer.

He and his wife, Annie, had eight children. He enlarged Marine Cottage into The Chase, a substantial property with a large garden, greenhouses, tennis court and formal gardens embellished with a fountain. Part of the weatherboarded old cottage still survives within the house. About 1870 JFTW moved the track to the sea wall and built for his oyster dredgers the three rows of cottages —Boarded Row, Shop Row and Brick or New Row. These continue to form the core of East End, although most cottages have now been extended or linked and modernised. The old track became The Chaseway.

James was a Past Master of the Rochford True Friendship Lodge of Freemasons. His many interests included writing and field sports. He wrote —with the Rev James Harris (Bernard Harris's uncle) and Rev H J Hatch, Rector of Little Stambridge, - *'The Paglesham Oyster, containing Tales of Fact, Fiction, and Romance, Music, Poetry, Charades, Riddles, Enigmas etc'* in 1870 and *'Logs for the Christmas Fire'* in 1876. The latter includes a historical poem, *'Isoline; A Tale of Hadleigh Castle'*, which runs to 84 pages. It has copious footnotes, and some lovely illustrations by him, showing both his serious and artistic sides. Neither book has anything of direct Paglesham interest! He only took up painting when he was 50 but had earlier attractively illustrated his reports of oyster surveys with sketches of houses on the shore.

Around the county, JFTW was known as a good shot. He kept a 'Game Book' listing the numerous birds he shot, from partridges to landrail, heron, woodpecker and even a glossy ibis. He spent many winters in Holland wildfowling, living at times on his own smack. He was sometimes accompanied to Holland by Zachary Pettitt or Zachary's son Robert.

He hunted with Mr Daniel Scratton's hounds from Prittlewell Priory, then a private house. On 4 January 1872, he invited Edward Jackson's Foot Beagles, which were kennelled at Smith and Chamberlain's Farm in Greenstead Lane, Hockley to The Chase. There was a large gathering including officers from the Shoebury Garrison who arrived in a *'brake drawn by 6 horses'*. The beagles came in a horse-drawn *'hound van'*. The account of this appeared in 'Land and Water' signed by 'Londoner' and included in a booklet in 1922, 'Edward Jackson's Foot Beagles, Reminiscences of Rochford Hundred 50 Years Ago.' The day was foggy to begin with but the hares took the hounds over the marshes of Clements Farm and Church Hall. They had a kill before 'returning to Mr Wiseman's, where a splendid oyster luncheon was served up to I would say over 100 ladies and gentlemen.'

After JFTW retired he went to live at Leys Villa, Plumtree, Nottinghamshire with his new wife Emma, née Falket, a cousin of Annie's, and his youngest son, William. He and Emma had another son, Samuel. Emma herself died about 1900.

JFTW died on 24 April 1903, aged 68, at Plumtree, 'from diabetes' and his body was brought back to Paglesham for burial. The newspaper reported that the weather was bitterly cold, and as

> 'the coffin, preceded by the Rector, the Rev T Lea, was borne into the church upon the shoulders of some of the oystermen who had been employed by the deceased, the sky was darkened by a heavy snow storm. ... Mr Arthur Wiseman [his cousin], was at the organ. The storm had ceased when the service was concluded at the graveside.'

As might be expected, there were many at the funeral. Four of his sons attended (two had gone to South Africa), as did his sister Jane Woodthorpe and her husband and a large number of his Masonic Lodge. Both his friend, Zachary Pettitt, and the man who was leasing his old house and oyster business, Mr Arthur Nicholls, were present. Bernard and Pet Harris were there, and 'there was a touching sight toward the close of the service, when the deceased's little son, Sam, who had borne up bravely until then, completely broke down.' JFTW's gravestone stands beside that of his first wife, Annie, not far from the gateway into the churchyard.

On his death, much of the village went up for sale. Arthur Nicholls bought The Chase and the oyster business he leased, as well as much of the rest. One of the less expected properties which JFTW had owned was the Plough and Sail inn. It was described in the catalogue, 'The Inn contains: Parlour, Keeping Room, Pantry, Bar, Taproom, four Bedrooms and cellar with bedroom over.' The sale also gives an idea of the cottages JFTW had built. 'The White Boarded Row —Each cottage contains 4 rooms with a semi-detached Wash House in the rear,

The Plough and Sail, c1909.

and there are four WCs for the use of the 8 tenants.' And of course their families! (Rosemary was born in No 1!) 'This lot is in the occupation of Mrs Fletcher, James Staines, and others at Quarterly rents amounting to £43.4.0 p.a.' This averages at about 2 shillings per house per week.

Arthur Nicholls also had the freehold ground rent of Milton Villa, which James Shuttlewood had built in Waterside Lane in 1899. The house had an extension on the east side from which surplus produce from the large garden and honey from their hives was sold.

ETHEL ADA

A happier occasion in 1903 was the launch of a new barge at the boatshed. *Ethel Ada* was a typical Thames barge, but it was to be the last full-size barge built at the yard. She was 80 feet long with a beam of 19.1 feet. The '*depth in hold from upper deck to ceiling at amidships was 5.42 feet*'. It was a tight squeeze to construct her inside the shed; it was said that there was only a foot clearance alongside. She was carvel built with a square stern, rigged as a spritsail barge and provided with six masts —main, sprit, mizzen, mizzen boom, topmast and bowsprit. Registered in London, she was given the official number 118352 (176 in 1903), with a registered tonnage of 47.75 tonnes (60.06 gross). The joint owners were George Edgar and Albert Edward Underwood both of Southend.

She was seen in 1970 at Manningtree, by which time she was out of trade and converted to a floating, but sailing, home for an IT man commuting (by train) to London. The details were recorded from the original Registration papers when she was seen in September 1993, tied up at Wallasea Marina, 90 years after she was built. She still sails today at well over 100 years old.

OYSTER DEPRESSION

A letter from Arthur Wiseman illustrates the problems in the oyster business.

Paglesham, Rochford, Essex
May 2ⁿᵈ 1904

'*Dear Sir,*

- Presentation Christ's Hospital —
Unfortunately not knowing personally any of the Governors having presentations to the above School it is quite as a forlorn hope that I am writing to you & the other Governors on the chance that perhaps I may be fortunate enough to find one who has not promised his presentation & would kindly consider my case & gives it on behalf of my

Son who will be 11 years old in a few weeks & whose only chance of getting into this School depends on his obtaining a presentation this May.

I am an Oyster Merchant or Grower & am suffering from the great depression in the Trade & for the last 3 years have been hoping it would improve so as to enable me to send my Boy to School; but up to the present it's a case of 'Hope deferred &', for this last Season just ending is the worst I have had & it's entirely owing to the generosity of my Brothers & Sisters that I am able to keep on my business. I feel I cannot ask them to educate my Son as well for I think they have done enough. If you

Fred and Arthur Wiseman at the oyster shed.

22

can in any way help me in this, you will be conferring an inestimable benefit upon me & by doing so relieve my mind of a great burden, the unfortunate part being, that only by a letter of thanks can I show my gratitude.

> *I am, Dear Sir,*
> *Yours obediently*
> *A. Wiseman'*

Arthur was clearly suffering more than his brother, Fred, at Buckland House, as he had a family and an expensive house to maintain. Unfortunately the business records do not survive to give better details of his financial problems, but it sounds as if he was unable to give any interest to Minnie and Percy on the mortgage.

RECTORS

The Rev Thomas Lea died on 19 March 1905 on the day that he gave his sermon on the text, '*Dust thou art, and to dust shalt thou return.*' He went home to dinner, felt unwell and later passed away. He had served the church in Paglesham for almost 15 years, having been inducted to the living following Zillah's great uncle on 30 June 1890.

He held services of 11am Matins, sometimes followed by Holy Communion, and 6.30pm Evensong, a pattern commonly used 50 years later. Evensong was brought forward to 3pm in the shorter daylight months, with a children's service to follow. He added an 8am Holy Communion and raised communicants at these from 400 in a year to over 1,000.

Arthur Wiseman had been organist since the start of Rev Lea's ministry in Paglesham. Ralph Wiseman, Arthur's son, recalled how his father would cycle to the church every Sunday, whatever the weather for the 11am service, returning to Redcroft for lunch. He then took the Sunday School at the Mission Room, came home for tea and then cycled back to the church for 6.30pm Evensong.

The Rev Thomas Lea was buried on 24 March 1905 on the west side of the church path. He was 72 years old. His wife, Penelope, lived for another twelve years, dying in 1917 aged 88. She had supported him in his work, and was remembered fifty years later as having often taken a Dorothy bag of sweets for the Sunday School children.

He was succeeded by Rev William Fraser, who, with his wife, did much for the village. He was Rector for 16 years, through the Great War. Mrs Fraser started the Mothers' Union and the Girls' Friendly Society. The school leaving age was raised to 14 in 1902, and girls of 14 and over joined the new Friendly Society. They met at the Rectory, had tea and learnt to sew.

During Rev Fraser's time '*Children's Treats*' are noted in the Service Book, along with '*Flower Service*'. Flowers and eggs were collected at these services. The July 1906 entry reads, '*Flowers sent to London Hospital and Southend SS Fund*'. The next year Shadwell Children's Hospital was also a recipient. In 1911, '*188 eggs and 50 bunches of flowers*' were distributed. Trees were planted to beautify the churchyard in 1908. Twenty-one donors gave a variety of species, including an avenue of limes leading up to the south porch. The limes and several of the others survive to this day.

Noted on 21 April 1912 was that the offertory was *'for Titanic Disaster Fund'* following the ship's sinking after hitting an iceberg on the 15th. A total of £4 2s was collected.

SYBIL BRAND

At the end of the decade, 1909, the year before Edward VII died and King George V came to the throne, John Brand, with his wife and youngest daughter, came across from West Mersea to take charge of oyster layings leased by a cousin from Zachary Pettitt. He was to get double his previous wage and a large house. Sybil, then 10 years old, later wrote an account of her time in Paglesham in a book, *Toasted Cheese and Cinders*. Her older brothers and sisters stayed behind as they were already working.

Well House.

The furniture was stacked on the smack, *Telegraph*, owned by James Hempstead, but when they were due to leave the smack was aground, and so they had to find a makeshift bed for the night. They got away between five and six in the morning with a higher tide, and a few hours later they were landed beside the boatshed at Paglesham. A piano was sent later. Their belongings were taken off and put on a wagon, which was then driven up Waterside Lane and across the recently cut cornfield to Well House. The road to Well House came past East Hall and would have been almost two miles further round.

Sybil loved the large wooden house which had been lived in by the Browning family since the eighteenth century. It was now owned by Zachary Pettitt. Zachary's father-in-law, George Fuller Browning had lived there from the 1830s to 1878 and had built the curved

Miss Emily Rice's shop, East End, c1910.
Barn Row on right.

brick wall to shelter the garden from the east winds. He landscaped the garden with box hedges, espaliered apple trees and roses. He had filled the orchard with mulberry, medlar, walnut, a sweet chestnut, apples and pears. Buildings on the north side included stables used to house chickens which Sybil's mother looked after. From the house there were extensive views over the 'marshes', where cattle and sheep grazed, to the river Roach and Paglesham Pool.

They were only a few hundred yards along the elm-lined path to the rest of

East End, Miss Emily Rice's shop and the Plough and Sail run by Miss Rice's widowed sister, Mrs Edith Kemp. Her husband, Alfred William Kemp, had been an oyster dredger before taking on the inn. He had died in 1906 aged only 39. His widow continued as landlady until the 1920s.

The butcher and baker delivered to the door, and Sybil wrote that the baker, Mr Moss from Canewdon, also brought milk as that from the cows in Paglesham went to serve Southend's growing population.

SHOPS

Miss Emily Rice took over the shop at East End when her mother, Mrs (Sarah) Rice, died in 1903. She had been famous for her sausages. The lean-to was attached to the end of Shop Row, next to Barn Row, and behind the Plough and Sail. Hams were hung from the ceiling and perishable goods were stored in the cellar. Her accounts show little change from her mother's of 1899. The famous sausages were still 9d per pound, lard was still 8d but pork had risen a penny to 9d. The goods sold are notably lacking in greengrocery and fruit, but most people would have grown these, or got them from a friend with surplus.

Many people kept an account at the shop, both wealthy and the poor. Names include JFTW and his son Charles, Fred Wiseman, Zachary Pettitt and son-in-law Percy Hutley, as well as Kemp, Forsdick, Lapwood and Fletcher. Not all were prompt payers; it is hard to understand how she could have managed when bills were not paid for twelve months or more.

Church End also had a shop at one end of a weatherboarded row of houses. Old photographs show that a shallow flat-roofed extension had been added to the frontage of the ancient timber framed building, with lean-to display shed at right angles. A closer view after it had been taken over by the Atkinsons in 1910 shows that it was also the Post Office, with a Victorian letterbox. 'ATKINSON'S SUPPLY STORES' had postcards, bottles and clocks in the window with a sign reading 'Watches & Clocks Cleaned and

Atkinson's shop, Church End, 1920.

Repaired, Cycles, Fittings, Covers and Tubes'. Cycling was a very popular pastime in the Edwardian period, and, as we shall see, an important form of transport a few years later.

The Atkinsons had come to Paglesham from Tottenham where William was already famous as a violin maker, having made his first in 1869 at the age of 18. He won several awards for his instruments, and his obituary read, 'He claimed to have found the varnish secret of the Cremonese masters. Although he had made over 300 violins, violas and 'cellos and though he could make an instrument in a fortnight, the varnishing and drying took nearly 2 years.'

However the secret died with him in 1929. Many villagers could recall half a century later seeing his violins drying on a line outside his shop and his instruments are still highly regarded. He was succeeded in the shop by his son, John. His grandson, Eric, became Postmaster there in 1956. Jim Cousins bought it in the 1960s.

SCHOOL DAYS

Sybil Priscilla Brand was enrolled at Paglesham school as entry No 595 on 18 October 1909 and stayed for three years, going on to *'Private tuition'* as noted in the School Register. Mr James Legge was schoolmaster, assisted by his sister, Miss H A Legge, and they lived in the School House. Florence Potton helped teach as well.

Hutley family and governess in a Daracq car at Cupola House.

There were two fatal accidents in Paglesham in 1911. The first was outside the school when, on 3 February, five-year-old James Powell ran across the road to a field opposite and was run over by a car driven by Henry Brown of Paglesham House. At the inquest it was stated that Jimmy had been chased through the hedge by another boy and Mr Brown was exonerated of all blame. This naturally caused much sadness at the school and the school attended Jimmy's funeral five days later. The Browns (who started Westcliff Bus Services) were not the only people to own a car; the Hutleys were photographed in theirs outside Cupola House in 1912.

'Southend Pleasure Brakes', horse-drawn buses, were run by Holmes & Smith of Southend. They came out to Paglesham on outings, and in June Henry Barnes was running beside the *Lord Roberts,* shouting for coppers outside the Punch Bowl, when he was knocked down by a horse. He fell under the iron-shod wheels of the brake and was killed.

Many children worked, when they could, to bring in money to keep their families, taking days off from school if necessary. In 1910, Walter Wood, then 10 years old, regularly worked at Redcroft on his way to school. He recollected in old age that he would get in coal and wood for the fires, clean shoes and do other jobs. Many helped at harvest time, stooking sheaves in the wheat field, gleaning ears or picking up potatoes.[6]

---

[6] See *'Children of Paglesham'* for more details of the school and the lives of Paglesham children.

7 RETURN TO PAGLESHAM

A NEW DECADE

The new decade continued the growing change of the previous one. Edward VII had shed his playboy image and had worked for peace, helping forge the Entente Cordiale with France and maintaining relations with Germany and Russia. Less than a month after his father's death in May 1910, George V was involved in constitutional talks, with the Liberal and Tory balance tipped by the Irish Nationalists and the growing Labour Party. Transatlantic radio was used to arrest Dr Crippen, later hanged for murder. The death of Florence Nightingale was another indication that the Victorian era was past.

Little of this filtered down into Paglesham life. It would take a world war to make a serious impact on the village. Meanwhile, King George's Coronation on 23 June 1911 was celebrated with typical exuberance with a Commemoration Service, a feast in the Church Hall barn and a fair. There had been much preparation in the field opposite the school for the maypole and the children enjoyed dancing around it. Tea and sports followed and it was another day that many would always remember.

RETURN TO PAGLESHAM

1910, however, was a turning point for the Harris family. Pet's mother, Rose, died on 13 February, six months short of her ninetieth birthday, and, in accordance with tradition, was buried alongside Fred, despite their having been separated over twenty years earlier. The polished red granite cross stands next to the double grave of their two children who had died so young of scarlet fever, 40 years earlier.

After Fred senior's death in 1897, Rose had gone to live at Woodham Walter. Minnie had joined her there, returning to Paglesham to look after her eldest brother, Fred junior. After her death Rose's two sons both married. Frank Buckland Wiseman married Edith Hope Dannatt on 27 July 1910 at Great Waltham, and Percy married Marian (Mamie) King a year later on 26 July 1911 on the Isle of Wight.

Also in 1910 Bernard discovered that he had tuberculosis and had an operation, after which he decided he could no longer continue to practise in London. He reasoned that sea air would be beneficial for his health and, having had experience of the sea back in 1887, presumably made the decision to become a ship's doctor quite soon. It was also decided to take the family back to Paglesham so that they would be in familiar surroundings, in the countryside the children enjoyed, when he was away. He brought Harry Gilmour into his practice – Gilmour is named jointly in the 1911 Kelly's Directory - and Pet and the children moved into a cottage Waterside, at East End, Paglesham.

They had found a cottage to rent in the middle of Shop Row, not far from Fred and Minnie at Buckland House and only a few hundred yards from Pet's other brother Arthur at Redcroft. Waterside was a small three-up and two-down in the middle of the terrace, with a wash-house and privy outside, across a passage which the others in the row also used to get to their back doors.

Shop Row and Waterside Lane, c1910.

Zillah Harris, c1910.

Before they moved there was much planning of what to do with all the furniture etc from 1 Holy Innocents' Road. Pet made lists of things to sell, of the silver to go to the bank, and of furniture to store with Fred at Buckland House. She also worked out the size of the rooms and what would fit in.

Pet recorded a few details of the move in a Boots diary, later recycled by Zillah for fuller use in 1944!

Tuesday 28 February 1911. 'Left Hornsey at 1 o'clock to drive to Liverpool St. B saw us off. Stayed the night at Redcroft as furniture would not arrive at cottage till tomorrow.'

Wednesday 1 March. 'Athelstan and I went and took flowers for a cross for Mother's grave. Furniture arrived about 5.30. Bedsteads did not arrive so stayed at Redcroft again.'

Thursday 2 March. 'Rest of furniture arrived early in the afternoon. Tottie helped us to get straight.'

Sunday 5 March. 'Church 3d [Collection] Tea & Supper at Redcroft. Sent off cheque to Hornsey bank. Kitty [the cat] caught in rat trap.'

Their neighbours in Shop Row, with Emily Rice at the shop, included the Browns, Rileys, and William Robinson, the village carpenter and coffin maker, at the other end. He had some land and a workshop on the other side of Waterside Lane, with the village pump at one corner.

Other entries indicate that she was buying supplies – *'Coal 2/8d'*, *'Fish 3d'*, *'Playle, cake & bread 1/3'*, *'oilman 4s 4½'*. On the 11th, *'Began with milk today from Paglesham House.'* This would have been the first time in Pet's life not to have servants, and one

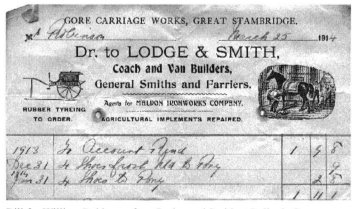
Bill for William Robinson, from Lodge and Smith at Ballards Gore.

28

wonders how much cooking she had done before! However,
Monday 6 March. 'Did a bit of washing. Got Mrs Fletcher to do the same 11½d', so she did
not go unaided. Mrs Popplewell was paid £2 *'on a/c'.*
Thursday 9 March. 'Marjorie's birthday, gave her 1/-. Went to tea & supper (leeks)'

The diary peters out ten days later after *'Sent card to EBH.'*
Bernard was still at Hornsey, probably staying at St Dunstan's if
Dr Gilmour had moved into their house.

Their home was much smaller and less private than at Hornsey
and Bernard, not a countryman, was not very happy there. He
wrote a sarcastic proposal to form *'The Patty Cake Club'* whose
intention was to start a subscription list to provide *'Creaking
Shoes for Curious Ellen Pry'.* He claims to be *'alarmed and
upset by a doubtless well meaning but very obnoxious Paul Pry
in petticoat array who ... is seen but not heard.'* Presumably
someone was walking along the passageway close to the
cottage.

So began Zillah's return to the Wiseman family village,
previously sampled as a holiday destination, and her life in
Paglesham which was to continue for another 64 years.

Christmas menu drawn by
Bernard, 1912.

SEA CHANGE

Over the next three and a half years Bernard sailed to many parts of the world, apparently
changing shipping companies to see somewhere new. His first appointment was on the
Royal Mail Steam Company's steam ship (SS) *Aragon* as surgeon, on 11 May 1911, sailing to

South America. On this trip he started
the habit of sending postcards to his
mother and sister at St Dunstan's, to
his wife and daughter at Paglesham
and to Athelstan, often at Ongar
Grammar School.

He uses the cards to keep in touch,
telling them of his ports of call and
future movements. He also passes on
the results of his curiosity as
geography lessons. The pictures give
an interesting view of the world at the
time, but the text gives little idea about
life on board. He of course lived with
the other officers enjoying the
luxuries that sea travel gave them.

Postcard of RMS *Aragon,* sent by Bernard Harris to
Athelstan, from Bahia, East Africa, 15 July 1911.

After South America, he visited the Mediterranean and spent a long time in Egypt. While
there in April 1912 he comments on the sinking of the *Titanic* and the loss of Dr Simpson,

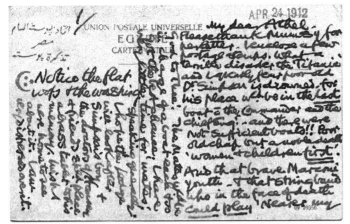

Postcard sent by Bernard to Athelstan about Dr Simpson, lost on the *Titanic*. 24 April 1912.

assistant surgeon on board, who lived in Hornsey and was well known to Bernard. Bernard wrote,

'*I greatly fear poor old Dr Simpson is drowned for his place wd be in the last boat with the Commander & Chief Engr. And there were not sufficient boats!! Poor old chap but a noble death. 'Women & children first.' And that brave Marconi youth, & that string band who in the face of death could play 'Nearer my God to Thee.' ... I hope the Lodge will look after Simpson's boy & the Doctors of Hornsey & friends should place a brass tablet to his memory. Wish I were home to see about it. I am very distressed over it.'*

No memorial was put up, but Dr Simpson had a long obituary in the local paper.

From Port Said, Bernard went on to Ceylon (Sri Lanka) and Calcutta. Other voyages took him round Africa, to Quebec and at the beginning of 1914 to Panama, twice[7].

No further cards were found until February 1915, so his activities until then are unknown.

8 THE GREAT WAR

THE COUNTRY CALLS

When the war started on 4 August 1914, there were 63 Paglesham men, from a population of 400, who volunteered. The school log book of September 1914 recorded the names of 10 boys who enlisted. Only Walter Forsdick was over 20, and Fred Farthing was just 15 and a half. They assembled at the Mission Room and were seen off in charabancs by Mr Meeson from Church Hall. This left a great shortage of manpower on the farms and in the oyster business.

Children had always helped out on farms, particularly at harvest time, and the school log books record a closure in September 1910, '*Closed for 2 weeks potato lifting*'.
In 1916 new laws made farm work by children legal. Children also helped by picking blackberries and in one year picked 114 lbs. The school log book records on 8 September

---

[7] See Appendix 2 for details.

1914, '*Children restless – territorials in the village & neighbourhood. Brothers were going into the Army & Navy.*'

Lord Baden-Powell, founder of the Boy Scout movement and Inspector of Territorials at the start of the war, immediately had Scouts on guard duty at bridges and other railway installations. The Territorials were soon mustered and, as the school log book shows only a month after the start, were being sent round the lengthy and intricate coastline of Essex coast to guard against invasion.

Children join men and women for potato picking, c1905.

The Territorials had been formed in 1908, each Volunteer Regiment having eight infantry companies and a company of cyclists, mainly used for scouting and intelligence services. The riflemen and some of these cyclists arrived in Paglesham at different times. J W Burrows'

Essex Regiment Cyclists at the seawall, c.1915.

history of the Essex Regiment (1932) gives the background. '*The personnel had to proceed to the war stations on their own cycles, other material being carried by motor transport impressed for that purpose.*'

On 10 September 1914, Athelstan Harris enlisted in the army, 11 days before his seventeenth birthday. He joined the Middlesex Regiment in the 1st London Rifle Brigade. On Sunday 20 September, there was a '*FAREWELL SERVICE to the 7th (Reserve) Battn. Middlesex Regiment*' at Hornsey Parish Church. The hymns sung were '*Brightly gleams our banner pointing to the sky*', '*Fight the good fight*' and '*Onward Christian Soldiers*', all very appropriate for the occasion.

Soon Athelstan wrote a card to his Aunt Frances, '*Having a good time here, only a bit wet now & again. ... Please send long arm vests to this addresss, Pte BAH..., 31 Armstrong Rd., Englefield Green in Surrey.*'

WAITING FOR ACTION

When the war started, Bernard must have wondered what to do. At the beginning of 1915, he was still undecided how he should balance his health with duty. Bernard was almost 50 years old, and still suffered from tuberculosis. Zillah began a diary and on Saturday 9 January, she noted that '*Dad had a wire to ask him to sail on a transport. He starts on Monday.*' A few days later, he wrote a card to Pet from St Dunstan's,

> '*... Refused the transport & Capt Burt (who came here this morning) thinks I did right – weather now awful in Aegean & Eastern Mediterranean. I <u>may</u> go to S. Africa in Durham Castle with Capt B. Mrs Gabriel's eldest son was killed at Dardenelles, so Miss G says, she is here to lunch today. He had been reported wounded & missing. It is truly awful the bad news all around.*'

On Thursday the 14th, '*Dad wants us to go to London on Sat to see him before he goes, & to have teeth done.*'   They duly went up on the Saturday and met Bernard in the afternoon, staying at '*Mrs Stones*'. They went to Holy Innocents' Church on the Sunday and '*Dad came about 3.15. Athel had not turned up but arrived just after tea. He stayed about 1hr & we saw him off at Hornsey Station.*' Both mother and daughter had dental treatment on the Monday and Wednesday. Athelstan came back unexpectedly with a three-day pass on the Tuesday, and '*Dad met us there* [the dentist's, on the Wednesday] *... came to dinner at Mrs Stone's & we went to St Dunstan's for tea.*' Bernard saw them again on the Thursday and saw them off home from Liverpool Street Station on Friday 22nd. They had seen a number of old friends from their time at Holy Innocents' Road.

On 26 January, they '*heard from Athel, perhaps he is going to Gib soon & is coming home for 4 days leave tomorrow.*' The next entries in Zillah's diary give other glimpses of their life. They frequently made a variety of cakes and puddings for the soldiers.

Wednesday 27 January 1915. '*I made a cake. T's* [Territorials] *had a treacle roly. We had tea fairly early so that we could go & meet Athel. We walked as far as the Gore* [2½ miles] *but not seeing or hearing from him we turned back. After we were in bed & getting dreamy I thought I heard a knock & presently Mrs R knocked on the wall & said Athel had returned. We let him in & he said he had left his purse at Egham so he had to go to St Ds to borrow money. We all retired again about 11.35.*'

Thursday 28 January. '*Athel stayed in bed late. After clearing away I made a beef steak & kidney pud. Also pastry for ditto pie for tomorrow. Also a roly poly. Aunt Tot* [from Redcroft] *came in during afternoon. We were not* [suitably] *dressed & Mum was writing to Dad. I ran up & dressed. In the evening we went to B House & stayed some time. Then Aunt M* [Minnie] *came in from Southend where she had been with the Tarbets* [at Paglesham House]. *The Ts brought back dish, they change again today.*'

OVERSEAS POSTINGS

A fortnight later, on 11 February 1915, Bernard sent Zillah a card from Valetta, Malta, '*Many Happy Returns of the 14th Febry. old lady.* [Zillah would then be 19.] *We arrived here early this morng. & sail this aftn. for Marseilles (query) & Avonmouth? Much love to you & Mummy.*' He was on board another Union-Castle steam-ship, now *HM Transport Galeka*, with Capt Burt.

'*Galeka*' had sailed with '*16 officers, 2 NCO, 937men, 2 horses* [of] *the 1st Reserve Battalion, City of London 3rd Royal Fusileers*' on Monday 1 February at 7pm with an escort. The next day found her '*sailing in company with Gratully Castle*' and a new escort *HMS Diana*. She had '*dropped one sick soldier at Gibraltar*' before steaming to Malta, where she exchanged her troops for '*29 Offrs, 4 WO, 922 men, 34 women, 37 children, 11 invalids* [of] *1ˢᵗ Btl City of London Fusil Ter,*' before sailing for home.

Also on 11 February, Athelstan wrote a card, '*Address: B Coy 7ᵗʰ Mx. Regt (Res) Gibraltar*'! Both father and son were now on active service, although Bernard was still a civilian. Athel wrote, '*Am quite settled down now & am enjoying myself immensely. We are in B'cks & pals together. It is now the end of winter*

Postcard from Athelstan, Gibraltar, 11 February 1915.

here yet some days it is as warm as our summer. Expect to go to Sandy Bay to guard shortly for about 3 months. Was unable to see Dad [who] *went on to Malta without stopping here. I was very sorry.*'

However, *HMT Galeka* called at Gibraltar on 15ᵗʰ, on the way home, to pick up a further '*1 man, 21 women, 37 children, 1 invalid*' and Bernard was able to entertain his '*his Lordship*' [Athelstan] to dinner on board. Bernard wrote home on the 16ᵗʰ February,

> '*Remind me I have 5/- of Athelstan's to hand you for safekeeping. We left this morning at 8am after spending the night at Gibraltar. Weather perfect & hope to reach Avonmouth on Sunday 21ˢᵗ Feb. Athel looks well & is very happy. Love from Daddy.*'

This was not the last time they were to meet in Gibraltar!

Having arrived at Avonmouth as expected, Bernard wrote to his mother at St Dunstan's, '*Expect to go to Barry* [South Wales] *for coal. Saw Athel at Gibraltar & he had dinner on board with me. He is well & happy. Did not run across any German submarines.*' He was on some of his pre-war routes, but sailing wasn't quite so carefree. Meeting Athel must have been a very happy occasion for them and for the families in England

Athelstan with mess-mates, Gibraltar, 15 April 1915.
Callan, Harris, Young; Nunn, Grainger, Webber; Hooker.

who would appreciate first-hand reports. On 22 February, to Zillah, '*Leave here* [Newport] *about Friday for an unknown destination. ... Hope all well, & bombs did you no harm!*

Thursday 24 February 1915. 'The snow was deep on the ground, 10 inches Willie said when he swept a path for us.'

Friday 25 February. 'We don't know if Dad will be coming down today as it is bitterly cold &
he says he is not well & must take care ... he came just after 6pm. We gave the driver a
cup of tea.'
Saturday 27 February. 'Although it was fine overhead it was dreadfully slippery underfoot,
so we decided not to go to church.'

Bernard was still at home on 8 March, before he returned to *Galeka,* by then at Cowes, Isle of
Wight.

HOME ROUTINE

When she was coming up to 19, Zillah had started her diary, which she kept for two years, at
times filling it in a few days later. She described the daily activities, including who got up
first, cleaning jobs done, dinner at 1 pm, what they wore and who they went to see in the
afternoon. Tea was at 4 to 5pm, supper later in the evening.

Washing up was done in a bowl on the kitchen table or in the wash-house as there was no sink
in the kitchen. There was no running water, and the water had to be heated on the fire, so
lighting the kitchen range was an early job. Pet had recorded buying a Beatrice oil stove for
'3s 3d' soon after moving in 1911. They would have used this for quicker cooking and water
heating, or in summer when the range might not be lit.

With no labour saving devices, there was the stove to be black-leaded, water to be carried
from the pump across Waterside Lane and kettles to be boiled on the stove. Zillah washed all
their smaller items. They usually sent them to a woman in the village who laundered them.
Each cottage in the rows had a small wash-house a few feet from the back door, with a
'copper' boiler in one corner, but Zillah doesn't mention using this. Rainwater, known as
'soft' water, was collected from the roof for washing clothes. Afterwards this would have
been used to water the garden or allotment. Behind the wash-house was the 'privy' toilet,
emptied by the 'night-soil men'. *'After dinner I made the starch but it wouldn't amalgamate*
properly. Still I did the job somehow.'

They kept their working clothes on until after their midday main meal, before going off for a
walk. They often called on relatives or friends and had tea with them, or invited them to their
own home. Sometimes they had supper at Buckland House. *'At 7pm we went over to*
Buckland House for a broccoli Supper by invite'.

Apart from the morning's household duties, Zillah did needlework, embroidering the WI
cloths (for their tables?), or mending clothes, which might be done in the evening, without
much light.

All three rows of cottages built about 1870 by J F T Wiseman, Pet's cousin, for his oystermen
were similar and had the same arrangements. They were linked to a drainage system,
unusual in Paglesham at that time, which ran 100 yards towards the river to a cesspit at the far
side of the field.

Meals were simple affairs compared with those that Bernard experienced during the luxury
of his life afloat, and one wonders how he reacted when at home. It is hard to know how the
war affected them at this time.

Friday April 16 1915. 'M woke me to say Maldon Station had been blown up- a Zep raid they say – Burnham & W Mersea were attacked. Most people in the village say they heard 2, 3 or 4 noises. I heard 2. It was such a lovely day we both felt inclined to go for a walk, so started about 2.30. We got as far as the Gore where we were surprised to see Ts & then we walked down to Creeksea. We had a talk with the guard.' They walked back across the fields.

Tuesday 20 April. 'Mrs Meeson [from Church Hall] *wanted to know if we could take in a convalescent soldier.'* They told her, *'we would be pleased to take a Tommy if circumstances would permit.'*

Saturday April 24. 'Southend full of Khaki.'

Sunday May 9. 'Went to BH to see the latest news about the Lusitania. ... There were 7 cars of wounded soldiers went down to the Chase' for tea.

Monday May 10. 'An aeroplane went over while M was at BH. We heard Zep has paid a visit to S/end.'

Zillah makes no further comment despite the fact that over 100 bombs were dropped on Southend. The newspaper reported it fully, but little damage was done although one person was killed. She also does not mention the contents of the letter they received the next day, despite its descriptions of Gallipoli!

Monday 17 May 1915. 'Had a letter from Dad, but it was not all there. It went from 2 – 19'. The next day they received *'the rest of the 24 pages.'*

Wednesday 19 May. 'Wrote to the Press Bureau for information regarding Prisoners of War.'

Friday 21 May. 'Heard from the Press Bureau, so now we can write to Wheeler.'

Sunday 23 May. 'At 3.30 went over to The Chase. The wounded soldiers were just arriving. We helped with the tea on the lawn & then afterwards the officers had tea in the dining room & 8 came altogether. When they had gone we had tea. Then I helped Mrs D bring in chairs etc.'

At this time the Metropole Hotel, Southend, (later the Palace Hotel) had been offered to the navy by its owner, Mr B W Tolhurst for the duration of the war, and had become *'Her Majesty Queen Mary's Royal Naval Hospital.'* During the summer, those able to travel were taken out by charabanc or cars to have tea at several of the big houses in the area. These included Loftman's, Zachary Pettitt's home in Canewdon, Clements Hall, Hawkwell, the Offin home, and The Chase at Paglesham.

Palace Hotel, Southend-on-Sea.

A booklet produced by 'E Kingsley Corke' pokes gentle fun at various aspects of the establishment with a poem for each letter of the alphabet and matchstick figure cartoons. Some of these read,

E's for Extras
Miss Sidney arranges.
Whist drives and motor rides.
What Welcome changes!

N is the Nursing Staff
Sisters and Pros
Ours are the very best
Every one knows.

R is for Rations
Meat, Veg & duff.
Even on meatless days
We'll get enough.

U is the Uniform
We've got to wear.
Treat it most tenderly
Lest it should tear.

These wounded all wore special uniforms, blue with a red tie, so Zillah may not have been aware in which service they served. However there was another hospital for wounded soldiers in Southend.

9 GALLIPOLI

TO WAR

On 31 March 1915, they 'Heard from Dad at Alexandria' with no further comment. Ignorance was bliss. HMT 'Galeka' had called at Alexandria to pick up Australian troops before sailing for the Gallipoli offensive, where Bernard had a ringside seat. His talent for writing and sketching came to the fore as he wrote a total of 87 pages of letter, with illustrations of what he was seeing, as well as cards.

Turkey was supporting Germany, and it was hoped to cut Turkey out of the war and to create a supply route to Russia by forcing a way through the Dardanelle Straits to Istanbul/Constantinople by sea. This was not possible – three major warships were lost to mines – and it had been decided to capture the Gallipoli Peninsular on the European side of the Straits. British troops were to land towards the southern end, with the combined Australian and New Zealand forces landing at a small bay further north, which would become known as Anzac Cove. The invasion fleet assembled at Mudros Bay, on the island of Lemnos, some 80 miles (120 kilometres) west.

Bernard sent the first letter of 24 pages to Zillah 'as I know your Mother doesn't like war.' Started on Sunday 25 April 1915 (now Anzac Day), it covered ten days of an experience he found exciting and depressing but, initially, patriotic. He was conscious that he was seeing history made, and collected souvenirs as well as writing a rare first-hand uncensored account of the action.

'The 'Galeka' had the honour of leading the convoy [from Lemnos].' Despite this he slept well on the crossing, 'but awoke when we cast anchor about a mile from the shore just before dawn. Hardly had we done so & I heard an ominous 'bang' quite close to me, & I sprang up & was in time to see a flash from a warship followed by ... an upheaval of *earth and more smoke. Bang Bang Bang in quick succession … soon 3 or 4 cruisers were in action & the replies soon came from the enemy batteries.'*

FIRST BLOOD

Troops were landed from *Galeka* using open boats towed by a tug, *'each tow consisting of 4-5-6 boat loads, possibly a complement of 300 men.'* *Galeka* had been shelled earlier, shrapnel passing between their masts but landing in the water. Bernard notes shrapnel sinking small boats, with two dead brought back *'without having set foot on shore.'* Bernard understates the effect, *'not particularly pleasant,'* without playing down what he was seeing. A Turkish prisoner was brought back, the wounded were

Australians being towed ashore from *'Galeka'*, 25 April 1915. Battleship and transports behind.

transferred to a hospital ship, casualties were frequent. But he was initially optimistic that progress was being made. *'At about 7.30am our men must have gained the first ridge some 300 ft high or more & could be seen silhouetted against the sky with the sun behind them, entrenching themselves…'*

A Turkish battery at Gaba Tepe at the end of the curving beach was causing problems. Bernard describes how *HMS Bacchante* had steamed close to the shore to cut off its fire, and endeavoured to silence it. He sketches what he means, with other diagrams showing where the fleet were, a map of the area, and the arrangements for burying the two unfortunate soldiers. Bernard philosophises about life and death, ending,

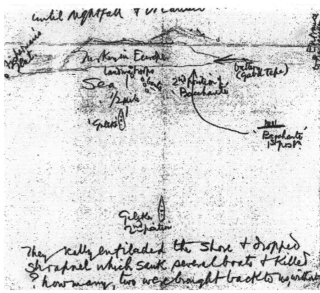

> *'Truly 'in the midst of life.' I do not know that I should have written these gruesome details, but having done so I will let them go. Perhaps as*

Sketch of 'Bacchante' manoeuvres by Bernard Harris, in letter from *'Galeka'*, 25 April 1915.

well to hear about them early in life – sadness is bound to come into all our lives.'

The medics were given orders to prepare for 50,000 casualties!

The *'booming of the guns'* reminded Bernard of Paglesham! There had long been a military establishment at Shoebury, and explosions from there or Foulness Island are still a feature of the whole Essex coast, although not as continuous or alarming as those he was experiencing!

On the Tuesday, *Galeka* was pulled back seven miles to the Greek island of Imbros,
> *'tucked away snugly with 6 other transports + 3 submarine parent ships in a little bay here, out of all danger, though we can clearly make out the ships (war & transports) + the balloon & hydroplanes.'*

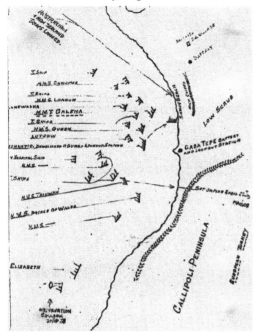

Plan of fleet positions drawn by Bernard Harris.

The balloons and seaplanes were used for spotting shellfire from the ships.

Galeka returned to Anzac Cove the next morning and a Fleet Surgeon (Bernard was still a civilian) came on board to arrange for the wounded to be brought on board with two surgeons, as the hospital ship was full up. The wounded *'did come – very quickly not singly – but a battalion! & no doctor'*, so Bernard went round giving brandy, or stopping bleeding, changing dressings and *'trying to be a ministering angel. The two chaplains & my steward were the most helpful.'* He organised a winch to lift stretchers straight out of the boats and on to the deck, *'fixed up 3 tables in the 2ⁿᵈ Saloon as an operating room'* and with two other surgeons *'got to work'*. The wounded were lined up on the promenade decks.

Just before they leave for Alexandria at the end of the month, Bernard wrote, *'When will daddy get home to see you both I wonder. I wish the war wld finish.'*

They arrived in Alexandria on Sunday 2 May and transferred the wounded ashore or to the hospital ship, *Goorkha,* which was going back to England. Bernard cabled his solicitor, Gerrish, expecting him to pass news on to Pet and Zillah, and sent the first letter via *Goorkha,* to be posted in England, which left on the 4th at 5.30 pm. This was the letter received in two parts on 17 & 18 May.

THERE AND BACK AGAIN
Galeka left an hour later and got back to Gallipoli on 9th May, having picked up East Lancashire Territorials at Port Said. In a second long letter, he continued to report events, movements of ships, his low opinion of the Australian doctors who congregate on *Galeka* with little to do, men's lucky escapes from drowning or bullets and the sinking by torpedoes of the *Goliath,* despite a screen of *'mosquitos'* (small craft): *'600 lost'*.

Some pages of this period appear to repeat others and may be copies made for his solicitor and friend Gerrish, rather than for the family at Paglesham. Bernard is conscious that letters can go astray and tries to cover such an eventuality.

On the 18th they left for Imbros and Alexandria, where he started a brief third letter on 27 May. He was delighted to find a letter from Pet at last, over two months old. *'You can hardly realise how much comfort a letter gives one when away from all one holds dear.'* He commented on a card to Zillah that he had seen about the raid on Southend in the *Egyptian Gazette*!

Alexandria *'harbour is packed, heaps of ships doing nothing & it is the same at Lemnos.'* Boredom sets in, in June, when they returned to Mudros Bay, as there had been submarine scares and the transports were kept in safer areas. There were British submarines with them, but he made no mention of enemy ships except in the Dardenelles Straits. Bernard (and his Captain) bemoaned the fact that *Galeka* was being used as a hospital ship. When Lady Carnarvon came on board with a General, Bernard was unimpressed by him. *'The old girl asked the Captain what he had in the way of comforts & stores for the wounded & he told her steam, coal and water. He does not mince his talk.'* Bernard was regularly critical of Churchill, the Generals, and the muddle – of stores, of instructions and of wounded brought on board, taken off and then returned. *'Oh for a Wellington or a Wolsey, or a Roberts and a Nelson. The men are fine but the heads are inflated fools.'*

Officers and nurses, HM Transport *Galeka*, Mudros Bay,
13 June 1915.
Capt. Bernard Bush, front. Dr Bernard Harris, back.

Bernard also complained that he was conned into coming, was underpaid for his role, technically only responsible for the crew, but had little to do as there were army doctors and nurses on board. He had not expected to be away so long, nor in this situation. He says his own health is *'good'*, although *'No cough or expectorant for days'*, suggests otherwise. He *'sent a letter to Pritchard* [of the *Union Castle*] *asking for a relief'*, without expectation, and made plans to be brought home *'on account of his health'*, but he told Pet that this was an excuse.

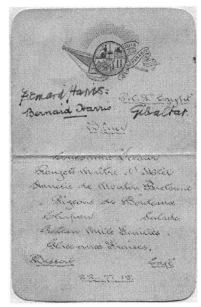

Menu card, P&O SS *Egypt*, Gibraltar,
22 July 1915. Signed by both (Edward)
Bernard Harris and his son, Bernard
(Athelstan) Harris.

Finally, with 450 – 500 wounded on board, *Galeka* went back to Alexandria. He sent off another long letter on 26th June, saying, *'the ship is in a perfect uproar after 3 or 4 days doing nothing. Lighters all around ... bringing 1000 tons of coal, and the same of sand.'* Carpenters were *'breaking up the 3rd & 2nd class* [with] *tons of wood being put over the side.'*

Whether Bernard returned to Lemnos is not known. The next surviving card was written on the P & O ship *Egypt* after calling at Marseilles on 19 July, and posted from Gibraltar, where remarkably he was again able to have Athelstan on board for dinner! They both signed the menu card on the 22 July 1915.

The Gallipoli campaign was a failure. After heavy losses, the troops withdrew from Anzac Cove at the end of 1915, with the British on the peninsular following soon after.

10 PAGLESHAM – 1915

ZEPPELIN LZ38
Paglesham became involved more directly at the end of May.
Monday May 24 1915. 'We sat in the front and read papers all afternoon. Italy has declared war against Austria. ... Mrs K brought the Ts' rook pie to show us.'
Wednesday May 26. 'Aunt came down after dinner. Of course Miss Rice [East End postmistress] *did not know the weight of parcels for Gib as Aunt wanted to send one.* [Athel was still there] *... Just before 11pm M woke me up to say a Zep was over Burnham* [less than two miles away]. *I dressed & went outside with the Rs* [Rileys next door]. *There was a lot of shooting over B'ham. The Zep seemed to be right over going towards S'end. We went over to BH* Buckland House] *to see how Aunt was* [Fred was away]. *We looked out of the window for some time then all retired to bed at 1pm.'*

Early War-time Zeppelin, LZ 43.

This was the same craft, the Zeppelin LZ38, as on May 10th, and it had approached down the coast from Clacton. Seventy bombs were dropped and two people were killed, one by fragments from a shell fired at the airship. A report on one of these raids, probably this one, was seen by Bernard in Egypt. Mr Legge put in the School log book, for Thursday May 27.
'The first time a Zeppelin appeared , it hovered in the neighbourhood and at times coming overhead. Villagers spent most of the night out of doors. 3 bombs dropped, 2 within a quarter mile of the school.'
This was a night long remembered in the village, both by young and old. Aunt Minnie decided to spend the next night with Pet and Zillah. They anticipated more visits from the Zeppelin each night.

Monday May 31. 'Cousin Agnes came down in the afternoon, did not leave until 5pm, so we were nearly late for tea at R'croft. ... We went up to Stannetts to look at bomb hole. ... I said, 'I hear a Zep or a motor boat'. It was a Zep & it seemed to be whirring over our heads as we ran down the road to Aunt M. When it had passed over we went home & got our coats and went back to BH. We heard it come back & then retired to bed – it went to E

London.

This was the first Zeppelin to raid London after the capital had been authorised as a target by the Kaiser.

This was followed in the school log book by, '*Children upset by another Zeppelin passing the area at 10.30 & returning at midnight. Shells from Shoebury whistled through the air quite near.*' And later, '*Everyone is worried by the war. Another bomb found near the school.*'

Friday June 4. 'Aunt M had been down to the waterside to ask Ts to tea tomorrow. 6 are coming.' Another Zeppelin was heard and they stayed with Minnie until it was quiet.

While they must have now have wondered if they would be attacked again, either by Zeppelin or by aircraft, life carried on as normal. [On 22 December, they '*heard a noise like a Zep and afterwards heard it was one.*']

TERRITORIALS

Saturday June 5 1915 'Made rhubarb pie & the old bread pudding for Gore.'
A section of Territorials was stationed there.

> '*Went to BH abt 3. Helped get tea ready. Saunders, Bird, Christian, Mac & Burr came, tea was in the garden & later adjourned to the drawing room. Christian played all the time, the others tried to sing. Later Sargt Curtis came up for Bird – had to go back – the former stayed and sang. I sat & talked to Saunders. They seemed sorry to go.*'

The following day several men had tea at Zillah's home. They were served cake and home-made wine, with Christian again playing the piano, not leaving until 10 pm. Both the troops and Zillah must have enjoyed these evenings. There were no army facilities provided for recreation.

Zillah went to stay with her Uncle Percy and Aunt Mamie at Wickham Bishops on 9 June. (Percy had married Marian Evelyn King (known as Mamie) at Ryde in the Isle of Wight in July 1911.) She bought a hat in Southend on the way and '*had a fish dinner at Garon's.*'

> '*M* [Mother] *came to Wickford* [by train] *with me and some person came to us on the station & offered to take me to Maldon* [a route now closed]. *I was very pleased. Auntie Mamie got in at Maldon Stn. When we got to Wickham Sta* [on the line to Witham, also closed] *we hung the luggage on our bikes & walked up to the house.*'

Percy and Mamie were getting ready to move to 18 London Road, Maldon and were clearing their house. Zillah went to help, but put little in her diary. They cycled to and from the new house, and Mamie was asked to tell '*the Stebbings* [that Zillah] *would not be able to play in the cricket match*'! A letter on 28 June called her home '*as we have a soldier billeted with us.*' She returned to Paglesham by train (during which '*it poured, thundered and lightened*),* having borrowed a '*mac*' from Shelley's in Rochford as it was still raining. '*Our billet came soon after 7 & we all had tea together.*' The soldier, Dick, had all his meals with them, except when he was on duty and they took them down to him on the seawall.

REG COOK

There is a regular note of Zillah receiving letters from Reg Cook and of her writing back, although his were usually addressed to '*Mrs Harris*'. Reg probably started as a friend of Athelstan. At the end of the war Reg's brother and sister were in Hornsey, so the friendship probably goes back to their days there, but he also he had been one of the Territorial cyclists

Reg Cook, A Coy, 18th Cyclist Btn, Essex Regiment. Southminster, October 1915.

posted to Paglesham. Reg sounds quite mature in his letters and was probably older than Zillah and Athelstan. There are hints that Zillah was fond of him, but it is unlikely that Pet would have encouraged a romance with Reg or any of the soldiers, even if Zillah had been interested. With her husband often away, Pet valued Zillah as her companion, which she continued to be for over 40 years.

Reg also came in at times to visit, bringing photos which they all spent evenings looking at. Like many of the soldiers he appreciated home cooking after army rations. On one occasion, Zillah noted,
'Had tea when Sgt Hatton came in & the sardines, chocolate cake etc were much appreciated. Reg sampled everything on the table. We sat round the fire and talked, looking at photos. We gave him mutton sandwiches, chocolate cake & lemonade & he left at 9.35. It was a very wild night.' Two days later a letter from Reg said, *'had to sleep at Creeksea Ferry as the night was too bad for him to get across.'*

The ferry – a rowing boat – had to be summoned by a semaphore arm from the opposite side of the River Crouch.

Reg wrote an undated letter to Athelstan from Southminster, where the cyclists were patrolling the seawall on the Dengie Peninsular, north of Burnham-on-Crouch. He *'went by motor boat to Holliwell'* at the mouth of the River Crouch, east of Burnham for a time. Then there was a spell in Burnham before going *'with the rest of the CT's to Headquarters where we were kept busy , cycle parades & attack practice nearly all day.'* They also cycled up to 50 miles a day as part of a fitness regime.
'I know the whole of the country well if you drew a line from Maldon down to Rochford. ... [We have] to keep a very strict gate guard (a couple of men day & night) at the post office to operate the switchboard and take messages from the outposts every 4 hours, because these outposts are not like those of the Rochford District, some of them being unapproachable by road, especially during wet & muddy weather.'
The seawall is several miles from the line of Dengie villages, and has little access even today. Reg was posted to
'Tillingham Coast Guard Station (in a cottage once inhabited by coastguards) and in spite of the weather here, I do enjoy the change from Southminster. ... It is altogether impossible for us to obtain leave for Xmas, [Conditions are] bracing! Too bracing at times. ... The seawall here is in many parts <u>rotten</u>! Well, we have to patrol this wall every high tide (that is once every 12 hours). The weather here soaks the ground & the wall is so muddy at times (especially at night when it is pitch dark) that it is dangerous to walk on it. ... It has been biting cold & winds howling always. This we don't mind so much. It is the rain we don't like. During the walk & although I carried a flashlamp to show me the way, I fell & got muddy dozens of times until I was glad to be indoors again! But for all

this I feel quite fit. ... I often think when I am tramping along the side of a seawall of the good times & kind folk at Paglesham.'

Tuesday 6 July 1915. 'I had a card from Reg to say he was at Southminster & would run over one day this week. I wrote to him in the afternoon & said we should be very pleased to see him.'

There were regular changes in the troops in Paglesham.

Monday 12 July. 'The first lot of Berks went off soon after 9am. More cyclists came down and relieved the others.'

Tuesday 13 July. '... Later the coal cart, with rations, came down ... the boy on it laughed ... the cart came back and the boy winked which I did not like.'

Sunday 18 July. '... an officer was around about billeting. ... Capt. [told us] we are to billet 2 men for meals from Wed next. Regulars.'

BERNARD'S RETURN

Thursday 29 July. 'The postman brought a telegram to say D [Dad] is coming back today. Auntie Tot & Marjorie came in after tea & while they were here D walked in & everything was wrong. Only the Sergt turned up for supper. When we went to bed it did not suit because of sleeping arrangements so he threatened to stay downstairs. Atmosphere thick.

Friday 30 July. 'D asked me to go down to the Waterside with him this morn, so we went & found Aunt Pollie [Bernard's sister, staying at Buckland House] and A Minnie there & presently all the tribe [from Redcroft] came down to bathe. ... I went to the Plough to get some bacca for Jack's birthday.'

Tuesday 3 August. 'Dad did not get up till after breakfast. The Sgt brought up the mushrooms [which the men had presumably picked on the marshes] *for me to pack for Granny & Dad took them up to London for me.'*

Friday 6 August. 'Mr Tarbet still complains about our light', so next day, *'when it got dark we went out to look at other people's lights.'*

Sunday 8 August. 'Dr & Mrs Gibbons called to ask if Dad would take his practice.' There is no further reference to this suggestion.

Despite his letters to them, Pet and Zillah would not have understood the trauma of Bernard's time at Gallipoli, nor the different conditions he had been used to on *Galeka*. Equally he would not have been aware of the routines they had developed in his absence. His experiences and his illness seemed to have changed him, as Zillah was always on edge when he came home. He was, however, often away which eased the strain. Conditions in the cottage, with the soldiers coming in for meals, must also have been difficult for him. He stayed at St Dunstan's at times and acted as locum, but Zillah often went for weeks without mentioning him.

Bernard returned 10 days later, arriving in Mr Nicholl's car, and stayed for five days. He made up Zillah's allowance book. On Thursday 19 August, Hornsby collected them all. Zillah quickly *'called at PO at R'ford & paid in cheque etc. [her allowance].'* They went into Southend, *'Did our shopping & had an oyster lunch. Saw Dad off at S'end, then waited for our train. Called at Smoothey's abt shoes then walked home.'* Smoothey had a shop in North Street, Rochford, and described himself as *'Boot Manufacturer'* in Kelly's Directory.

If the war seemed distant most of the time and occupations trivial, there were reminders of the realities which must also have raised the Harris's concerns for Athelstan. On 20 August, Taylor, the housekeeper at Buckland House heard that her brother had been '*dangerously wounded & in hospital, so she is going off to see him.*' Next day she '*telegraphed to Uncle to say she will be back tomorrow.*' Her brother did not come from Paglesham, so he does not appear on the village's Roll of Honour in the church.

The Harrises often had Territorials in to eat their meal or took food to them. They were always paid an allowance for this, but one suspects the men fared well! Sgt Ryan and Jack were their responsibility, but they at times did not turn up. There is no suggestion in the diary that Zillah was annoyed about this, knowing that there was some good cause for it. Only occasional glimpses of a more personal nature are recorded by her. On one occasion she says, '*Only Jack came to tea. He says he is going out with Lily Cottis this evening because his girl won't write.*' Jack also told them '*how disagreeable the men are down there* [at the waterside].' But there was also the entry '*Jack came in to tea having had too much beer.*' Not for the first time!

Sunday 29ᵗʰ August 1915. 'The men came in late & did not finish breakfast until 10am, so we could not get to Church as we should have liked. We cannot go this even as Dad is coming. ... Presently we heard knocking at the door but thinking it was next door took no notice. Then we heard Auntie Edith's voice at the foot of the stairs. She, Cousin C, & Hugh had come to Pag for the day. [Edith Hope Wiseman was the wife of Pet's brother Frank.] *... Dad came down in the taxi.*'

It had been an unusual day, but there was more to come. Bernard may have been stirred by the earlier offer of a practice, and he came back with an alternative job.
Monday 30 August. 'I have decided to go to Wales with Dad while he does a locum at Haverford West. ... Dad pulled out the Sgt's tooth.'
Tuesday 31 August. 'We went by taxi to Rochford taking Jack & his boots with us. M came up to London with us & we went to Selfridges where I bought a new coat & skirt, macintosh and hat. (M also bought one.) & a trunk. Saw M off at Liverpool St & then Dad & I went on to St Ds. Aunt F ... arrived soon after. Saw the Vellacots for a minute. Had a bath & went to bed.'

To bath without having to prepare it would have been a luxury for Zillah. She would usually have had to heat the water for use in a tin bath in front of the kitchen fire. They would each have bathed in turn, although Zillah never mentions this. It would have been difficult if there had been a soldier billeted with them.

On the Wednesday, Bernard and Zillah went by train from Paddington, arriving at Haverfordwest at 6 pm. They briefly met the doctor for whom Bernard was standing in, and next day he started work following a telegram '*to go to Clarbeston Rd.*' Zillah went with him by car. On other days they walked to see patients and Zillah was asked in by '*Mrs Davies at Prendergast.*' It must have been pleasant to have people call, and Bernard must have been used to new situations after moving between various ships.

The next day, Zillah '*found a letter from Reg waiting for me, also a few lines from Mother.*'

Her diary entries peter out until they had returned home via St Dunstan's.

Friday 17 September 1915. *'Had a bathe before breakfast. Walked into the village during the morning. Had lunch early & walked slowly to the station. The train was very full but at Welshpool several people got out. There were some very rude men in the carriage but they got out at Stafford. We had the carriage to ourselves from there. At Nuneaton we got a luncheon basket...'*

Saturday 18 September. [At St Dunstan's] *'Had a bathe before breakfast. ... After dinner I got ready & we caught the bus for Finsbury Pk & then tube to Moorgate St, then to Liverpool St. ... Drove from R'ford in the taxi. Aunt Minnie was at the cottage when we arrived.'*

Sunday 19 September. *'...a figure at the gate. It was Reg who came round to the back door. I met him & then M came & welcomed him. We took him to the front room & I entertained him until Dad came in. Then we set the dinner & D got rather cross over the cutting up of the meat in the kitchen. We looked at Reg's photos during the afternoon, then went down to the waterside where he took our photo. ... He left at 7.30.'* Reg sent the photo ten days later on 29 September.

Zillah, Bernard and Pet at the Waterside. Taken by Reg Cook, 19 September 1915.

WALKING

A fortnight later Zillah and her mother had a break at Ongar, staying at the Kings Head for the weekend.

Sunday 3 October. *'After breakfast we went to Church but none of the OGS* [Ongar Grammar School, where Athelstan had studied] *were there. Had chicken for dinner & then up to Moreton village. On the way home nearing Ongar, we overtook a young soldier who limped. We walked as far as the camp with him. He came from Jersey & is in the 6th City of London. ... We walked to the school but Mr Wiseman had gone to service, so came back to Kings Hd & waited until 8.30. He was in that time. We had a long talk & they gave us a wicker basket which Mr W insisted on carrying to our hotel.'*

Monday 4 October. *'[After breakfast] Don Mason came in with the school magazine. Finished packing & then started on our walk to Brentwood. Looked at Kelvedon Hatch church en route.'* Then by train to Colchester and motor bus to West Mersea, where they stayed at a guest house run by Mrs Wood. *'Mersea is growing fast.'*

Tuesday 5 October. *'We strolled out and met a native who knew Grandfather* [Fred Wiseman, who sailed his smack up from Paglesham and often visited West Mersea] *Then we ordered some mussels from D'Wit. ... we walked down to the Victory after dinner.'*

Wednesday 6 October. *'Left Mersea at 10.30 for a good walk. Went across Strood* [the causeway linking Mersea Island to the mainland] *then to Peldon, on to Gt Wigborough Church.* [A piece of the Zeppelin brought down nearby is now hung in the church.]

Found the 'Kings Head' & asked for bread & cheese & tea. The woman was dubious at first but let us have it & thawed a lot. The house was most unhomelike. Saw her parrot in the wash house. Walked back to Peldon ... church which was locked. Got back to W Mersea in time for a late tea.'

Thursday 7 October. 'After dinner we went down to the beach & walked a long way along the sea wall towards E Mersea. Passed an out post of soldiers making tea.'

Friday 8 October. '[Caught] 9.10 bus which took us to Langenhoe Schools. [The church had been destroyed in the 1884 earthquake.] *From there we walked to Wivenhoe Ferry stopping in Fingringhoe village at the pond & looking over the church, then took the train to Brightlingsea. Walked about the town there to find a place to have something to eat. At last after wandering some time we came back & had tea & buns, then wended our way to the water where a man ferried us over to E Mersea, where we walked back to W Mersea, 5 miles. We went a little out of our way but reached home about 6.30.'*

After a fairly strenuous holiday, they left Mersea on the Saturday by bus to Colchester, looking round, visiting the museum and then going to Capel Road in the rain to try and meet Sgt Curtis, who had been in Paglesham. They encountered Sid Chapman, *'who seemed very pleased to see us'* and the sergeant, who *'did not seem very pleased to see us, only surprised.'* Then they took the train to Rochford, changing twice on the way, hiring Hornsby to drive them home. *'A letter waiting for me from Reg. He can't come down tomorrow but will next Sun if possible.'*

The Harrises had groceries delivered from Willan's at the bottom of West Street, Rochford. They did not, at this time, often use the shop run by Miss Emily Rice in the same Row, except for the post office service, preferring to walk the mile or so to William Atkinson's shop at Church End, even for a single item, such as vinegar for pickling. This entailed walking past Redcroft and Paglesham House, or along East Hall lane. Then there was a choice of footpaths, either behind East Hall, or across the field near the corner on a path known as the *'Caution'* [now lost], or carrying on down to the school and the shortest footpath which arrived in Church End opposite the church. Pet and Zillah would have used the same route to walk to church. The footpaths would have been wet, if not muddy in bad weather, and the roads were not tarred at that time so would have been rough and uneven underfoot. But the Harrises were seasoned walkers. Their regular walks into Rochford and the walks they did at Ongar and Mersea prove that. On the other hand they were happy to accept lifts or use the train or a taxi.

DISSENTION

Life continued for Pet and Zillah, with the *'Ts'* taking meals, visits to *'BH'*, plum and walnut picking, *'taking M U* [Mothers' Union] *magazine,'* crotcheting and reading. The Territorials featured more often.

Wednesday 13 October 1915. 'The Sgt had to hurry off to Shoebury for medical inspection. ... A Coine came down to take the Sgt's place. We think he is a detective, anyhow he spoke like a gentleman. He takes snuff. ...' Zillah sounds like a detective too!

Friday 15 October. 'Lieut Hutton & Col Ravenscroft came & paid the billeting money. Had an argument with Jack at dinner about the rich & poor volunteering as soldiers... [Jack] asked for some sandwiches to take on his journey to R'fd tomorrow. Sgt came in as he ought to have been on guard. He had had too much to drink.'

Saturday 16 October. *'Jack ... did not come in to dinner. The Sgt is very worried today & wants Jack to go on guard as they are very short of hands.* [Later] *As I passed the Plough I heard Jack's voice ... Sgt tried to persuade him to go down to the waterside, so did we, but he was a bit tipsy & as obstinate as a donkey.'*

Sunday 17 October. *'Sgt had to go to Shoeburyness to see what could be done about the dissention* [sic]. *He came back with Joe Catterell & Anderson. He is quite relieved now & able to enjoy his dinner. I wrote to Reg, 6 pages.'*

Sunday 24 October. *'The Sgt* [Hatton] *taking Sgt Ryan's place came up to breakfast, he seems very nice.'*

Friday 29 October. *'Some new soldiers came down, also a gun carriage affair with Officers etc & we heard the Borders are to go. Sgt Ryan came up* [from the waterside] *in a hurry for some sandwiches to take & he gave us his photo.'*

Saturday 30 October, *'we had nearly finished the washing up* [after the soldiers had had their dinner]. *Dad came home & had his. Got thro' tea all right. A little friction over frying some dabs for supper.'*

Again there is no mention of where Bernard has been, or why. He continued to be in the way and critical. On another occasion, she wanted to get to a cupboard in the small room, but couldn't *'as the chair was occupied.'* Again, *'We walked as far as the school with D* [Dad] *but we were wrong all the time.'*

Sunday 31 October. *'The Church was full of khaki. The Sgt & 5 Lincolns, A Shuttlewood, Cpl Heywood & Eric* [Arthur Wiseman's son]. *Also one of the Sailor boys.'* Afterwards they called at Buckland House and borrowed the *Essex Weekly*, the only paper which Zillah seemed to read.

Bernard went up to London on 4 November, *'to see about his birth certificate'.* He missed Pet's birthday on the 11th but *'sent her a parcel.'* He returned on the 13th without warning as his letter had not been received. *'We had oysters for supper. I wanted to wash down in the kitchen, but thought he was never going to bed.'*

Pet, Zillah and Minnie were always concerned and helpful to others in the village and this comes through in November.

Friday 26 November 1915. *'M made a custard at Mr Samson's* [next door] *request & Ethel baked it* [at Buckland House]. *Mr S went to Rochford after dinner to see about getting his wife into the Infirmary. M took tea in to Mrs S & sat with her sometime.'*

Saturday 27 November. *'Much excitement prevailed in the village during the morn as the ambulance came to take Mrs S away. We filled the* [hot] *water bottles for her.'*

Unfortunately she died early in the New Year.

Wednesday 1 December. *'There were 40 cyclists in Pag. Some visited the shop but I don't know what Coy they were.'*

Saturday 4 December. *'The Cpl came in for his high tea soon after the Sgt. The Officer who told them to come up separately has gone to S'end so they think it is safe to come up together.'*

Friday 10 December. *'M & I both heard from A* [Athelstan] *who is now in Alexandria. D is not coming down for a while.'*

CHRISTMAS 1915

It was all change for Christmas. Reg Cook came about dinner time and stayed for tea.

Sunday 12 December. '[They all] '*sat around the fire and talked. About 8pm, M set about getting some supper for him while I talked to him & then AM came in & talked her talk. Reg left about 8.45. Aunt never said a word about him but we had said nothing but S'end talk.*'

This does suggest that Zillah was more than just polite to Reg, and others may have wondered! Reg was moved the next day from Wickford to Southminster, which may have been why he stayed so long.

Monday 13 December 1915. 'The men never came [for breakfast] *till 9.15 & we had to leave for S'end at 10. So we had to hurry. Had to call at R'croft for a message.* Mr Hutley [Cupola House] *picked us up at the hill & put us down at the Anne Boleyn* [public house, on the Sutton road junction – he was probably going to North Shoebury House where his parents lived] *and we walked across the fields. Shopped all day. Had cocoa & crumpets at Garons. Caught the 6.4 train home & drove back in the taxi.* ... [They had a] *bloater supper at BH, ... the Cpl came up to tell us they were leaving & the 8th Essex are relieving them.*'

Wednesday 15 December 1915. 'At 8am the transport came down for the kit bags & soon after 7 cyclists of 'H' Coy 1/8th Sx [sic] relieved them. Sgt R & Cpl R came in for their provisions & wished us good bye. The latter said it was like leaving home. Mrs R then buttonholed 2 cyclists & gleaned all she could.'

The village grapevine was at work! Pet '*wrote Xmas letters*' on the 19th, and on the 21st received a '*box of chocolates from Mrs Stebbing... After tea we cut out 4 pairs of knickers & started making them.* ' Their Christmas season had started.

Thursday 23 December. '*Had little presents from Miss Stebbing & Aunt Mamie. Mrs Fraser called during the morning & gave me a little calendar. I made a cake for ourselves & got the pastry ready for mince pies for Terriers tomorrow. After dinner went to C End for a few things.*'

English-French Dictionary 'in every packet' of Black Cat cigarettes, 1915.

Friday 24 December. '*Granny & Aunt* [Harris, at St Dunstan's] *sent me an apron & 2 handkerchiefs. I made mince pies & cooked the beef. ... We had just finished our tea when Dad arrived in the taxi.*'

Saturday 25 December. Christmas Day. It poured with rain so they were unable to go to church. '*Later it cleared up and we 3 went down the waterside with cigs, apples, chestnuts, mince pies. ... Went to BH to spend the day. After dinner we retired to the drawing room. Just before tea M & I won a pr of gloves* [?] *by kissing the gents asleep.*'

Sunday 26 December. '*We were a little late for Church. It was almost too windy for Dad. Aunt M walked back with us by road.*'

Monday 27 December. '*M & I went down the waterside as we thought there was some spray to be seen but we were disappointed & the wind was so rough we could hardly stand.*'

Wednesday 29 December. '*Dad had dinner early as he went back to Redbourn,*' where he was presumably acting as locum.

11 THE GREAT WAR – 1916 - 1919

On 25 Jan 1916, *Notes for Guidance* were issued by the *Local Emergency Committee* for the Rochford area under the chairmanship of James Tabor. While stressing that the likelihood of invasion was no greater than earlier, it gave instructions *'in the event of a hostile landing.'* Nothing was to be done except *'on the orders of the Military Authority of the Police.'*

All *'mechanically propelled vehicles'* were to be handed over to the Military if required, and disabled if not. Animals were to be removed or destroyed. People were *'to be prepared to move along such roads and to such collecting centres'* as directed. Special Constables *'and other trustworthy persons'* had been appointed to give the necessary warnings and instructions. Railways *'will not be available for the civilian population,'* and most major roads would also be closed except for the military.

Collection centres were North Benfleet Hall for those living *'South and West of the GER'*. Everyone else was to go to Wickford. Those living south of the River Roach were to cross at Stambridge Mills and join others, including those from Paglesham, at Ashingdon. *'From Ashingdon both parties will proceed by Lower Hockley Hall, Hanover Hill, the Rawreth Lane, Rawreth Church and Shotgate Farm to Wickford, where they will receive further instructions.'*

The Notes for Guidance ended, *'All civilian inhabitants are strongly advised to take with them their money and valuables and, if possible, blankets and enough food for themselves and their horses for 48 hours.'*

Pet and Zillah had emergency bags ready to take with them in such an eventuality.

BREAKS IN ROUTINE

Typical party entertainment was enjoyed at Paglesham House.
14 January 1916 '[They walked] *calling for Aunt & Uncle on route. The first game of guessing names of celebrities written on our backs. Then we danced several dances including the Lancers, which was murdered. Later we adjourned for Supper which was very nice. More dances, a game or two, more dances, a cup of tea & cake & then adieu.'*

Soon into the New Year of 1916 they heard from Athelstan *'in the desert'*. Also, Bernard was offered a new boat to South America which he declined, as two weeks later he came home. He brought Zillah a *'cooking book'*. On 26 January *'a telegram came from Dr Owen, Fishguard, asking Dad to go there tomorrow for a week as it is urgent so he is going.'*

On Tuesdays a Working Party met at the Mission Room. A sewing machine was taken along from Buckland House. Pet (but not Zillah) went and she knitted socks for the troops.

Comforts for the Troops, from Leach's.

49

When she needed help *'turning the heel'* she went to see her sister Minnie at Buckland House. A leaflet, *Knitting Patterns for Troops* survives from those days.

Friday 7 April 1916. 'Uncle Arthur came in & said Mr Hutley said we might have first offer of Chez Nous. The rent would be £25' The Brands were due to leave Well House and this could have been the place meant. However they never lived there.

April was time for spring cleaning.
Friday 14 April 1916. 'We began M's bedroom directly after breakfast & after scrubbing floor and paint we went to BH to beat carpet which we laid again before dinner. Finished off the room in the afternoon.'
Carpet beating was done with a cane 'bat' and would have spread dust across the neighbours if carried out in their garden or yard. On another day *'Spring-cleaned the staircase'*. John Popplewell did some wallpapering and whitewashing for them.

Easter was late in 1916, and Uncle Frank, Pet's younger brother, was coming to stay at Buckland House. After church on Good Friday morning, 21 April, Zillah and Pet went over *'to help mow lawns etc.'* With so many men at war, there were few about to do gardening. The next day, *'Went to Church for decorations. Marjorie & I did the Reading Desk & Lectern'*. On Easter Sunday they went to *'Early Service'* at 8am, and *'church in the evening & supper at BH'*, walking both times. *'A parcel of sweets, tea & eggs arrived from Dad'* on Easter Monday. *'I cleaned a few bits of silver & china & put them away for when we trek.'* Were they thinking of moving to Well House?

Thursday 27 April. 'Mrs H Raison (from Clements Farm) *had a long chat with M & told her of a mysterious letter they had received from Gold Coast which they think is spying. We are going to Clements tomorrow evening to read it.'* The next day, *'After tea we went down to Clements Farm. We had a long chat with Mrs Raison about Paglesham as it used to be, then she showed us the letter which is most mysterious & finally we*

Clements Farm, 1907.

went round the garden. We walked [back] *round Pound* [Pond] *home to bread & cheese & spring onions.'*

In May they had a trip to London. Potton's trap had been ordered from Church End to pick up Zillah and Pet at 7.45 am to take them to Rochford Station for the train to Liverpool Street.
Tuesday 2 May. '...We took a bus to St Paul's Churchyard, then walked to Bettymans where we bought a carpet, hearthing & mat. We walked to Regent & Oxford Streets, it was

raining all the time. Took the bus back to St Paul's Churchyard where we bought a coat & skirt & ordered a dress. Then we went into the Cathedral for an hr.'

They caught the train back to Rochford where the horse and trap was waiting for them.

Potton's trap at the Causeway, Church End.

Some of the bigger houses – The Chase, Redcroft and Buckland House among them – had tennis courts, and held '*Tennis Teas*'. Zillah did not play but went to help. She often put in her diary what she wore (as she did for churchgoing). On 19 May, '*Wore my blue colienne & new champagne shoes & stockings. We helped hand round tea.*'

On Saturday 20 May, '*Summertime*' was introduced for the first time under a daylight saving scheme to save coal. '*Before we went to bed we advanced the clock 1 hr according to the new summertime*'and the next day, '*We overslept ourselves a bit according to the new time!*'

Tuesday 30 May 1916. '*After tea we started out with the intention of going to Church End, but as we passed Mr Brand* [at Well House] *in his garden we were invited to have a look round & then Mrs B asked if we would like to see over the house, which we did & were charmed with it. After supper we walked to BH but Aunt was too absorbed in gardening to be interested.*'

There is little reflection in Zillah's diary of the effect of the war on Paglesham, although those with sons or husbands in the services must have been worried for them. However, on 3 June 1916, '*There was a great naval battle in the N Sea*'. A few days later, '*Aunt M came down with the news that Kitchener is drowned.*' The Army Chief's ship had hit a mine. A Memorial Service was held in Paglesham church on Sunday 18 June for Lord Kitchener and for the sailors lost at the Battle of Jutland. The battle at the end of May had seen the loss of two British capital ships, five destroyers and 6,900 men, but it was still considered a 'victory'.

After church on Sunday 2 July, Zillah and Pet '*went to BH to pay our respects to Dr Doak. We like him very much.*' Frank Doak had come over from Australia to study in Edinburgh. Pet had corresponded with his sister, Margaret (Madge) Doak, as a youngster in the 1890s. Madge may also have been over before the war – a single postcard posted in Colombo, Ceylon (now Sri Lanka) probably in 1910 or 1911 said, '*We are now half way home. Love to [Mother] & yourselves from Stella & your M Doak.*' Madge had always wanted to visit England, while pressing Pet in vain to travel to see her own country. Stella was another Australian cousin, either Stella Wiseman (born in 1889), a grand-daughter-in-law of the original Wiseman settler, Charles, or more likely, Mabel Stella Doak (born in 1895), Madge's unmarried niece. Unfortunately, nothing else is known of these visits.

In July, Zillah again went to stay with her father, when he was a locum in West Wycombe. She went up to London by train.

Tuesday 4 July. 'I met Dad & Aunt F at L Street. We had dinner & then Dad & I went to the Mansion House to afternoon tea. Met Aunt at Padd in good time to catch the train for W Wycombe. We saw some wounded soldiers arrive, also some Sinn Feiners.'

This was only a week after Sir Roger Casement had been convicted of treason for his part in the Irish 'Easter Rising' which had occurred in April. These were presumably prisoners, possibly the wounded.

Wednesday 5 July. 'Dr S had gone before the following breakfast. ... at 11am we went out in the big car for our round [of patients]. *In the evening we went round to 3 patients in the village & I was permitted to hold a baby 22 hours old in my arms.'*

Friday 7th July. 'I had a card from M to say Reg came over last Wed. as he is leaving England for Egypt.'

Sunday 9 July, 'I heard from Reg if he was not sent away before Sat, he will come over. We [Bernard and Zillah] *meant to go to church this morning but did not like to in case His Lordship came. In the afternoon Louie asked me to go for a walk but I did not as it is always the unexpected that happens'.*

Zillah had been writing to Reg Cook regularly and continued to do so while he was away in Egypt for three years. Six weeks later, on 25 July, Reg sent a postcard of Gibraltar, posted in Egypt.

'Dear Zillah. Spect you have heard all about this place. Am now somewhere in Egypt. Just landed. Am sorry I was unable to say 'Au revoir' but it has been a bit of a rush. It's gloriously romantic here except for the filth of the natives & the sun. Still I am quite happy, so is my brother… Yrs as ever. Reg'

Zillah was away for two weeks, returning for a dental appointment with Mr Archer in Hamlet Court Road, Westcliff, on the 17th.

ZACHARY PETTITT'S DEATH

Zillah's diary entries are intermittent in July or she might have recorded on the 8th the death of Zachary Pettitt. Oyster merchant, farmer and benefactor to Paglesham in many ways, Zachary had lived at Loftman's just in Canewdon for many years, but had been a major figure in Paglesham ever since his marriage to Alice Anne Browning in 1870.

His passing was greatly mourned and the press reported,

'By the wish of the deceased the coffin was borne from the house to Paglesham in a wagon drawn by a pair of his favourite horses, and dredgermen acted as bearers. Long before the hour for interment every blind in the village was

The Pettitt family. Alice Ann (far left) and Zachary (behind). Percy and Eva Hutley (2nd & 3rd from left). Hector (far right).

lowered [as a token of respect] *and most of the villagers attended the obsequies.'*
The bearers included Edgar Clarke, aged 62, George Fletcher, 50, Alfred Kemp, 59, Fred
Kemp, 57 and young George Popplewell, 30. His sons Hector and George were at their
father's funeral, but Arthur was serving in France and was unable to attend.

Apart from his work as Churchwarden in restoring the church in 1883 and in providing the
Mission Hall in 1894, Zachary had been Overseer for 40 years having resigned because of ill
health only 10 months earlier. He had been the first Chairman of Canewdon Parish Council
and one of the promoters of the Southend Conservative Association, and he was a Mason
with the Lodge of True Friendship in Rochford. He had built three pairs of cottages for his
men – at East End, Paglesham, at the Gore and at Loftman's Corner in Canewdon – each with
ZP and the date on their fronts.

Other hobbies included shooting. Sparrows and pigeons were considered as vermin, and
boys employed to scare them from crops in the fields. Sparrow shooting clubs were popular,
and in 1881 two teams had shot over 100 between them in a competition. Zachary was in one
team, and at a pigeon shooting match in Chelmsford he tied in the fifth round with a Mr
Phillips. Zachary won the shoot off with 9 birds in succession, Mr Phillips missing his nineth.
He was also elected President of the Rochford Hare Coursing Club and *'generously offered
the whole of his fine estate to the Club for coursing purposes.'* Times were different then.

In 1898 he had also been President of Rochford Bicycle Club, with his two of his sons, Hector
and George, as Vice Presidents. At the annual races on 21 September 1898, held in a meadow
near the board schools, George was named as Starter, but he also took part. Races were held
between 3 and 5.30 pm, with the Annual Dinner at 7 pm at the Old Ship Hotel. Tickets were
2/6 each. Prizes were presented at 9.30 pm. Paglesham had its own Cycling Club at the time.
Zachary also supported horse racing at The Lawns, Rochford, giving one of the cups.

Most notably, he had put in the two stained glass memorial windows in the church in 1883.

CHRISTENING

A highlight for Zillah was the christening of Vivienne, the daughter of Pet's brother Frank
Wiseman and his wife Hope, on 30 July 1916. They lived at Broomfield, having called their
home *Paglesham House*. The day before, Zillah and her mother had gone by train from
Rochford via Shenfield to Chelmsford, where they visited friends and where Zillah had her
photograph taken. *'Then we caught the motor bus for Broomfield,'* where they stayed for the
Saturday and Sunday nights with the Wisemans. The christening was in Broomfield church
on the Sunday afternoon. Some walked there, others of the family went in the trap. Zillah
noted that she *'held Baby for a long time'* and on the Monday, *'I held the baby until it was
bathed, which performance I watched. Then I helped Joan* [Vivienne's five year old sister
and in due course the mother of Margaret Pinkerton] *tidy her drawer and played with her till
dinner.'*

Returning to Rochford by train, *'we were surprised to see Aunt Florrie step out of the train
with Dad. However she had only travelled down with him & went on to Southend. Dad is not
at all well. A letter from Athel on our return.'*

53

On 2 August more wounded were entertained at The Chase. Pet went to help, but Zillah had to stay at home to get her father's tea. Pet said, *'The soldiers were an exceedingly nice lot,'* presumably because they appreciated the attention they received. On the fourth a service was held to mark the second anniversary of the start of the war.

FAMILY TRAGEDY

Bernard was clearly not himself. On the Sunday, Zillah recorded *'D felt depressed all day'* and on the Monday, *'Dad did not know how late it was, so did not get up till after dinner.'* A fortnight later, on Sunday 20 August, *'We did not go to Church in the morning. ... Dad did not get up, but his foot is not so swollen. ... M took up Dad's tea just in time to see him drink some brandy & collapse on the bed. She gave him ether.'* There are few entries in Zillah's diary after this.

While Bernard was so ill, straw had been put down on the lane outside the cottages to deaden the sound of horses' hooves and wheels. Bernard died on Friday 1 September 1916, but Zillah, not surprisingly, did not record anything for over a month. The burial register shows that he was cremated at Little Ilford on 6th September. The ashes were interred on the south side of Paglesham church next to the remains of his grandparents, George and Grace Gibbs Harris, and those of Elizabeth Harris. Bernard's memorial reads,
> *'Here lie the ashes of Edward Bernard Harris, who died 1st Sept. 1916, Aged 52 years. I believe in the resurrection of the body and the life everlasting.'*

After Bernard's death, H M Hospital Ship *Galeka* returned to England in 1916 and then went to pick up medical staff from Le Havre. While waiting to enter, she struck a mine and sank. Her Captain, Commander Bernard Bush, who had been a great friend to Bernard, was lost along with 18 others.

The few remaining entries in the diary tell us that on Monday 9 October, Zillah and Pet returned *'home after staying a week at Hornsey and a week at Broomfield.'* On Sunday 15 October, *'Found an official postcard on our return from Church to say Athel is wounded'.* This must have been a dreadful shock, coming so soon after her father's death. On 8 November, *'Went to London having had a lift to Rochford from the Rectory. Saw Athel at the Hospital, then went to Mrs Stone's arriving in time for supper.'* This must have been some relief, but there is no mention of how badly Athelstan was injured!

On 21 November, Zillah briefly states, *'The East Surrey left this morning and Lowland Scottish Cyclists have taken their place.'*
Sunday 3 December, 'saw a Lowland Cyclist ... asked him to call for the cake. He came after dinner & seeing he was prepared for a chat on the slip invited him in as the neighbours were about. He was very chatty & stayed 1½ hrs. At 4.45 another came for him so he had to go.'
Mon 11: *'M had a card from Peter McLean from Greenock'.* On Thursday 14th, *'P McLean [came] to ask for a piece of rag to prevent his sock from touching a burn. He stayed & talked for some time & then M came in.'* The next day *'P Mclean came up to say he is going to Wickford for Medical Inspection & will not be able to come to tea on Sunday'.* Zillah certainly attracted the soldiers, and she may have appreciated the male company, particularly as Reg was so far away!

A final entry, on 28 December 1916 makes one realise that her thoughts were on the wider scene, where Athelstan had been, and where Reg Cook was still.

> '*As Napoleon wrote (1797), "The time is not far distant when we shall feel that truly to destroy England we must take possession of Egypt". '*

ATHELSTAN RIFLEMAN

Having signed on in September 1914 and been posted to Gibraltar the following February, Athelstan was moved to Egypt after six months, having had an interesting and relatively quiet time so far. '*At Sea*', he wrote on a postcard of Malta harbour to Zillah on 28 August 1915 but said '*Mustn't tell you any news as it will be censored*'. The card was passed by the censor, '*Capt Kingston Sennett, 2/7 Middx Rgt. ',* and posted at the '*Base Army Post Office Y'* two days later.

Postcards of the Sphinx, from '*Cairo, '* were sent on 23 September and 3 October, a week or two prior to his being wounded, but said little because of censorship rules. The injury cannot have been life-threatening, although serious enough for him to be shipped home – a 'Blighty one', as they were called. However, he was frequently unwell after the war, and unfit for further service in 1939.

Athelstan wrote a week before Christmas 1916 from his hospital at Brentford that he wouldn't be home for the festival. He hoped to be home on '*the Thursday after Xmas ... I shall travel with a "pass". We went to a Concert last night in aid of Serbia.'*

Having recovered from his injury, he was posted to Dawlish, Devon, at the beginning of 1917 with G Coy, 3rd London Rifle Brigade, and billeted at 12 Landsdowne Place. On 10 January, he told his mother, staying at 21 Harvey Road, Tottenham Lane, Hornsey, that '*Several of the old 2/7th M'x here. '* On 5 February he asked his Aunt Frances,

> '*if she would mind sending down the money out of my box, as I should like to get Zillah something for her 21st Birthday, and I cannot afford it out of my pay as 3/6 goes for suppers & washing. '*

He expected to be home on leave on the 23 March, having recently seen some of his Harris relatives in Exeter. A month later he thanks his aunt for a parcel and clothes he had received, tells her that he had been to a good Battalion concert, and anticipates that he would be moving on. On 27 April, nine days later, he writes a card to her,

> '*304211 S Section. 3rd LRB, Blackdown Camp, Aisne Bcks, Nr. Farnborough. ... Not a bad camp where we are, but give me good old Dawlish again. I may have a chance to go over to my old billet at Egham shortly & perhaps to Reigate. '*

The barracks were back in the heart of the military establishment, but it sounds as if he had learnt how to live with Army rules.

ATHELSTAN RADIO OPERATOR

In December 1917, Athelstan transferred to the Royal Flying Corps as '*A/C2 Harris'* having taken a Wireless Telegraphy course at Farnborough from August to December 1917. The Royal Air Force was created from the RFC and the Royal Naval Air Service on 1 April 1918 and Athelstan was posted with the RAF to France only a month after the start of the final German offensive. He was sent his mother's photograph on 8 August and carried it with him,

'Mrs M B Harris, Next of Kin'.

Peace post-card, 1918.

labelled *'Next of Kin'*. He also wrote on the back *'402830 AM, B A Harris, Wireless Operator DA HqS, 47 Div, France.'* August 8th was the day the Allied counterattack began, stiffened with the first American troops. Athelstan's activities were not recorded, but he brought back a trench map of Albert, which suggests he might have been in that part of the front.

The Armistice on 11 November goes unrecorded in the family papers, but the church service book notes the signing, with a *'Thanksgiving for Armistice'* service on 17 November. At the end of the year there were *'memorial services for the fallen'* on 29 December. On Sunday, 23 March 1919 there was a service at 3 pm when the *'Memorial to Dead & Living was unveiled by Col Smeaton GB.'*

1919 is notorious for the influenza epidemic which killed more people worldwide than the war had. It had been preceded by a note in the church service book on 1 December 1918, *'Epidemic of Influenza.'* But 1919 also saw a near major revolt by the soldiers still on active service in France. In January 1919, two months after the Armistice, Athel was at Abscon, near Valenciennes and the Belgian border. He came across Harry Brown, who had lived at Paglesham House, who *'saw the riots at Harfleur, in fact took part in them.'* Harry was then at *'Marchiennes, about 10 kilos from here.'* Athelstan began the letter to his mother,

> ' ...ever so many thanks, also, for the lovely parcel received a few days back. The cakes were lovely, and the big cake was quite all right this time and not heavy at all like the last one. The Jelly I made this time as I was in the cookhouse and so could easily get the water. Your letter also enclosed I found. At the same time I received a parcel from A Frances, consisting of a tin of biscuits, café au lait, cocoa, milk, candles, Oxo. The following day at 10pm I was told to pack up my kit etc, as I was going back to the Squadron, the usual occurrence moving if I ever receive a parcel, and things had to be gobbled up somewhat as they would take up too much room and be weighty. Still I, and the cooks, enjoyed them very much. Of course only one person set eyes on the little pudding, and that was not for long.'

Athel was moved to '*1/ A.S.D RAF,*' between Calais and Boulogne, to a windswept site and into

'*a fairly big hut, which was conspicuous for the holes in it, and which had ice on the floor, where it came from I do not know. There was not even a stove in the place, and the snow was thick outside. … They are only asking for riots to take place.*'

42 Squadron was returned to England later that month, and Athel was demobilised and transferred to the Air Force Reserve on 29 March 1919 after four years, six months and 18 days' service. He received £26 10s War Gratuity, and 28 days '*furlough pay @ 2/3 - £3 3s. and 28 days ration allowance*', making a total of £32 11s 4d. He had had a '*plain clothes allowance*' but was charged £1 for an overcoat! 42 Squadron RAF was disbanded in April.

The Peace Treaty was finally signed on 29 June 1919.

War Memorial in St Peter's Church, Paglesham.

12 BETWEEN THE WARS

REMOVAL

The Harrises' cottage, *Waterside* in Shop Row, was quite small and must have been very restrictive when Athel was at home. Within a year of his return in 1919, they moved to a larger but older one at 2 The Chaseway. Three cottages had been built about 1620, according to the date over one door, beside the track to the river, but since the three Rows had been erected by J F T Wiseman, the track had become the approach to The Chase. The present Waterside Lane became the new river access. Number 2 consisted of two of the three cottages, giving much more room for the Harrises. They rented it from the Nicholls family, who still owned much of East End, at £3 19s 3d a quarter.

The ground floor consisted of a living room, parlour and kitchen. Up the stairs (two sets) there were four good-sized bedrooms. The wash-house and w.c. were still outside, and there was still no water supply, but there was a well in the front of number 1. They had a much larger secluded garden than in Shop Row, with walls on the east and south to The Chase and with fruit trees in it.

Whether Zillah and her mother's interest in history, and the family's history, was the result of living in this older house is not known, but she kept a sketch of the old house which had been alongside until JFTW's expansion of The Chase and the reordering of its drive.

ALICE PETTITT and HECTOR

Soon after Zachary Pettitt's death in 1916, and with three of her children in the services, Alice moved back to Cupola House, while Percy Hutley and Eva went to live at Loftman's in Canewdon. Loftman's was a much more spacious place for their family, with 80 acres of grounds. There was a tennis court, and the large hall with its organ on a gallery saw many parties. Zachary had given his grandchildren a boat to row on the large lake there. Alice at Cupola House must have felt like coming home after 30 years. Fortunately, all her three children survived the war. A brief newspaper cutting tells us,

> *'George went into the 9th Essex, but unfortunately broke his leg, and is now for home service only'. Arthur is in the Mechanical Transport, ASC. Hector, the eldest belongs to the 'Artists,' and is in training at Richmond; he served for three years in the same Corps some time ago.'*

Hector Pettitt came back as *'Lt (Retired) 10th London Regiment'* and went to live with his mother at Cupola House. By then he was nearly 50. Some 40 years later, when Rosemary's parents were living in the house, the authors investigated a small half-hidden cupboard in the cellar and pulled out various catalogues which give us an insight into Hector's interests at the time. [8]

Hector clearly wanted to improve the lighting in the house where oil lamps were the norm, and wrote to *'The Dargue Acetylene Gas Co. Ltd, Newcastle on Tyne.'* He was also interested in office equipment and received booklets from *'H J Ryman Ltd'* of London in

---

[8] (There were also two diaries of 1845 and 1846, written by Ann Patience Browning before the birth of her only daughter, Alice, - part of the *'Paglesham Natives'* story - and a scrapbook of Victorian newspaper cuttings.)

1920 and from '*Libraco Ltd, of 62 Cannon St., London*' with a letter describing their '*Portable Bookcase*' and '*Portable Shelving.*' N M Rutherstein of Northampton sent him details of '*Reliable Footwear also Hosiery, Clothing, etc. Direct from the Manufacturer,*' while Barbour (still trading today) offered their range of clothing.

Most of the catalogues were for gardening, which was to become Hector's passion for the next ten years. Between 1919 and 1926, many well known firms sent their catalogues. Carter's of Raynes Park, Bees of Liverpool and Rowntree Bros of St Albans were all received over the years. Another firm, Cants Roses of Colchester, is still in business.

The one nursery local to Hector, which he might have visited, was Lant's at '*The Aviaries, 31 Southchurch Road, Southend-on-Sea.*' Mr Lant himself lived at 11 Tyrell Drive. He sold a large variety of seeds, many at 2d a packet or 6d per ounce. He also advertised that he '*had Aviaries of Foreign Birds for Sale, Puppies, Rabbits, Tortoises, Monkeys etc.*'

Hector must have made a lovely garden. Receipts show that he bought plants for the herbaceous border, which was backed by an old red-brick wall, roses for the rose garden by the side of the house and fruit trees for the walled kitchen garden.

Alice liked to sit in the front bedroom to do her needlework and watch people go by. She died in 1929. Appropriately, as Zachary had done so much for the village, a beautiful window was installed '*by their sons and daughter*' in the chancel of the church,
> '*To the Glory of God and in loving memory of Zachary Pettitt Born 27th July 1838 Died 8th July 1916, and of Alice Anne his wife. Born 18th January 1845. Died 20th February 1929.*'

Cupola House herbaceous border.

They are buried together beside their children, on the south side of the chancel, with the added inscription,
> '*To live in hearts we leave behind is not to die.*'

Percy and Eva Hutley sold Loftman's in 1927 and went to live at North Shoebury House, the Georgian-fronted Hutley family home, but they came to Cupola House two years later when Eva's mother died.

Hector became a monk for some years, possibly in Germany, but returned in 1935 to stay for some weeks at Cupola House. Some of his plants, trees, and roses particularly, were still thriving in the 1940s and '50s. He died at Walsingham, the place of pilgrimage in Norfolk.

Loftman's was destroyed by fire in October 1932 and not rebuilt. It was then owned by the Phelps family. Vera Woodward, daughter of the then Canewdon vicar then, recalled in 1990,
> '*I remember her* [Mrs Phelps] *waking us at midnight, "Mrs Woodward, Loftman's is blazing." They stayed with us for several months, & then moved.*'

The Phelps had heard explosions from the gun room and had discovered the house already well alight. Mr Phelps climbed down knotted sheets and then returned with a long ladder to help his wife and child escape.

CHANGE OF RECTOR

Rev William Fraser and his family left Paglesham in 1921 after 16 popular years. A *'Farewell Presentation'* was made to them at the school, which had been *'tastefully decorated by Miss Peacock, the headmistress. ... A plated tray, an umbrella stand & a handsome cushion and wool rug worked by the scholars was presented.'*

The new Rector was Rev Courtney B Jennings. He was inducted on 13 January 1922. He came with his wife, two sons and two daughters. In the late 1960s, the elder daughter, Ada, recalled her memories of their arrival.

> *'It must have been a very different place in 1922 when we first went there than now. Then it was indeed truly rural, quite at the back of beyond – very, very quiet even for the country. All the people, either at work on the land or fisherfolk at East End. A bus just twice a week* [run by Westcliff Motor Services]. *'*

The benefices of Canewdon and Paglesham were united in 1923, but the two parishes retained their separate incumbents until Rev Jennings left in 1946. He had been a familiar sight with his bushy white beard, riding his bicycle. He also kept a donkey and cart. His long sermons, commented on by Zillah, were also remembered. The vicar of Canewdon, Rev Woodward, who lived in the Georgian vicarage beside his church, retired at the same time and Rev Arthur Harriss (no relation of Zillah) moved from Stambridge to Canewdon Vicarage and looked after both parishes from there.

Paglesham Rectory was sold to Mr and Mrs John Burrows, the owner of the Southend Standard, who renamed it 'Ingulfs' after the Saxon thegn who had given the church to Westminster Abbey prior to fighting for King Harold in 1066. After the Second World War, it was bought by Mr and Mrs Judge, who ran an equestrian centre there. The rotunda used as a riding school came from the Kursaal Amusement Park in Southend

POSTWAR BLUES

Neither Athelstan nor Reg Cook found it easy to settle down after the war, a response typical of soldiers returning from war service after a period of widened experience, often traumatic.

Reg was still in Egypt in April 1919, having been out there for almost three years. He was still writing letters to Zillah, her mother and Athelstan in turn, and looking forward to getting home – *'Oh to be in Blighty, now that April's there'*, he wrote to *'Mrs Harris'* on 13 April. Having heard that Athel was demobbed and interested in engineering, he sent a letter of introduction to his old firm in London for him in a letter to Zillah. He sounds philosophical about staying in Cairo a little longer.

> *'The lives of other Europeans here depend on our presence in this sun-dried place & for this reason we shall not grumble at a few extra weeks after 3 years out here already.*

Despite this attitude, he found little to keep him at home once he had been demobbed. A year later, he replied to another letter from Mrs Harris, while in Tampico, Mexico.

25 May 1920. 'Essex for me will always be the home of my happiest recollections, however much I may roam over the world ... I have been here 6 months & dislike the place. ... I came here full of aspirations, to "make good," but have not found the right berth for my enthusiasms.'

He was about to come home, but had '*practically accepted ... a good post in Yokohama*' at the end of the year. He expected to have six months training in London, living in Hornsey with his brother Billy, who had been with him during much of his army career. He ends by being '*sorry to hear Athel not happily settled to his new job.*'

Frustratingly, that is the last heard of him.

FRED AND ARTHUR RETIRE

The Wiseman family had been in the oyster business for over 150 years when the brothers, Fred and Arthur decided to retire in 1924. Fred was 66 and Arthur 64. Business had been declining, and there had been a '*death*' in the oysters in 1921, which had set them back further from the hard but profitable days of the nineteenth century.

They were still in debt to Percy and Minnie, and so they put Buckland House and Redcroft up for sale. It must have been an emotional time for the whole family. Buckland House had been the family home since 1784, when James and Susannah Wiseman – Fred, Arthur, Minnie and Pet's great-grandparents – started their married life there. It had been enlarged in 1854 and was too big for Fred and Minnie. Fred went to live with Pet and Zillah; Minnie rented the coachman's cottage from The Chase which she called 'The Cot.'

The Cot (right) and The Chase Stables, 1953.

Arthur received an '*illuminated*' testimonial which beautifully summarises his life,

> '*We, the undermentioned members of Paglesham, desire to record our feelings of regret at your removal from our midst, and your lifelong home.*
>
> '*Your manner of life, in your going in and out amongst us, will ever be cherished by us, for your kindness of heart and unselfishness of character, and your readiness to lend a helping hand.*
>
> '*Your work in respect of the Church you so much love, as Organist for over 35 years, Churchwarden for 25 years, Superintendent and Teacher of the East End Sunday School and the Monthly Services there, together with your licensed Lay readership of the Parish, has been much appreciated by those who have come under your care and influence so ungrudgingly given.*

Arthur Wiseman at Redcroft.

'We ask you to receive these accompanying presents, and trust Our Heavenly Father's blessing will ever attend you and Mrs Wiseman and your family in your new home. March 24th 1924.'

Almost 150 names follow testifying to the effect he had had in Paglesham.

Mrs Anfilogoff and baby Alexander (*Sasha*), and Redcroft staff. Nurse and Housekeeper, with Housemaid standing, 1933.

All the Redcroft children had grown up and Arthur and Tottie went to live in Bury St Edmunds. Redcroft was bought in January 1926 by a Miss Mary Robson, who sold it in 1930 to Mr and Mrs Anfilogoff. He was a director of London and Coastal Wharves Ltd, and was responsible for their construction of public oil storage on Canvey Island. Mrs Anfilogoff took an interest in the village and in 1933 became the first President of the WI, soon after the birth of their son, Sasha (Alexander).

Walter Keeble, who was landlord of the Punch Bowl, and his sons, Hubert and Alf, took over some of the oyster business, which recovered somewhat in the late 1920s, but it was, however, never on as great a scale as it had been and suffered a further series of setbacks over the years. Walter was one of seven children who produced 35 in the next generation. Between them they married into many of the other families in Paglesham.

FARMING

Farming had had a bad time at the end of the Victorian era. Some land in Canewdon and elsewhere had been allowed to grow derelict, and other fields were sold off for plotland

Wedding of George Keeble (3rd son of Walter) and Annie Rawlings. Group outside the Punch Bowl, 24 January 1931.

development in the new century. Paglesham had better soil and so survived that difficult time. The 1920s and 1930s saw another depression, which, with the decline in the oyster industry, resulted in harder times in the village as they employed much of the labour force. Apart from the bailiffs, stockmen and '*agricultural labourers*', women were employed at harvest time at jobs like potato picking.

The biggest farms remained those based on the original four manors – Church, West, East and South Halls.

South Hall had long absorbed the twelve acre holding of Stannetts and was farmed by the Davis family. It was sold at Michaelmas, 1925, to George Perry by '*the executors of the late Mrs C D Davis.*' The sale catalogue showed that at that time the farm had '*13 Horses and Colts, 85 Head of Cattle, ... 220 Head of Swine, and 280 head of poultry*' as well as running to

550 acres. The horses and '*milch cows*' were all individually named. The number of horses indicates the big requirement for ploughing, sowing and harvesting, although the dairy round accounted for the '*Milk Cob.*' No fewer than 12 ploughs were for sale – seven of them from Bentall's of Heybridge (though some of these were probably old, discarded ones) plus a '*Maldon Ironworks potato plough*' and an '*iron sub-soil plough.*' There were horse hoes, harrows, a ring roll, cultivators, seed

South Hall or Paglesham House.

drills, mowing machines for the hay, and reaping machines for the cereals . There were eight '*tumbrils,*' two '*Iron arm road wagons*' and three harvest wagons. There was also a '*set of Sea Walling equipment*' as farmers were expected to look after their walls.

The cows were mainly shorthorns, with some '*Dutch*' and two Guernseys for their cream. Only the pigs were anonymous, not even given a breed. To round off a picture of a fairly typical mixed farm of the time were the stacks of wheat, barley and oat straw and of hay, mainly in the yard, but with stacks in the meadows where the hay had been made.

George Perry arrived from Cornwall in 1925 with his wife and two daughters and brought the Devon breed of cattle with him for fattening. The animals arrived at Rochford station and were driven along the road to Paglesham. Peter Whittingham helped with this at the age of about 13. In 1992 he recalled the cattle drive.

> '*The word would go round that Mr George Perry was having some Devon Curly steers sent up from his brother in Devon by the iron road. That was Mr Perry's definition of the railway. This train comprised of six large cattle trucks holding twenty steers in each truck and a guard's van. ... a London & North Eastern engine brought these trucks to Rochford railway station to be unloaded, fed and watered ready to be driven to Paglesham marshes.*
>
> *These trucks would be unloaded in the early hours on Saturday morning and I, with several other boys, would report to Mr Perry and he would give us strict orders of what we had to do, run ahead of the herd and make sure all the gates were closed and be at the road junctions to ward them off. There were three or four drovers, K T Marven, Wacker Arbin, Bob English and Mr Vic Cardy, Mr Perry's herdsman, and their dogs and about ten or fifteen boys.*
>
> *As we came back from the marshes Mrs Perry would be at the gate with her maid, handing each one of us a cheese roll and a glass of home-made ginger beer, and Mr Perry would go round to each boy and give him a sixpenny piece. After being refreshed we would prepare ourselves for a five and a half mile walk back to Rochford.*'

Mr Perry continued the dairy and sold milk from '*South Hall Dairies*' round the village. Tom Keeble and Vic Cardy were both photographed with the delivery tricycle which survived in the village for over fifty years after these first days.

Brian Fletcher, who worked on the farm after the war, retiring as one of the two foremen in

Tom Wood with the South Hall milk delivery tricycle.

West Hall Dairy's milk float.

East Hall, c1910.

2008, also wrote in 1992 about the farm in the Mr Perry's time (1925 to about 1965).

'There were 10 full time men + two casuals employed which included a foreman, 2 cowmen & a milkman, looking after approx 400 acres mainly of grass meadows which were used for fattening Bullocks and Sheep, plus feed for the Dairy Herd of about 20 milkers.

There were about 100 acres of Wheat, Barley and Oats, plus 8 acres of potatoes & 8 acres of Sugar Beet grown each year. All ditching, cleaning of sugar beet plus carting of all crops was done by hand.

Threshing of stacks, riddling potatoes and cleaning out of cattle yards, again were all done by hand, in the winter months.

The only chemical used up to about 1950 was DDT–coated bags pulled over the sugar beet to kill black fly etc.

The Milk Round served both East End and Church End seven days a week. Milk was also collected by Howard Dairies of Southend in churns.

Wheat yield in 1930 was approx 1 ton per acre, in 1960 approx 1 ton 30 cwt.'

Tonnages now would be double that, with increased use of fertiliser.

Mr Meeson, who had been at Church Hall there since at least 1891, died and in 1924 the farm, with East Hall and Clements, both of which he also owned, were sold to A D Martin. Mrs Meeson continued to live at Church Hall until her own death over 30 years later, while 'Rawty' Martin lived in the old timber-framed East Hall with his housekeeper, Miss Murdoch. Clements was a smaller farm along the East Hall lane, later shown as 'North House' on maps. The wooden house was set back from the lane and lived in by two families, with two more cottages at the roadside. The 200 acre Clements Marsh was once part of Hockley, and like other fields by the seawalls was grazed by cattle and sheep.

Church Hall, 475 acres, and East Hall, 471 acres, were again on the market in 1933, but Rawty Martin failed to sell them. They were described as '*good for growing potatoes and market gardening.*' There was a wharf on each farm, '*suitable for barges.*'

West Hall continued to be farmed by Percy Hutley from Loftman's with his bailiff in the Hall. They too had milking cows and ran Paglesham Dairies. The 20 acres at Finches on the way to Church End (now Finches and Maules), once owned by the Wisemans and Quys, were farmed by George Hymas. He sold the farm in the 1930s to Mr Bilham, who sold it to John Smith, who farmed it during the Second World War.

LUNTS FARM

The 30 acres that went with Cupola House were owned by the Hutleys, but from Michaelmas, 29 September 1929, they were tenanted by Alan H Boardman, Rosemary's father, then just 22 years old.

Alan was not from a farming background. In 1870, his grandfather, Clement, had founded the department store, Boardmans of Stratford, which became known as the Harrods of the East End of London. Born in 1907, Alan became a pupil of Hugh Hutley at Sutton Hall, at a time when parents had to pay for pupil experience. He then went to the East Anglia Institute of Agriculture in King Edward Avenue, Chelmsford, from 1926 to 1928. This moved to a new site and became Writtle Agricultural College, which is now affiliated to the University of Essex. He also went to Canada for experience and became very interested in farm mechanisation.

After this he worked at Hampton Barns, Great Stambridge, and while working there heard about Lunts Farm. The middle of a countrywide depression was a bad time to be starting out in farming, but he was determined to go in for market gardening, and also kept pigs. He had good land for the purpose and by 1933 he was doing well enough to have a lorry and his own wholesale shop at 53, West Road, Southend-on-Sea.

He was featured in *Town and Country News* on 13 January 1933. The article pointed out that '*if there is one bright spot ... it is perhaps Market*

Alan Boardman's shop in West Road, Southend.

Gardening.'

> *'Corn growing is certainly not* [a paying proposition], *while with livestock ... one is faced with the prospect of having to sell at a loss to obtain ready money, or keep laying out capital and "holding on, in hopes".'*

It gave his *'wide range of produce'* as including

> *'beans, peas, late spinach, lettuce, parsley, cabbages, Brussels sprouts, cauliflowers, among other items, while in the flower department, tulips and anemones were a speciality. The outdoor tomato crop (7000 plants) was exceptionally successful last year owing to fine weather and favourable prices. The previous year's crop was a total failure owing to disease.'* [Probably blight.]

He also bought in other growers' produce to meet demand when necessary.

> *'His greatest difficulty is getting really expert labour ... despite the fact we have millions unemployed.'*

He also grew and sold potatoes, something he was still doing thirty years later.

In 1938 he expanded his rented acreage by taking a tenancy of the land which belonged to Mr Nicholls around The Chase. This surrounded East End, and linked to that at Lunts. It also included the farm buildings which JFTW had put up in the 1870s and stables with a horseman's cottage. He later took on the twenty acres at Finches and Maules, rented from John Smith.

DOGS, CATS and NATURE

Zillah had been fascinated by animals and birds since her early visits to her 'Granny Wise' in Woodham Walter and holidays at Paglesham and West Mersea. Both she and her mother were interested in all nature. She mentions hearing the first cuckoo in April and the swallows returning. She did not like animals or insects to be killed and cannot have been happy to note on 12 May, the first legal day, *'Rook shooting – first of the season.'* There was a large rookery and heronry at The Chase farm buildings, and the rooks were felt to do a great deal of damage when corn had been sown. She sowed candytuft in the cracks of the brick path. Her mother wrote a letter to her MP to get him to support a *'Protection of Animals'* Bill in Parliament. Zillah even puts down that she caught 109 slugs in one day – one wonders what she did with them!

They acquired a sandy kitten in 1935, and there are numerous entries about its health in her diary. A pet dog, Pal, also features frequently, with walks such as on

Wednesday 24 July. *'We went down Waterside & round wall to Pool and back. The wall sides were dotted with courting couples – early closing day* [in Rochford] *I suppose.'*

In the autumn Zillah describes walking near Clements Farm where she *'filled a carrier bag with mushrooms'* which were plentiful on the marshes.

Exceptional weather is also noted as on 17 May 1935, *'Ice as thick as a penny in wash bowl this morning.'* That was in her bedroom. Papers the following day *'full of abnormal frost on night of 16/17. Tremendous damage to potatoes, fruit, etc, everywhere. Such frost is unknown in living memory.'* Rosemary's father always said that frost could be expected up to 18 May, and it must have been a worrying time for him.

Whether Athel had taken up Reg's earlier letter of introduction we do not know, but ten years later he too was still unsettled. For much of the 1930s, Athelstan was in Australia, also suffering the world-wide depression. His cards home, some of which survive, indicate that he enjoyed the heat, was *'puddling about'* with radio sets, collecting stamps for *'Uncle Fred'* (including in April 1932, *'Bridge stamps'* – the new Sydney Harbour Bridge had just been opened in March), and seeing people presumably of common interest.

He was in Hobart, Tasmania in 1931 (where he had *'a one valve set now, & have raked in 26 stations including Perth & Wellington, NZ'*), in Goulburn, near Canberra in April 1932, and then in Sydney from November for 16 months. One wonders what he did to bring in an income. He takes short flying trips and attended *'an Aerial Pageant at Mascot, about four miles out. It would probably be tame compared with Hendon* [then London's aerodrome] *but I enjoyed it.'* This may have been when he met some of his Australian cousins. He sent an aerial picture of Sydney Harbour Bridge in 1933; the southern approaches necessitated the demolition of the house in Prince Street which his grandfather's elder brother had lived in until his death in 1873, sixty years earlier.[9]

Athelstan went on to Coogee on the coast south of Sydney in March 1934, by bicycle, *'but the luggage nearly made it buck, so I am having a front carrier put on'*! He was probably carrying some wireless sets as he proposed *'to leave them behind pro tem & make up a crystal set.'* He then headed for Moruya, 200 miles (320km) further south, *'on a new adventure'* with a prospector's licence, trying to make some money gold mining. He was *'back again at the shack, after just the week in Hospital'* in June – had he had an accident, or had he been ill? But he *'had a nice! walk of about 23 miles after leaving hospital to get back here.'* Athel is not as consistent as his father had been about giving his address! He was back in Sydney by August.

Athel returned home from Perth on 15 June 1936, sailing via
'Colombo, then Suez, Port Said, Malta, Plymouth, & then Tilbury. Due about 16 July I believe, so see you at the wharf.' He was *'looking forward to seeing you & Z again.'*
If they thought that he might have travel out of his system, they were wrong.

He wrote to his aunt Minnie from Sydney again on 2 November 1938,
'Just a line to let you know I still AM in the land of the living.'
He sounds as though he had found life tough.
'I suppose things will look up a bit some day ... Judging by the paper a few days ago, we are as good as back to normal times, at least before the "depression." But it certainly makes one wonder when looking around.'
He came home again just before the Second World War started.

VILLAGE CHANGES

The twentieth century had already seen changes to people's way of life and attitudes. The motor car had arrived before the Great War. The war itself changed people whether on active service or at home. Horizons were broadened. Women began to exert their rights.

---

[9] Charles Wiseman settled in Sydney in 1840 as a paddle-steamer captain. See *'Paglesham Natives'*.

Education had been made compulsory up to the age of 14.

Paglesham was not immune to change, although hardly in the forefront, and the 1930s saw various improvements to life. Zillah was very family orientated and both friendly with and concerned about the other villagers. However, without Arthur Wiseman's family at Redcroft, and with Uncle Fred living with them, visiting family in Paglesham was limited to seeing Aunt Minnie.

The start of the Women's Institute (WI) in March 1933 widened people's contacts, with its intention '*to improve and develop conditions of rural life by providing opportunities for educational and social intercourse and activities.*' Not surprisingly it was immediately embraced by Zillah and her aunt, although Pet was never a member. Meetings were held in the Mission Room and presided over by Mrs Anfilogoff, of Redcroft, with a committee of eight. They had to overcome several difficulties, one of which was the lack of electricity in Paglesham and no means of heating. So one member brought the coffee over from Church End in a can, by bicycle! Fundraising started with a rummage sale and in July, a '*Fete and Sale of Work*' was held at Redcroft.

This was a major event, raising £48, with a marquee on the lawn, gymkhana performances, dancing displays, and lots of stalls. WI membership cost two shillings which could be paid in two instalments. (It was £10.50 in 1993 and £28 in 2009!) Zillah was Secretary and organised a coach outing to Brighton in 1934. This left at 7 am and got back at 11 pm! She also enjoyed making things for the monthly competitions.

WI outing to Brighton, July 1934.

A Men's Club had started in the 1920s, with billiards, darts and cards in the Mission Room, and outings as well, and the WI were at first not too welcome when they also started to use the corrugated iron building, then 40 years old. It was barer then and bore little resemblance to the cosy room of today. A wooden floor and stage, a cubby-hole beside that for storage, and heating from a large round stove opposite the door, contrasts with the present carpeting, extensive cupboards, curtains, electric light and heating, running water and even an indoor loo!

Zillah also widened her involvement with the community by starting a library in their house, open every Saturday for three hours. A van came every three months to renew her stock, with two or three readers asked to choose the new books. It was in a cupboard under the stairs, with the book ticket tucked into a holder for each borrower, a system still used 37 years later when she finally closed.

Another change begun in the 1920s was the advent of wireless to the village. Reading books had been Zillah's pastime previously. Her diaries from 1933 show that she continued to read, but she now also enjoyed listening to the wireless, to the news, to talks, music and generally *'listening in.'* They bought their first one in 1925 for £3 11s 6d and had a new one in 1934. As there was no mains electricity, the wireless sets were powered by glass accumulators, which had to be recharged regularly. For many years this was done by Mr Watkins who lived in Boarded Row, who after the Second World War had the first television in the village.

Telephones were also being acquired, although there were few in Paglesham. The Plough and Sail had one, which was used by the village in emergencies, both for incoming and outgoing calls. Zillah recorded on 13 July 1935, *'Telephone laid on today at 1 Boarded Row.'* Alan Boardman had one for his market gardening business. There was a manual exchange at Rochford at first, and then Canewdon had one to cover Paglesham as well. In 1938 this exchange had only 44 subscribers! Alan Boardman's number was Canewdon 239. The exchange became automatic for local calls after the war in 1945 and Subscriber Trunk Dialling was introduced in 1970.

OUT AND ABOUT

The No 10 motor bus service had started in the 1920s, enabling easier access to Rochford and Southend for everyone. The early buses were quite small. Running between Southend and the Plough and Sail, they also went round to Church End. Despite the fare of 1s 6d, the service was popular and they sometimes had to run several journeys so that people were not left behind. The driver before the war was Stan Galpin who recalled that the bus did not have a windscreen wiper, so he rubbed a cut potato on the screen to help shed the rain.

No 10 bus. With the driver are (l to r) Vin Wood, George Fletcher, Lol Bradley and Vernon Mills.

The Harrises certainly made use of the bus and enjoyed going into Southend to shop, or make an appointment. They would then have lunch or see a film. If they had to wait for the bus back, they might walk along the cliffs, or go into the library. They also used it to go into Rochford, or sometimes round to Church End.

On 16 June 1934, Zillah and her mother went on holiday to Rievaulx Abbey, Scarborough and Knaresborough and back through Castleton in Derbyshire and Kenilworth. Their week's Glenton tour cost eight guineas. Her diary is blank except for the cost of entries, snacks and guides.

In September 1935 they stayed at the Osbourne Hotel in London before going up to Liverpool by train and catching the *Mona's Queen* to the Isle of Man for a week.

DROUGHT

The weather is naturally a cause of comment, although Zillah does not record it every day as her grandfather had. There was a drought in June 1934 and Zillah commented, *'The drought is serious in many parts of the world besides England.'* Despite welcome rain in July, *'almost tropical in some parts,'* there was still not enough. *'15 inches is needed to fill springs etc.'* Mains water was not laid on until 1949.

Village pump, Waterside Lane, before new pump, c1933.

There was a pump in Waterside Lane opposite Brick Row. Zillah recorded on that a new village pump had been installed,

Saturday 26 May 1934. 'Several weeks [ago]*, a small one with a wheel. Alfred Kemp goes down twice a day to unlock it & pump water for everyone so that none is wasted.'*

It was rationed to two buckets a day. The well at Buckland House

'is practically dry only 2 feet of water in it, so they are digging a new well in a little lawn having had a water diviner to locate water.'

Another service generally taken for granted was the subject of a meeting in the Mission Room in November 1934,

'to discuss how we empty our lavatories now that [the] *Col has given up. Mr Martin* [East Hall] *was there & it will be done for us but each house will have to pay abt 6/-.'*

This was not to be done by a proper sewerage system until 1969, and then only as far as Cupola House for East End, when a sewage works was installed near the boatyard.

ROMANCE – ALAN BOARDMAN

At the end of April 1935, Alan Boardman went to Holland to see the bulbfields. There he met a girl from New Zealand who was making a world tour. Phyllis Oldbury Jones had been left some money by an uncle and, like many 'Down Under' decided to travel and see the *'home country'*. It was a whirlwind romance.

King George V celebrated his Silver Jubilee in May.

Monday 6 May 1935. 'Listened to Silver Jubilee Thanksgiving service at St Paul's ... Hurried to catch the 1.45 bus for the Bowl Meadow Jubilee Celebrations. Started with a thanksgiving out door service at 2.15. Then sports, Children's tea, ditto Adults. More sports & entertainment at intervals ... Mrs Meeson presented mugs to the Children.... Got home for the King's Speech.'

Zillah spent the rest of the day spring cleaning the china pantry!

On Tuesday 9 July, *'Mrs Riley told us Mr Boardman was marrying by special licence to a NZ lady.'* It sounds as though Alan had kept quite quiet about it. They were married at St Marylebone Church, near his parents' flat in London. After their short honeymoon on the 12th (also noted in Zillah's diary), they returned to live at 1 Boarded Row. It must have been quite a culture shock for Phyllis after living in Wellington with all the modern conveniences of a city of the time. She had no tap water, no sewerage and electricity did not come until the early years of the war!

YEAR OF ROYAL CHANGES

1936 brought momentous events to the Royal Family. King George V's illness had been on the news on the Saturday and Zillah recorded,

Monday, 20 January. 'The even brought disquieting news of the King at 9.25pm. A bulletin was issued, "The King's life is moving peacefully to its close". This was repeated each ¼ hr till one at 12.15am announced the end at 11.55pm.'

There were no wireless programmes on the Tuesday, '*only Big Ben every ¼ hr with announcements, no general news… Mr Baldwin gave a nice homily at 9.30.*' Zillah notes that the King's body had arrived at Westminster Hall from Sandringham on the Thursday, a '*Memorial Service for him from Broadcasting Hse with an address on him by the Arch B of Canterbury*' had been held on the Sunday, and that '*throngs of people*' had been at the lying in state. She listened to the wireless on Tuesday 28 January from 9.30 am, to the arrival of the Royal Family at Windsor about 1 pm when '*the funeral service was broadcast.*' They all went to a memorial service in Paglesham Church at 4 pm. '*A good congregation. A proper form of service and 4 hymns, including 27, the King's favourite* [Abide with me].'

Zillah continued to record village events, including the funeral of Alfred Kemp on the 27 January 1936, to which Pet, Fred and Minnie went. He had been an oyster dredger and a well-known figure in the village. Later in the year, James Shuttlewood, the boat builder, died on 5 November. He too was a prominent person, having taken over the yard 40 years earlier. He had built Glenthorpe, beyond New Cottages, in 1926 for himself and his wife Harriett who lived there for another 20 years. Fortunately his son Frank was ready to continue building traditional wooden boats.

At a meeting at The Chase, Zillah recorded,

Thursday 12 March 1936. '[Mrs Dixon] *drew a very dismal picture of possible future war. How aeroplanes could bomb all ships (food) going up the Thames. Oil wd be stopped so no boats, lorries etc could run. Possible treaty between Germany, Italy & Japan. The last named is supposed to have designs on Africa. They conquer India, Austr. & finally Britain, dominating the world! V nice tea…*'

An event of different importance was entered in April. '*Daughter born to Mrs A Boardman during the night,*' across the road from Zillah at 1 Boarded Row. This was the arrival of the author, Rosemary, with the help of Nurse Chant!

Nurse Chant was well known, riding on a bicycle to see her patients in the large area she had to cover – Canewdon and Stambridge as well as Paglesham. She lived next door to the Police house in Stambridge Road, near Ballards Gore. There were several babies born around the same

Rosemary outside 1, Boarded Row, 1936.

time as Rosemary, and after the births she would visit them daily for a few days. Zillah also later mentioned Rosemary getting measles and then mumps.

Apart from his first broadcast to the Empire on 1 March, King Edward VIII does not feature in the diary until

Monday 17 November 1936. 'AM ... brought back a USA paper with an a/c of Mrs Simpson's divorce and friendship with King Ed VIII.' It was over a fortnight before

Thursday 3 December 'Cabinet Crisis over King Edward's wish to marry Mrs Simpson. Some papers publish pictures, ours does not.'

Friday 4 December 'Mrs Simpson left today for France.'

Monday 7 December. 'Wanted to listen to Mr Baldwin's statement to Parliament on news but accumulator had run out...' On the 8th, *'Had tea with Mrs Anfil in writing room, got on to thin ice with regard to King's marriage as she upholds it.'* On Thursday 10 December *'we adjourned to dining room for announcement by Mr Baldwin re King Edward. He has abdicated.'*

They listened to the King's farewell speech on the Friday and finally on

Saturday 12 December. 'Prince Edward (late King) left Eng late last night after broadcasting & arrived in Boulogne.'

It had been a dramatic ten days.

A final, more local, change was augured by the death of Percy Hutley of Cupola House on 27 December. His death at North Shoebury House at the age of 59 was sudden and a great shock to all.

CUPOLA HOUSE

A month later, Zillah recorded, *'Cupola let to the Boardmans'*. There was a sale of contents on 15 April 1937, and it would be interesting to know which lots the Boardmans bought to help furnish their new house, which was so much larger than the tiny Boarded Row cottage.

Post-card of painting *'Ancient Mariners of Paglesham'*.

Lots 16 and 17 in the *'Outside'* section were probably Rosemary's future high chair and dolls' house! They fetched three shillings and one shilling, and are still in our possession. Lot 159 was an *'Oyster still life £1'* and Lot 160, *'oysters dancing round a barrel'*, which sold for 14 shillings, which Pet had *'rather wanted.'* A postcard reproduction of the second picture exists. Minnie had been *'most interested in Cupola chairs'*, six *'Chippendale style'* chairs which sold for £126!

Cupola House was built by Thomas Browning in 1803 on the site of an earlier property called Lunts, and the Boardmans continued to call the farm *'Lunts Farm.'* Their new house was a tall Georgian brick house with an attractive semi-circular front porch with two classical pillars. In plan it was T-shaped, with the main rooms facing south and the service wing at the rear. The dining room facing south and east had French doors to the side, while the lounge had an office behind it with its own door to the garden on the west. Alan Boardman continued to use it as such. Up the stairs with their elegant mahogany banister rail were two main bedrooms on the first floor and two more rooms at the top, one described in the sale catalogue as a '*Writing Room.*' The stairs continued up to the ceiling where the cupola had once been.

There was a large bathroom off the half landing, with the '*Maid's bedroom*' behind that. The bathroom must have been a joy to the Boardmans, although they didn't have any live-in maid to bring up hot water! Winding stairs went up from the maid's room to further maids' bedrooms in the attic and others went down to the kitchen. The kitchen was large, but dark, with doors all round; to the servants' stairs, down to the cellars, out to the storeroom, to the scullery and to the yard outside. Two steps led up to the hall through another, baize-covered, door. There was a lovely corner cupboard and the window had a sliding shutter which pulled up from below.

The scullery had a stone sink under the window which had bottle glass in some panes and was between its yard door and a lever hand-pump from the well. Water had to be pumped up to a tank by hand until electricity arrived at Cupola House in 1942. A built-in 'copper' wash boiler filled the far corner, and there was storage on a floor over part of the room.

Altogether this was a very attractive house to live in, even though it was built for people with servants and money – not readily available in 1937. The Boardmans moved in on the 20 April and it was to be Rosemary's home until her marriage.

It rained all day in Paglesham for King George VI's Coronation.
Wednesday 12 May 1937. 'Did all little jobs that would keep us close to the loud speaker for the Coronation Ceremony. ...
The Service was impressive, the King's responses loud & clear, but hesitating. The cheering was wonderful.'
Zillah and her mother went off on the 1.45 pm bus to the usual village celebrations – church service, then tea in the Church Hall barn, with fancy dress and entertainment. They were home at 7.45 pm '*in time for Empire Broadcast culminating in a speech by King George VI.'* They went to Garon's Cinema in

Church Hall barns, 1940.

Southend on 1 June, '*Enthusiastic audience for Coronation films.'*

Seawall breaks and flooding were a regular, if not frequent, feature of Essex. Another occurred when, as usual, strong winds and high tides coincided. Zillah wrote,
Friday 13 February 1938. 'High tide broke through sea wall & over marshes... The tide

comes as far as the ditch across middle of field.'

This was one of The Chase fields, which Rosemary's father was renting.

Saturday 14 February. '...walked along the sea wall to the breach which was being repaired by 10 men with sandbags & a palisade of stakes. It was high tide but it didn't go over [again].'

There were plans to strengthen the seawalls, but events prevented this.

IMPENDING WAR

Zillah noted in March 1938 that '*German Army has marched into Austria to help the Nazis there (so they say).'* Chamberlain had become Prime Minister the previous year, and was

endeavouring to avoid a war. However, a new aircraft carrier, the *Ark Royal* had been launched, the government had decided to issue all children with gas masks, and work was progressing on radar. Although their purpose was secret, the construction of tall masts at Canewdon must have caused speculation all round. The four 360 foot steel pylons carrying transmitters and the 240 foot timber receivers could be seen for miles around. In fact Chamberlain's trips to Munich at the end of September were tracked from Canewdon, one of the first five 'Chain Home' radar stations to be built.

Zillah noted Chamberlain's flights and the worsening demands of Czechoslovakia by Hitler. Pet, Minnie and Zillah were all put on the ARP (Air Raid Precautions) Committee. They attended meetings about gas attacks and noted that there were 14 volunteers for first aid classes. At the same time Zillah continued her activities for animal welfare, getting signatures for a petition against the docking of horses' tails. There was also a meeting about trench digging, '*one at the school and one at East End. The ditch will be used at Church End.'*

One of the Radar transmitter pylons at Canewdon, c1940.

Despite Chamberlain's claim of '*Peace for our time,'*

Wednesday 28 September 1938. 'Athel 'went trench digging in field opposite Shop Row.'

Thursday 29 September. 'Caught 9.40 bus to Rfd to get our gasmasks.'

There was a '*Peace Thanksgiving'* service in the church on 2 October, but peace would be short-lived.

The year ended with a chilly Christmas, with comments by Zillah,

Tuesday 20 December 1938. 'Coldest spell in England for 10 years. Ice in both our jugs, flannels frozen on the washstands.'

Wednesday 21 December. 'Snowing gently all day.'

Thursday 22 December. 'Went to Southend. Men busy clearing away snow & loading it on

lorries, everywhere sloppy & nasty.'
Friday 24 December. 'M & I took Pal in jungle.' The 'jungle' was the 'nut boughs' behind
Buckland House, where they exercised their dog.
Saturday 25 December. 'A White Xmas, but not cold… glassy roads. [Minnie] *came to dinner
& spent the day, she brought a dish of home cured ham & a sweet for supper… A went to
take Presents as we couldn't get to church & milkman couldn't take them as he had to
walk.'*

This was the Boardmans' second Christmas at Cupola House. Photographs show Rosemary
on a sledge in the snow. It must have been difficult to keep warm in that large house.

13 WORLD WAR II

EVACUATION

At a meeting on 21 January 1939 in Rochford, Miss N C Flynn (*NCF* in Zillah's diary), who
was headmistress of Paglesham school, was put in charge of arrangements for receiving
evacuees from London, *'in the event of a war with Germany.'* She asked Zillah to help her
with billeting. On 3 February 1939, Zillah went round Paglesham with Miss Flynn *'making
arrangements for billeting children in wartime. A slow job as people want to talk & NCF was
in no hurry.'*

Zillah listened to the news *'from France re Spanish refugees … pouring over the frontier,'* and
to *'the launching of the battleship 'King George V'* later in the month. In March came news
of Germany's annexation of Slovakia and Hungary, and of Messel being given up by
Lithuania. On 8 April, *'Italy invaded Albania yesterday,'* and 11 May, *'England & Turkey
have concluded a military pact.'*

Evacuation plans continued.
*Monday 22 May 1939. 'Evacuation Committee … 9 Paglesham people present … Most of the
people who refused to billet children have had adults given instead.'*
After a quiet period in her diary, Zillah noted the recall of Parliament to pass an Emergency
Powers Defence Bill on 24 August. They looked at the Glenton tour brochure and doubted if
they would go on one, *'owing to the situation.'* A WI tour planned for the Sunday was
cancelled.
Saturday 26 August. 'May Cardy says there is a searchlight 2 fields from OBS Cottages.'
*Sunday 27 August. '…Intercession Services today. Ours was not inspiring. … Mrs Sam
[Hutley] said there were 200 soldiers & lots of guns not far away. S'end hotels deserted
even by permanents.'*

During the next week the Harrises continued their normal activities under the cloud of worry
– going in to Southend, *'while we still can,'* vacuuming in case they had an evacuee and going
to first aid meetings. On 1 September Zillah *'went to School House – stayed the night there
as NCF was feeling v nervous.'*

Saturday 2 September 1939. 'Billeting Meeting in Rfd. All billeting officers were told to expect the children next day. ... Went round to all billets telling people what time to expect the children. Everyone seemed smiling & anxious to do their best for them all.'

Sunday 3 September. 'War declared at 11am against Germany. Sunny & Warm. Went on 11.40 bus to school after hearing Mr Chamberlain's speech. NCF, Miss Bright, Mrs Kemp, Lapwood, Keeble & I were on duty all day expecting the children any minute but they didn't turn up until after 5pm on a double-decker bus, 32 children, 3 teachers & 3 mothers or helpers. [They came from Chingford.] NCF filled up all billeting forms & I had a list of vacancies. Being low down on the list there were few girls left so AM [Aunt Minnie] & we were offered a brother & sister & could only concur as AM said she must have a girl... stayed at the school house.'

Phyllis and Rosemary, '*the day war broke out*', 3 September 1939.

Monday 4 September. 'Stayed in school in case anyone came. Only Lionel & Elsie Allen [evacuees] came. Elsie in tears as she didn't want to go to another billet. ... Walked home in even, met M outside Mrs H Keeble's, Robert Bell was called out to speak to us. M [mother] said Barry & Thea [Barber, aged 10 and 6] had settled well, felt they had known them a long time.'

Having written to Mrs Barber on Wednesday 6th,

Sunday 10 September, 'Mr & Mrs Barber & Gran Barber ... arrived. All v nice people. After chatting awhile we inspected 'The Cot' & Chase grounds.... They left at 5.30, Mr B wanted M to take 5/- to buy herself something as they all seemed so grateful & are so glad to find children so happy & looking so well.'

In the following days, the children were taken out for walks both by their teacher and with Pal by Minnie. They went to play at Redcroft or out with Zillah on her various jobs, for example when Zillah took '*a bundle of books to the Bowl for 2 evacuated mothers,*' or into Southend where she '*took B & T into the 3 chain stores to spend the 6d I gave each.*'

Ration books were issued at the end of September but did not come into use until 8 January 1940, when Zillah noted, '*Rationing for Butter, Bacon, & Sugar started today.*'

Not all the evacuees were as lucky with their hosts as Barry and Thea. Miss Flynn told Zillah, '*One lad's landlady wants to get rid of him, wants his room! Says he is greedy, gave him salts & he was always wanting to stay in bed, which she won't allow, tho' he had to later as he had a cold, which he gave to her children. If he goes out, she locks door & he can't get in, if he goes for a walk & is late, he has no tea or supper.*'

On Sunday 26 November Robert Bell came to join the household. He was more unruly than

Barry and Zillah put in her diary that day *'Considerably more commotion with another inmate!!'* She did enjoy having them, but now had to set rules. *'I wish R were not so disobedient as it makes A & Un cross with him.'*

The boys started making paper chains for Christmas decorations on 3 December, Pet made puddings on the 13th and they played charades and sang carols. Evenings were spent playing games, *'Happy Families'*, *'The Minister's Cat'*, *'the Grand Mogul'*, or *'My Love begins with an ...'*, roasting chestnuts or reading.

Robert Bell, Thea and Barry Barber with paper decorations, Christmas 1940.

Saturday 16 September. 'caught 1st bus to S'end. ... to Woolworths where the boys & Thea did most of their shopping ... All met at Garons for dinner. The boys had a good tuck in, tomato soup, 2 sausages & chips, pineapple & cream, & a raspberry drink.'

On Thursday 21 December they went to school for a breaking up party. *'B wore my short fur coat for 'Cat & Fiddle' & Mrs Watkins made a headdress & wire whiskers for him. R was 'Old King Cole.' Thea was a fairy in 2 things.'* The Barbers visited on Christmas Eve. They were expected all day, but

'only arrived at 3.30 after a trying journey... and they had to leave by 5.40. ... They brought presents for everybody as well as crackers and novelties. ... After they were in bed we had a busy time doing up parcels for the tree. I filled their socks with walnuts, cobs, an apple, some sweets & dates & an inflated thing each.'

Christmas Day started with a white frost, *'with a few peeps of sunshine.'*

Monday 25 December. '. ... A[Athel] got up & lit the fire. Busy morn with hot dinner, turkey spuds & sprouts, Xmas pud. The boys went round and round the tree, a great temptation to wait for 3pm... Dinner much enjoyed by B. I got 3d bit & bachelor's button in pud... A cut presents from the tree. B v pleased with pen & pencil from M & my book [a dictionary costing 2/6]. Thea was here too & AM came later. We had Christmas cake & after tea the boys & I acted 3 charades, all guessed. Mr Barber had brought pork pie, novelties & firework crackers etc. & they seemed to have a happy day & were only in bed shortly before 10pm.'

Such were typical Christmases of the time. Putting silver 3d coins (thrip'ny bits') in the puddings and waiting until after lunch for presents was widespread. The 'phoney' war had little effect other than to split families. They even received a *'lovely hamper from the Doaks,'* their Australian cousins.

WINTER 1940

The winter of 1940 was exceptionally cold with ice and snow. Photographs show salt water in the River Roach at Paglesham frozen into ridges by the cold and the movement of the tides. Ice was thick enough on the marshes to walk on. Zillah put on a '*Notes*' page,

'The winter was the coldest since 1895 and January the coldest since 1938. The Thames was frozen in the upper reaches. It interfered with shipping in the estuary ... Trains took a week to get to Glasgow from London. Snowdrifts were reported 16ft deep in outer London.'

Keebles' oyster smack, Caroline, 1940.

Zillah had grown fond of her charges and was very upset when they had a letter from Mrs Barber saying that she would be taking Barry and Thea home.

Sunday 21 January. '*It made me terribly sad to think of parting so soon with Barry. I really love the child.'*

Mrs Barber had said, '*Please do not be angry with me for this decision, it has been very difficult to take them away when you are all so fond of them.'*

Barry wrote the day after he left to say he missed Zillah, continuing,
'*We all arrived home safely at 8.45pm. It was snowing very hard & we had to wait 1hr at Rochford Station because we just missed a train.'*
The Barbers had decided that Chingford was as safe as Paglesham. Many evacuees went home, as a result of parents missing their offspring and taking them away. The expected heavy raids on London had not materialised.

Fifty-five years later, Barry Barber fondly remembered his time in Paglesham. He had slept under the south window in the sitting room, with Robert being under the north window. A small-lean to off the room was used for washing.
'*We got drinking water from the pump in the backyard, washing water came from the rain butts. ... Auntie Pet & Zillah would spend 1 – 2 days making their preserves, pickles & various wines including potato. We used to collect mushrooms the size of a saucer... Uncle Athelstan had dug his own air raid shelter between the kitchen and the outside wc. It was only shallow & only had a sheet metal cover. It was not used while I was there.'*
Miss Betty Nicholls, Arthur's daughter, let them have baths at The Chase. Cooking was done on double paraffin burners, bread came from Canewdon by van and fish was bought from the Keebles.

The dreadful conditions, snowstorms and icy churned up roads meant that on Monday 29 January 1940, '*only 5 children put in appearance*' at school. Mr Willans, the grocer, came round on horseback, and when Mr Anfilogoff died unexpectedly on the 27th, his body had to remain at Redcroft before it could be removed. His death was a great shock to all.
Thursday 1 February 1940. '*Thawing all day but roads like glass under a layer of water. Not cold. We had a scramble to get out about 10am to go to Redcroft for a short service before Mr Anfil was taken away for cremation. There were over 20 people there. The*

coffin was plain wood & mauve, & stood on a small chrome table.'

Another evacuated to Paglesham was Vera Britton, who in 1994 also recollected the time. She was 12 and her sister Thirza was ten when war was declared.

'All our things were packed ready ... with labels on our coats, & enough corned beef sandwiches to last two days. ... It seemed like hours before we reached Paglesham. ... Mrs Meeson at Church Hall took four of us girls ... we were all very frightened and everything felt very strange.

'We were taken in the back way into the kitchen which was quite big, and we were met by Audrey Quy the cook and Eileen Kemp the parlour maid. We were taken up to our rooms, which were obviously

Church Hall, with Mrs Meeson's car and Chauffeur.

the maids' and very basic. We were told we couldn't use the bathroom, that was for Mrs Meeson's sole use, and when we were shown the outside toilet (which was not supplied with running water) I received a culture shock...*

'Some of the village children thought we had never seen a tree. This amused us as we lived a short walk from Epping Forest. ... Then came our second culture shock: No buses, No Cinema, No Fish & Chip shop, and No Library. Nothing but one small village shop cum Post Office, and what passed for a library was down at East End...'

The other two girls went home quite early on and in January Vera and Thirza moved to another billet before going home at Easter. *'Neither of us ever forgot Church Hall and the people there who were so kind to us.'*

One change which made life easier was that the Harrises now sent off their major washing to the *'Princes Street Steam Laundry',* Southend. The 12 or 16 items before the war went up to 18 or so when the evacuees were with them. Sheets, towels, underwear and a variety of other items were the norm. They were charged at a flat rate of 2½d per item until May 1940, when their laundry book advised them that after 3 June 1940,

'Owing to the great advance in working costs, especially the recent proposal to increase wages for workers in Laundries throughout the country, Launderers have been compelled to raise their charges by 1d in the 1/- (ie ½d for every 6d or part thereof.)

The Harrises' bills therefore had a *'War Increase'* of 3d or 3½d added each time. In October 1939, a *'War Risk'* disclaimer against losses had been added, *'whether war be declared or not,'* which sounds as if the war came sooner than they had expected!

News of fighting is missing from Zillah's diary until the 10 May 1940, when *'Germany has invaded Holland, Belgium & Luxembourg today.'* However, Churchill's takeover as Prime Minister the same day went unreported. The next day they were able to get a *'new wireless battery as ours gave out a few days before the new invasion.'* The wireless was their main source of news and light entertainment. Zillah noted *'the last night of Garrison Theatre with J Warner, Arthur Askey & Stinker Murdock,'* names familiar to all of that generation.

ALL CHANGE

The German expansion resulted in the evacuation of British troops from Dunkirk at the beginning of June. Small boats from Essex were among the many which went across to rescue troops. The *Grace Darling* had been built in the 1920s in Shuttlewoods' boatshed, and had been used at Southend as a pleasure boat. She failed to return. *Vanguard* was an oyster smack which picked up troops from the beaches. Another vessel, *Ma Joie*, ferried troops to larger vessels until its propeller got fouled, her crew joining *Vanguard* to return with a complement of soldiers, leaving their boat behind. *Vanguard* was later bought by the Keeble family for their oyster business during the 1960s and '70s.

Dunkirk was a turning point at home as well as in France. With the retreat from Europe, the threat of invasion became real, and the Essex coast was once again a potential invasion area. Any evacuees remaining were told to return home (under their own arrangements), and children in the area were evacuated further west. Zillah saw George Cox off with others from Rochford station on 2 June. Robert Bell, one of the last to leave, was taken by bus to Rochford station on 6 June, his mother due to meet him in London.

Children in Rochford were evacuated to Bream in the Forest of Dean. Mrs Doris Sime, later headmistress at Paglesham, recalled that about 70 children with six or seven teachers and a few parents set off on that long journey, with more children getting on the train at various anonymous stops. *'The worst journey I have ever undertaken,'* was how she described it. Noise and cheerfulness gave way to boredom and hunger after the sandwiches had gone. *'One train toilet per compartment of 30 – 40 children definitely was not enough.'* The youngsters, including some four-year-olds travelling with older siblings, began to miss their mums and dads and started crying. After 10 hours they reached a final stop not knowing where they were. Then came an hour of medical inspections for the children before even a cup of tea. Even then their travels were not finished. They were bussed from Lydney to Bream, where the villagers, waiting to do their bit for the country, grabbed any child, weary and frightened, that they fancied.

> *'Brothers and sisters got separated and the crying was indescribable. Then the miracle happened. In walked the small figure of the District Nurse. She summed up the situation, she knew her village people and they listened to her. The large houses took the large groups, and most children found a good home. We finally left the Village Hall at 11 o'clock. The people of Bream made us more than welcome.'*

Rosemary and her mother, Phyllis, went to Stapleton in Shropshire on 28 June 1940 to stay with two cousins who were also evacuated there, but they did not stay long. Phyllis felt that she could be of more use with her husband. When they returned she looked after 1000 chickens and 100 ducks, which she did very well. They lived in outdoor runs and the collecting, cleaning and packing was a big task. The eggs could only be sold to the packing station, who called every week for the wooden boxes each holding 30 dozen eggs. Phyllis wrote in a letter, *'Rosemary is the greatest help to me with the chickens and can tell a sick bird at a glance.'*

CLOSE TO HOME

Southend had already had areas cleared for the shore establishments of *HMS Leigh* and *HMS Westcliff*. The Royal Navy organised outgoing convoys from the pier. Thames Naval

Control initially operated from the Palace Hotel, and after March 1940 from Royal Terrace. Alan Boardman had had to clear 300 pigs off the farm in January due to swine fever, and now the evacuation of Southend and Rochford had a disastrous effect. He was left with many vegetables, including 12 acres of lettuces which were ready to cut, and no market. He had to plough them in. He then turned to wheat, potatoes and root crops, which could be stored – or fed to the pigs after he bought ten from Cottis's at West Hall in August.

Alan Boardman hoeing lettuce crop, 1940.

There had been soldiers manning two searchlights since the beginning of the war, one near Stannetts, the other at Clements, north of Cupola House. Zillah now refers to the '*Kilties*' in the area – shades of the Great War. These were men of the Black Watch, billeted or under canvas at Church End, whose duties included manning four anti-aircraft Bofors guns there. Notes of German aeroplanes overhead and air raids in the area were so frequent in Zillah's diary that '*no guns or raids*' became newsworthy. In Paglesham there was a bomb at West Hall on 20 July and flares on the 5 and 8 of August, the latter with '*single and bunches of bombs.*'

Monday 19 August 1940. '*A ... cld see the [sea]wall alight in places from incendiary bombs. We found it blazing in spots so I got water in a bucket from a boat & he put it where it was needed. A German bomber came over so we got down the side of the wall.*'

Phyllis Boardman wrote to a friend in America about this time, describing events. The censored letter was returned later. It read,

'*The Nazis started dropping bombs in earnest and ... dropped three in this village about a mile from this house. We did not worry unduly and continued to sleep peacefully until the night of* [censored]. *We suddenly wakened to hear a dive bomber screaming past our window flying very low. He dropped flares and lit our* [...] *and then dropped 70* [...]. *We flew to the window and looked out on a most devilish scene – brilliant fires in our precious* [...] *on which our hopes were pinned, with the weird flares overhead impressing a never-to-be-forgotten picture in our minds. Alan tore on his clothes and rushed to extinguish the fires, whilst I flew to the telephone to call the Fire Brigade. A few minutes later, to my horror, I heard the bomber returning. He screamed down and the next moment we heard the hateful whistle and crackle of the bombs as they dropped through the air – eight high explosives this time. He was aiming for the villagers who had rushed out to extinguish the fires. Fortunately they fell short and the men saved themselves by throwing themselves down flat. This house heaved and rocked, but stood up to the shaking like a veteran. Our men and the villagers had put out the fires before the Brigade arrived, which was wonderful. Alan could not speak too highly of their pluck – the villagers I mean.*'

Phyllis said she was glad that the three of them were together, rather than separated like so many. She applauded the bus conductor in London who, in the midst of devastation said to her, ' '*Itler 'as a long way to go yet*' and the humour in the signs, '*Business as usual in spite of certain structural alterations.*'

Monday 3 February 1941. 'A lone plane came over this afternoon & dropped 2 bombs near Church Hall. The blast killed Ernie Cardy who was driving a tractor.'
Ernie had been ploughing a field with two others, who stopped at the edge of the field when they heard the plane. Ernie's tractor kept going after the bomb, and it wasn't until it stalled in the hedge that the others realised anything was amiss. Less seriously,
Saturday 3 May 1941. 'At 4.25am we were awakened by a v low plane. A could see a light in its cockpit as it was three times the height of the house. ... Sun morn we heard it came down in a field behind East Hall; it had returned from bombing Cologne, got shrapnel in the engine. 3 members baled out, landed safely at Southminster, & 2 came down [safely] in the plane. Harold Brown threatened them with the gun he used for protecting lambs from foxes. They put up their hands & asked where they were, he said, "somewhere in England." When he realised they were English, he directed them to Mr Perry's to phone.'

ZILLAH'S WAR WORK
Having joined the ARP Committee in April 1938 and become Miss Flynn's billeting assistant in January 1939, Zillah did everything she possibly could to help the war effort. Looking

after Barry, Thea and Robert in 1939 was followed by becoming a blood donor in July 1940, in which month she also became the village's official salvage collector, arranged through the WI. She took aluminium into Southend and organised collections of paper, rags, bones and old clothes destined to be remade for evacuees. The ornate cast iron railings in front of Cupola House were also taken '*for the war effort,*' although the gate was left to keep out stray animals.

Cupola House, with railings removed in 1940.

At a salvage meeting in Southend, '*We had just started when 2 sirens went but as no one wanted to return to the shelter we continued the meeting.*' Although she often refers to '*disturbed nights*' this sangfroid also comes through. '*A Jerry about and bombs being dropped both N & S. Lay down on bed under eiderdown in clothes and coat. Went to sleep and never undressed.*'

Zillah was a regular collector on fund days, Spitfire Week, for the local hospital and many more. In fact, on 20 September 1941 she noted that someone she asked,
'*said Flag Days were blackmail! But was more affable when he heard I had not had breakfast & it was nearly 10am. Was asked to do a collection for Comforts Fund on Tuesday but said no – too many Collections just now.*'
She listed these days in 1944 – '*23 February – Aid to Russia; 14 March – Aid to China; 4*

April – Sailors' Day; 6 June – Red X & St John; 19 June – Rose Day; 26 August – Gen Hosp Day; 14 September – District Nurse Fund; 13 October – Aid to Russia; 31 October – Ld R[oberts'] Workshops; 11 November – Poppy Day.' For each one she usually collected about £3, sometimes with the help of others and on Poppy Day, with the aid of Ada Jennings, £6 8s 11d was raised.

She continued to take old jars into the Public Dispensary for Sick Animals (PDSA), and also held collections for Our Dumb Friend's League (ODFL). The family grew vegetables, as many did, both in their own garden and in an allotment in the one acre *'Garden Field'* near them, opposite the Plough and Sail. Uncle Fred liked to grow lilies there. They continued to preserve produce, even though sugar became a problem. Athel was a keen beekeeper, and honey may have been used as an alternative.

HOME GUARD

In May 1940, with the retreat from France imminent, men between 17 and 65 were asked to enrol in the Local Defence Volunteers. After Churchill spoke of them as the Home Guard, this became their new name. A dozen Paglesham men joined the section of the *'Rochford*

Company of the 1ˢᵗ Essex Battalion Home Guard' based at Stambridge, under Capt Percy Bentall. Athelstan joined, but his poor health prevented him from taking part in all the activities. They had a series of lectures in December 1940 on topics such as *'Camouflage,' 'Musketry – Firing Positions,' 'Messages and Reports', 'Map Reading,' 'Patrols,'* and *'Fighting in Woods and Villages.'*

Paglesham Home Guard. (Left to right) Back: Vin Wood, Jim Thorogood, George Fletcher, Lol Bradley, Arthur Sharp, Bill Fance. Seated: Benny Sharp, Tom Keeble, Tom Hines, George Kemp, John Killick, Vic Cardy.

Home Guard duties included checking identities on the buses. Canewdon and Paglesham buses were stopped between the Royal Oak public house at Stambridge and the Gore. They also guarded ration books, kept in a house near Rochford Fire Station.

The medical corporal, Reg Suttle, was a humourist, who wrote songs which they sang on the march. One, sung to the tune of *Onward Christian Soldiers,* went,
    'Onward Stambridge Home Guard, Marching to the Gore,
    Lt Harry Barker going on before,
    With old Percy Bentall Bringing up the rear,
    Praying for 'Parade Dismiss', So we can get some beer.'
Another, to the tune of Abdul Abulbul Amir, poked fun at *'Lt Hypes Barker'* who was the baker in Stambridge.

RESTRICTIONS

A large area east of Wickford became a restricted area. Only people with permits were allowed in from other areas and identity cards were checked. For her wedding in Canewdon, May Rollin had to get passes for her bridegroom's parents and relations. One girl was omitted and was not allowed in to attend. Alf Lane, the bridegroom, was in the Artillery, and on emerging from the church, Alf and May were amazed to find a Guard of Honour of the Royal Artillery, who were stationed nearby. Alf and May spent their honeymoon at the Plough and Sail, Paglesham, for the remainder of Alf's 48 hour leave!

When Rosemary's grandfather came to visit, he also had to obtain a permit. There were checks at the railway stations and at other significant points such as Warners Bridge over the railway on the way in to Southend.

Pill box at corner of Paglesham Pool, 1990.

Concrete defence points were built in 1940, known as 'pillboxes' after their shape. Two were built in Paglesham, on Paglesham Pool and at the Pool's junction with the River Roach. On 1 August, Zillah and her mother '*walked across Pool to the new Watch house. M took cigs and choc in case it was occupied. It was not.*' These were more for observation and rearguard action than serious defence; a major defence line ran north from Canvey Island to Chelmsford and Cambridge. This was the middle of three lines protecting London from invasion on the east coast.

An important check point was at the top of the hill at Ashingdon, where two pillboxes guarded the road and were reinforced by coiled barbed wire and weapons trenches around the church. A plan of April 1942, prepared by the 9th Devonshires, shows proposed additional wire entanglements. Some of the large open fields in Paglesham had tall poles erected (as elsewhere and including beaches) to make an airborne landing more difficult.

RATIONS

Rationing of petrol started on 22 September 1939 and of food in January 1940. An allowance of 4oz (100 gm) of butter, 4oz of bacon or ham and 12 oz (300 gm, later reduced to 8 oz (200 gm)) of sugar was allowed. These were the first items to be rationed, with meat rationing starting in March (1s 10d worth, later reduced to 1s 2d) and tea, margarine and lard in July.

Jam, marmalade and syrup were added in January 1941, cheese in May, eggs in June (only one per person per week) and milk from 1 November. Clothing and furniture had been added in June as well, with the famous CC41 mark. Only Utility furniture could be made from November 1942 in order to save raw materials.

Utility Mark, 1941.

Saccharine was a substitute for sugar. It had a metallic taste but did help sweeten food. It was not always readily found. In January 1941 Zillah went to Southend, *'walked to Hamlet Court Road to try for saccharine for AM, none to be had at 6 shops.'*

In January 1941 when the meat ration was reduced, Zillah commented on various days,
> *'This is the first week of reduced meat ration (I forget whether 1/6 or 1/2) so we had a sheep's head for dinner and there is a hock in pickle.'*
> *'Cooking means much brain racking these days.'*
> *'M cooked rabbit, back of pork etc,'*

Thereafter it was taken as normal and not mentioned!

MACFARLANE LANGS
BISCUITS

29th March 1941
St Peters Church
Bought of **J. B. ATKINSON,**
Grocery, Provisions and Drapery,
Post Office Stores, Church End,
PAGLESHAM, Rochford

1 14 Apl 1940	2 Galls Oil		2	1
2 27 May	2 Galls Oil		2	4
3 30...	2 Galls Oil		2	4
4	Ripe		5	6
5 31 Aug	2 Galls Oil		2	4

The Ministry of Food gave out many recipes as advertisements, in booklets or on the radio to help with ideas. Woolton Pie was one such recipe, named after the Minister for Food, Lord Woolton. This was a concoction of cooked vegetables topped off *'with potato pastry or mashed potato and a very little grated cheese.'*

Zillah *'tried a wireless recipe. Raw potatoes cut small and fried, then a beaten egg poured over. Not bad especially if one had more eggs.'* Meals could still be bought, but were small. *'Dinner at Garons. Mother & I had boiled Cod. Minute portions now cost 1/-.'*

Firms like Stork margarine also produced helpful booklets. Recipes included *'nourishing sandwiches for ARP workers',* cakes without currants and puddings without sugar. There was advice on *'What you can do if an air raid warning interrupts cooking – the first thing to do is to stop the heat.'*

One of the Ministry's posters had the slogan,
> *'Reflect whenever you indulge,*
> *It is not beautiful to bulge,*
> *A large untidy corporation*
> *Is far from helpful to the nation.'*

It is now considered that those times produced a country fitter than today's!

WAR-TIME MEMORIES

Rosemary was three and a half years old when war was declared. Her earliest memory is of seeing a German parachutist coming down near Stannetts, while she was pedalling her tricycle up the road. Her father talked about another who was lost in the River Roach on 3 September 1940. Alan was working not far away and ran towards the man, who was shouting in German as he drifted across the seawall. By the time Alan had run to the top of the wall, all traces of the German and his parachute had disappeared. He was amazed how quickly this had happened. Only recently the story was confirmed by Bill Pavelin, whose father also witnessed the event from the Barling side of the river, also mentioning a man – presumably Alan Boardman – looking from the Paglesham side. Zillah also recorded the incident, adding that two other parachutists came down.

Alan strengthened one corner of the cellar with sleepers as their air raid shelter, making a cosy place to sleep. Unfortunately the cellar flooded occasionally, so the large deal kitchen table (Lot 40 in the 1937 sale, 5/-!) became their next shelter. Windows were criss-crossed with brown paper tape to reduce splinter damage and were covered with blankets when they were blown out. The window shutters added to the family's safety.

Rosemary's mother also talked about a red glow illuminating Cupola House. This was a moving light on the East Hall lane, deployed as a decoy to divert away raids from Rochford airfield. During the Battle of Britain Rochford was the forward base for RAF Hornchurch, and afterwards it had its own 264 Squadron of two-seater Defiants as 'RAF Southend'. It was unnerving to think that they were encouraging bombs to be dropped on Paglesham! The light was there for a fortnight at a time.

A Guernsey heifer and calf came in by LNER from Reading to Rochford for the Boardmans in January 1941. 'Primrose' provided rich milk and cream. Phyllis gave much away and provided the milk for WI teas. She also made the cream into butter, and one of Rosemary's jobs was to turn the handle of the butter churn. The rest of the milk was used to rear calves.

On Rosemary's fifth birthday, in April 1941, she suffered a bronchial asthma attack, brought on, it was believed, by the shock of landmines exploding nearby two days earlier. In another letter to her friend in America, after Christmas 1942, Phyllis wrote,
> *'It was the night London was so badly burned and for hours the Germans were passing overhead, dropping landmines round here like snowflakes. Our tall house shook, heaved, groaned and creaked and we felt sure it would topple down, but apart from windows* [blown in] *nothing happened. Alan (who is an ARP Warden) was blown against the house and felt badly winded for several days. ... Since then we have had a great deal of trouble with Rosemary's health and last April she had bronchial pneumonia and asthma together and we had to rush her to hospital.'*

Rosemary became very fond of Dr Southwell. She remembers him carrying her in his arms through the corridors of the Children's Ward of Southend General Hospital, before being put in an 'Iron Lung'. She had not been expected to last the night. Rosemary got to know him very well over the years as she had *'bronchitis 7 times, but that was the worst,'* as well as recurring asthma for the next 20 years. She wrote in 1995,
> *'Dr Southwell became a legend in the Rochford area. He was very caring and terribly busy, often arriving at an outlying patient late in the evening. He drove around in a little car and carried a basket of tablets for emergencies, as it was 6 miles to the nearest chemist.'*

The iron lung had been invented in the 1920s to help people with polio to breathe, and seven hundred had been made and distributed by Lord Nuffield. Rosemary still wonders if it was one of those! But it was the M & B (May and Baker) tablet, which had only recently been brought on to the market, which was also the reason for her pulling through at other times. M

& B tablets were also said to have saved Winston Churchill when he was ill in Africa.

After the war started, Rosemary shared a governess with Jeremy Squier at Apton Hall, Canewdon.

Mrs Boardman and Rosemary in the trap, at Apton Hall, 1940.

'With petrol rationed, my mother took me in our horse and trap. After my illness I was not well enough to go to school, and Miss Ada Jennings, the Rector's daughter, came in and taught me at home. To me she was an elderly lady with white hair and she would arrive on a bicycle. I did well with her and by May 1944 I went to Netherfield in Westcliff on Sea so I could take the Scholarship examination to a Grammar School. (In 1947, I passed and went to Westcliff High School.) The journey to Netherfield was a long and difficult journey. The bombing was not so bad by then, but we occasionally used the air raid shelters – Andersons outside for the older children and Morrison table shelters inside for the younger ones.

'At Netherfield we kept a 'Nature Record' and one May I wrote, 'I saw three rooks chasing a heron, it just looked like three fighters chasing a bomber.' We children soon adapted to our circumstances, from the problems of getting to school, to war overhead!'

One of Rosemary's contributions to the war was to pick rose hips for their Vitamin C content, getting 3d a pound for them. She also collected salvage; in July 1943 Zillah wrote, *'helpers enraptured by Rosemary's salvage & coveted it'*! Children were also encouraged to collect cabbage white butterflies. There were competitions to see who had the most, and they were mounted on a board with a pin.

Rosemary's father, Alan Boardman, continued farming during the war. He was always interested in mechanisation, so he had a tractor to work the land and pull trailers. He employed local women when extra hands were needed, and later a Land Army girl came to help for a short time. The Women's Land Army had first formed in the Great War, but recruiting began again in May 1939. At its peak there were some 90,000 members, often town dwellers having their first taste of country life. They were paid three pounds per week but had to find their own digs.

WW2 diaries, gas masks, ration book, identity card, paper flag, window tape in tin, Land Army doll, basket made by German prisoner-of-war.

'*I* [Rosemary] *was given a hand-made Land Army doll, complete with jodhpurs, which I was very pleased with and which still causes interest today.*'

Towards the end of the war Alan also had German prisoners of war. They were brought over from a camp at Wakering by lorry. Rosemary recalls,

'*I remember taking out a large enamel jug of tea and jam sandwiches to them in the fields. We got to know quite well a few who came over at Christmas time, possibly in 1945. My father picked them up and they sang 'Silent Night' in German for us.*'

AIR RAID SHELTERS

Several people had Anderson shelters in their gardens. These had been designed before the war and were made of corrugated iron sheets bent to curve over at the top. These were bolted

together to form a six foot high shelter, 6' 6" long and 4' 6" wide. These were dug 2' 6" or more into the ground and the soil was piled over them for further protection. They were designed to resist nearby blasts but not a direct hit. They were issued free to those with an income of less than £250 per year, which would have applied to most labourers. Others paid £7. The one in the garden of 1 Boarded Row is still there almost 70 years later. Many grew vegetables or flowers over them, but being partly underground they were damp and uncomfortable to use.

Air Raid Shelter at 1, Boarded Row, 1994.

In 1940 the new Home Secretary, Herbert Morrison, ordered a new shelter for use indoors. This was an angle-steel box with a steel top and mesh sides, which could be used as a table as well, as it took up a lot of room. It was designed to absorb the impact of the house falling on it by deforming a few inches, but not enough to harm those inside. This technique saved steel in its construction.

There were no shelters at the school at first – children hid under their desks – but later a brick shelter with a concrete roof was built, as were many like it in the streets of towns, which could hold the numbers necessary. Children going to school from East End walked along East Hall Road where there was a ditch to jump into if necessary, and a railway sleeper shelter was built in a ditch near East Hall corner. School hours were changed so that children were not on their way to school in the dark. It was quite exciting for the children if a siren went off, but parents must have been very worried.

RAIDS AND BOMB DAMAGE

The frequency of air raid warnings is clear from the entries in Zillah's diaries. Many of these were false alarms as far as Paglesham was concerned, with the planes dropping their bombs elsewhere. She records some of these as '*heard afterwards were dropped at Maldon*' or Foulness or Warners Bridge. But many were more local, and Zillah records in 1940, for example, a time bomb near West Hall in July, '*more cannon fire than we have experienced* *before '*at the end of August and a procession of planes going over in September.

The Battle of Britain, as it became known, was apparent in Paglesham, with sirens going on most nights and planes going overhead. Zillah recorded the effects on London heard on news broadcasts. Three examples were,

Saturday 7 September 1940. 'London was very severely bombed. Waves of aircraft, est at 400 – 500 started big fires in docklands… Berlin had a 3 hr raid & large fires…'

Tuesday 17 September. 'All London's famous places are being bombed – Strand, Piccadilly, Bond Street, big hospitals.'

Wednesday 2 October. '2 sirens during the day, both of short duration, it has been v quiet here lately, they seem to be going a different way to London.' The next day she *'went round the village asking for 24 – 48hr billets for bombed out people if they should ever be sent here.'*

The lull seems short-lived as planes or bombs were recorded on most of the next ten days, including bombs falling at Church End, Canewdon and Hampton Barns, not far away. Three bombs fell in a field opposite Jubilee Cottages on 19 November, across the river near the boatshed on the 20th and behind East Hall on the 29th. More dropped near South Hall on 11 December and Redcroft was fortunate when a bomb failed to explode nearby on the 14th.

Just before Christmas, Zillah *'had a letter each from Barry and Thea'* to say that *their street* [in Chingford] *'was wrecked by a landmine opposite,'* but they were safe.

There are fewer mentions early in 1941, but in March, East Hall suffered severe damage one evening in an air raid.

Wednesday 19 March 1941, 'A said a lot of incendiaries had been dropped at Burnham and could be heard popping. We went upstairs to look & while there, bombs were heard whistling down, which proved to be at East Hall.'

Thursday 20 March, 'We hear East Hall is unsafe pro tem. One of the RAF men was blown into Pound Pond while passing, he had been ordered to put out red light as they were bombing lights that night. The bombs fell on the edge of moat at back.'

Friday 21 March, 'AM went up to E Hall to inquire of inmates. Miss Murdoch is sleeping at South Hall & Mrs Quy at Cupola as house is unsafe if more bombs fall.'

Sunday 23 March, '… looked at damage at E Hall. Most of the plaster blown off at the back, windows out and tiles off.'

The bombs killed several pigs and injured others, and the vet, Mr Harry Sparrow, had to be called to put twenty-eight down. Interestingly, he kept his records in a 1915 book designed for treatments for horses. Farmers were compensated for such losses.

Paglesham was generally only under the flightpath, while London was suffering.

Wednesday 16 April 1941. 'A v large no of planes went over … It was the biggest raid on London yet.'

Thursday 17 April. 'We had a few planes over & 2 heavy ones passed at 5am.'

Friday 18 April. 'Soon after 9pm, German planes began coming over, there seemed to be swarms of them… bombs dropping within hearing.' After a lull, they *'started all over again. A went up the road to see if any bombs had fallen about… he met Mr Boardman who had a window broken by blast, finally he called on Mr Loader & got to bed at 4.30am.'*

Entries about disturbed nights, as Zillah had called them, are intermittent thereafter, but other interesting pieces of national news are included. Rudolf Hess's landing, the sinking of *HMS Hood*, one of our biggest battleships, and fighting for and the evacuation of Crete are mentioned alongside investing '*£50 for Hornsey effort in London War Weapons Week*' and another £100 for Rochford's War Weapons Week.

UNCLE FRED

On Saturday 29 November 1941 Uncle Fred Wiseman died. He had been very ill for a long time. Eight months earlier, Dr Southwell had said, '*Un was a perfect picture of senile decay & he couldn't patch him up.*'

'*Mrs Chamberlain and Mrs Fletcher ... came and did the needful. ...*[The Chelmsford undertakers] *brought a shell to put him in, & when they had finished we saw him. He looked v nice & AM exclaimed at his length & the undertaker said he was just 6ft. The 3 men had a glass of Ginger wine.*'

Fred Wiseman, Minnie Wiseman, Pet, Zillah and three cats, No 2 The Chaseway, c1940.

Uncle Fred's cremation took place on 4 December at the City of London Crematorium, and the ashes were scattered there an hour later. They '*went to an ABC* [café] *for tea and biscuits,*' while they waited.

The world situation changed dramatically three days later.

Sunday 7 December 1941. 'Japan has dropped bombs on Hawaii without declaring war.'
Monday 8 December. 'We are at war with Japan'
Thursday 11 December. 'USA at war with Germany and Hitler.'
The following Monday, Zillah took some of Uncle's things
'*to Mrs Fletcher for her to cut & contrive for her family, & odd fishing tackle to Hubert Keeble,*' and she was '*renovating some old crackers to go with the new for the school. ... Miss Bright was v pleased.*'

They went to church on Christmas morning, had '*turkey etc, Xmas pud, mince pies & tarts,*' for dinner, '*opened what few presents we had and read letters after the King's speech at 3pm... did needlework as we sat round fire.*'

The new year, 1942, started with a surprise visit from '*a smiling Australian Sergt Pilot – Richard* [Wiseman] *Dick & Stella's son.*' He was a second cousin, but Athel '*recognised him at once*' from his time in Australia. They made up a bed for him at Minnie's and showed him landmarks the next day before he left by bus for Southend and Grantham.

Mrs Anfilogoff moved to Stambridge and rented Redcroft to Mr and Mrs Wilson. Zillah went to a WI Group Conference in Rochford, first aid lectures, meetings for billeting officers, and the WVS. In June, Zillah and Pet went up to London to see their solicitor, Mr Gerrish, who had been bombed out at Hornsey, to make their wills, but they also looked round at the damage. *'Great devastation all round.'* In July, *'M & I went out starting our collecting for Lord Mayor of London's Air Raid Disaster Fund.'* No doubt seeing it for themselves helped their powers of persuasion. They returned in August to sign the wills, noting, *'St Stephen's* [by the Mansion House] *is the only building left in Walbrook.'*

In the autumn, Athel *'picked 6 ¾ bushels of cooking apples which Mr Willans took away.'* A 'British Restaurant' opened in Rochford, where simple meals could be obtained; Bill Robinson *'disposed of his largest* [onions] *to it.'* *'M & I ... spent a day gleaning* [wheat]. *We got 3 baskets full (more than 3 pails) and enjoyed our sandwich lunch.'* There had been one of the few mentions of *'Jerries round this way'* before they went out! They picked and bottled Victoria plums. *'AM has 3½ dozen peaches to dispose of.'* *'After dinner we went blackberrying.'* The Harrises and others made the most of the harvests.

BETTER NEWS

The old year ended with better news from North Africa, and the new one started well with the relief of Leningrad on the 18 January 1943. Minnie went as a guest of Mrs Anfilogoff to a *'reception'* at her inauguration as President of the Rochford WI. One casualty of the war effort was J F T Wiseman's personal papers. On 4 February *'M & I went to one of the Chase outhouses to sort some salvage recently found by Lapwood, business papers of Cousin James.'* Two and a half sacks were later taken away by the salvage men! Being a very successful farmer as well as oyster merchant in the 19th Century, JFTW's records would now be very valuable sources of information. Fortunately, Zillah did not consign her own branch's papers, which went back to the eighteenth century, to salvage! An indication of Zillah's interest in her family history (although it had failed to save JFTW's papers) was an entry,

Friday 30 April 1943. *'Then to Benfleet, walked about trying to find an old inhabitant who might know of Jas Wiseman who died in 1869, but no luck.'*

Barry and Thea Barber came to stay for a week over Easter. Zillah said, *'It seemed quite like old times to tuck* [Barry] *up in bed & kiss him.'*

On 17 May she noted from the news, *'Last night our Lancasters bombed 2 large German dams, & now floods are destroying bridges, power stations etc'* – the famous Dambusters' raids.

On the fourth anniversary of the start of the war,
3 September. *'I went to Cupola House 3 times, first with our beetroot, then took Mrs Watkin's apples and lastly some marrows, which Mrs Boardman took up* [to the church] *in trap… There was a Harvest Festival combined with National day of Prayer.'*

Zillah had been helping at a Rest Centre in Rochford, and when Mrs Hubert Keeble took over from Mrs Ellis, Zillah volunteered to be Information Officer, *'but it needs a lot to learn!'*

With two relatively quiet years and better news on the front line, the year ended on an optimistic note. Another invasion of Europe was in the air,
30 December. *'Great aerial activity overhead today. A counted over 200. I thought invasion must have started but it was over N Germany and N France.'*

MOST BOMBED VILLAGE

Having been invited by Mrs Boardman on the Friday,

Monday 31 January 1944, 'M, AM & I went to Cupola round 6pm for high tea. We had some of their own ham, butter and cream. There was also cake, jam and mince tarts. The meal was in the kitchen, then went into the lounge to chat while Mr B did the milking. R took me to her bedroom to see dolls etc. We all sat around a nice log fire till past 9pm, mostly in firelight as it is pleasant and saves electricity. They gave us the rest of the cream to bring home.'

There were advantages in being on a mixed farm!

Around this time there was renewed German activity in the local area, with incendiaries and phosphorus bombs causing the death of animals and the loss of straw or hay stacks.

Saturday 5 February 1944. 'Mr Shuttlewood said several bombs were dropped near his house, some are unexploded. The baker said 500 incendiaries fell at West Hall.'

She confirmed a few days later that *'W Hall had narrow escapes from incendiaries last Fri. They fell near stacks.'*

Sunday 13 February, 'They dropped 2 flares in field opp Buckland House & 3 bombs near Clements & incendiaries in the distance as well as 2 near Well House.'

After another alert on the 20th, Zillah added *'The blitz on London is pepped up a bit.'*

Monday 21 February. 'caught 3.40 bus to school. We did Red X. Mr Smith discussed various air raids – they picked up 2 – 3 sacks of incendiaries. **Paglesham, for its size, the most bombed place in Essex – Official.** *We saw bomber which came down yesterday almost in same place as the one nearly 2 years ago, it was home from a maiden flight over Germany.'*

Unfortunately, Zillah's 'official' source is not known.

Paglesham saw a different aspect of the war when streams of army vehicles came down to a small, water-filled gravel pit near South Hall. The site is now hidden by trees. Lorries and Jeeps went through the water, testing – as it was later realised – how waterproof the engines were. What was not known was that they were preparing for D-Day.

Zillah recorded on 6 June, *'INVASION DAY'* and briefly that *'We landed in Normandy early today, fighting in Caen* [an over-optimistic report]. *The King broadcast at 9pm and Churchill made statements in House.'* There were few further reports of the fighting. Paglesham had more immediate concerns when doodlebugs started.

SCHOOL

Paglesham School, 1920s.

Having been used as the distribution centre when the evacuees first arrived, the school then became very busy with the extra pupils. Of the 32 evacuees who came, some will have been old enough to go to the Rochford senior school and which was also attended by several Paglesham children. Numbers at Paglesham were much fewer than at its peak of 97 at the turn of the century, so they managed.

Although Rochford was evacuated in 1940, the school

registers suggest that few, if any, Paglesham children left the village. Thirteen Paglesham children registered in 1940, five after Dunkirk, and others joined them as they became old enough (4½ or 5 years old), or when their family came to the village. Those who left school during the war generally did so to go to Rochford Senior School. However, in May 1940, the Rochford school closed and pupils had to stay at Paglesham until 1944, when those old enough transferred back to Rochford. That year six of them left in July, being '*of age,*' ie 14. 1947, there were just 28 children on the school roll.

Miss Flynn, who lived in the School House and had been headmistress since 1924, became ill in 1940, and retired to Stambridge. Zillah wrote on 2 August, '*Heard from NCF that she is resigning from the school.*' Caretakers lived there afterwards. Mrs Dorothy Davies took over, coming each day by bus from Benfleet. She recalled that quite often they had to get off the bus and take cover when the sirens went for an air raid.

The children had school life disrupted by air raid warnings but otherwise made good use of opportunities to collect spent bullet cases, anti-radar foil or pieces of Perspex from aircraft windscreens. These were made into souvenirs, or polished and made into rings. Incendiary cases would be sought, dead or alive, and dismantled for the aluminium discs which made wheels for model cars. When a Liberator bomber crashed behind Church End, it became a playground – complete with live ammunition – until guards turned up to spoil their fun!

The schoolchildren also helped the war effort by saving money through National Savings. Miss Bright sold them the Savings Stamps which she got from Atkinson's shop at Church End. In January 1941, during War Weapons Week, they increased these savings to help buy a Bren gun, and later in the year saved £56 in 12 weeks. With weekly wages being well under £5, this was a remarkable effort. In October, the school log book noted '*During this month the children have been making Blackberrying Expeditions in order to assist Jam Making Programmes of the Women's Institute.*' The playing field at the back of the school was turned into allotments for the children. Savings Stamps were also sold once a week at the Mission Room by Ada Jennings.

In 1943, anti-personnel bombs were being dropped. The children were given a lecture by a Bomb Reconnaissance Officer, as these were often made to look interesting to pick up before exploding. It is not thought that any were dropped on Paglesham.

The war drew to a close with a final drama for the pupils. A bomb fell within range of the school on Monday 12 March 1945 and failed to go off. The next day Zillah noted, '*The rocket that fell near Stannetts yesterday is still in the ground, although they have dug down 18 ft.*' The school was closed for a month.

ROCHFORD HOSPITAL

Zillah took on more war work.
Wednesday 31 May 1944. 'Got to WVS for meeting at 2.30. Mrs Swire [asked] if we were sufficiently staffed for taking in Air Raid casualties?, etc. A Mrs Cook of Ashingdon asked if we wld undertake work at Hosp if necessary, no night work or scrubbing, so we agreed.'
Thursday 15 June, 'Mrs Mercer conducted a party of WVS to interview Matron re our work

there when required. She thought of attaching one of us to each ward...'

Monday 10 July, After *'taking a load to PDSA'* in Southend, *'I caught 1.15 bus to R'fd for my 1ˢᵗ days work at Hosp. I helped make beds with patients in, otherwise helped with the tea & washed umpteen bowls with monkey soap & left at 6.10pm. I am in Chalkwell Ward, mostly elderly men.'*

Zillah did a variety of small jobs such as preparing bandages. *'I cut up more than 3 rolls of cotton wool with the aid of a new young nurse,'* or *'cut over 200 gauze dressings.'* Tea making was a regular job, serving it, and washing up, or emptying ashtrays, wiping over lockers or sewing on buttons. She spent time talking to patients and commented on whether some of them looked better or otherwise.

'One old man who only whispers & is rather helpless took my hand, thanked me for what I had done & said "God Bless You".'

Although Zillah and the nurses went to a canteen for their own tea, she was often left on her own, which she clearly did not like. She sometimes helped with suppers before leaving at 6.30 pm after 4½ hours' work to catch her bus home from Rochford Square.

These visits always followed an hour spent at the Citizens' Advice Bureau with Mrs Mercer, dealing with a variety of queries. In July 1944 a bombed-out family from Stoke Newington came in. They were staying in Ashingdon and were *'fitted out with American clothes.'* This took longer than usual, and Zillah *'Finished at 1pm. Ate sandwiches in Hall Road,'* before going in to the hospital at 2 pm. In August a *'bombed out mother'* was sent to the Assistance Board and Mrs Mercer dealt with *'someone in lodgings.'* Permits for sheets for an expectant mother, the validity of some clothing coupons and acorns were also dealt with. In September 1944, Zillah felt that enquiries *'seemed to be slacking off with no bombing now.'* Mrs Mercer lived at Little Wakering Hall.

Zillah continued to go in to work at Rochford Hospital for a long time, changing (along with the Citizens' Advice Bureau work) to Tuesdays after twelve months. By 1946 she was mainly preparing bandages and sewing on buttons, or going through the linen cupboard to find what was needed. She was still there in 1952!

DOODLE BUGS and ROCKETS

Only ten days after the D-Day landings on 6 of June, which she entered as *'INVASION DAY,'* Zillah noted,

Friday 16 June 1944. 'Wakened at 7am, I think, by our first experience of Doodlebugs. It passed very near, making a loud thrashing noise and appeared to go up the road between Cupola and Redcroft.'

An alert at 6.45 am woke them on the 19ᵗʰ, *'followed soon after by a pilotless plane ... making for Chelmsford way. ... later we heard the explosion.'* The next day *'Mrs Boardman told M a pilotless plane came down in Chelmsford near Saracen's Head.'*

Another who saw them was Mrs Olive Redfarn, working at *HMS Leigh* in Southend. She said *'How weird to see them, like fiery chariots. When the light goes out, they fall to earth and explode.'*

94

Other references to 'Buzz Bombs' or 'Doodlebugs,' as they rapidly became known, occur in Zillah's diary in the next few weeks, followed by

Thursday 20 July. 'Awakened just after midnight by buzz bombs, followed by 6 more in ¾ hr ... 4.25 ...4,'

Friday 21 July. '... we counted 11.'

There appears to have been a lull in August, but

Tuesday 12 September. 'About 5pm there was a mighty bang & A saw pieces go up in the air. ... supposed rocket exploded in field near Clements making a crater about 20ft deep. No damage or casualties. Police, fire engines and military soon on the spot.'

Another came down without exploding on Clements Marsh. George Perry went to see it and realised it was different from the V1. Officials soon came to take it away, and would not discuss it. It was thought to be the first of the many V2s to be directed at Britain.

While V2s were aimed at London, they regularly fell elsewhere. Zillah noted one falling in Stannetts Creek on 2 December and another at Scaldhurst in Canewdon on the 8th. They were fired from northern Europe. Rosemary always remembers that,

'My father took me upstairs to an east window in Cupola House and, looking towards Holland, we could see the vapour trails going up. Five minutes later they would be passing over the house. He told me that this was an important part of our history.'

'Usual V1s and V2s' were still being mentioned in March 1945, but by April Zillah was including headlines in block capitals, on consecutive days.

Friday 27 April 1945. 'AMERICANS AND RUSSIANS HAVE MET.'

Saturday 28 April. 'HIMMLER HAS OFFERED UNCONDITIONAL SURRENDER.'

Sunday 29 April. 'MUSSOLINI HAS BEEN EXECUTED.'

Monday 30 April. 'SNOWING.'[!]

Tuesday 1 May. 'HITLER IS DEAD,'and

Wednesday 2 May. 'GERMANS IN ITALY UNCONDITIONALLY SURRENDER.'

All this among spring cleaning, *'Usual Sat work & Library'* and *'Flags out at the Borehams to celebrate John Boreham's return last Thursday from POW camp.'*

WOMENS' INSTITUTE AND KALORAMA

History was again the theme for the WI's 12th birthday meeting in March 1945. To brighten up the dull, drab days of the war, members dressed up in clothes of historic times. Zillah's were probably historic in their own right.

Wednesday 7 March 1945. 'AM dressed me in crinoline pink & blue dress ... The Parade was quite a success, 15 in all. Rosemary B presented a posy to each. ... the Birthday cake made by Mrs Bowen [one of several noted cake-makers over the years] *who gave a prize for the one who guessed its weight (7½ lbs).'*

Paglesham Women's Institute, 12th Birthday, 1945. Mrs Bowen (far left), Zillah Harris (4th from right), Rosemary Boardman (far right).

Members from Stambridge and Barling WIs had been invited and the costumes were photographed in the road outside the Mission Hall.

Before the war Paglesham WI had made a link with the CWA, the Country Women's Association, of Australia, its equivalent organisation. Mrs Myring, from the Kalorama branch, just east of Melbourne, came for a visit in June 1939. She stayed with Mrs Anfilogoff at Redcroft and gave a talk to a Paglesham WI meeting.

On her return to Australia, Mrs Myring made a broadcast referring to the visit.
'Early in the afternoon we drove to the tiny hall, beautifully decorated with flowers, where about 50 members were assembled. After being introduced to this friendly audience I spoke of our CWA branch & its work in the lovely Dandenong Ranges, of our berry, flower and vegetable gardens, our birds & our sunshine. As I concluded my little talk there was a strange silence suddenly broken by the ringing tones of a Kookaburra, which laughed and laughed. I joined in its mirth with some difficulty as I was quite overcome by the kind and welcoming touch of home…'
Zillah commented on the occasion,
'A's Kookaburra record was put on which quite surprised Mrs Myring.'

In 1945, when British rationing was getting worse, and after a national appeal to help Britain, Kalorama began sending food parcels to Paglesham, both to individuals and to the WI. Zillah had a parcel in April 1945, and wrote her thanks,
'…I felt like a child with a Xmas stocking as I took out one by one all the varied articles it contained. It was a real surprise packet, and all so neatly packed like a jigsaw puzzle.'
After describing British rations, she added, always grateful,
'Nevertheless, I shall never complain & think we have much to be thankful for that we never starved as some countries did.'
In January 1946 she received cake, jellies, cheese and a calendar. In 1947 it was tinned dripping, raisins, dried apples, pastry mixture, jam, dried milk and a jelly.

Zillah thanked for the dripping and added *'most housewives find the scarcity of fats very trying to cope with, each person receives ¼lb marg, 2ozs butter, 1 oz lard or suet.'* Mrs Myring said that their branch had sent 200 lbs of fat to Britain. Individuals in Kalorama rendered it down and sent it to Head Office to be tinned as part of a *'CWA FAT FOR BRITAIN'* campaign.

Paglesham WI also responded with thanks and books for the library in Kalorama – surely Zillah's suggestion? Kalorama CWA were always pleased by the thanks they were given and for the books. Zillah kept in touch with Mrs Myring and their correspondence was discovered in a shed forty years later! In 1995 Mrs Myring was sent copies which were read out to their CWA members who were surprised and delighted to hear about those earlier times.

These parcels were certainly well received and widened outlooks in the village, as the war had been doing as people followed the battlefront news.

In 1945 Rawty Martin gave his whole estate of 1,000 acres, including Church Hall and East Hall and '*over a dozen cottages*' to the nation '*in the hope that the Ministry of Agriculture will use these farms as an Agricultural Training centre for ex-servicemen and women,*' as the Farmers' Weekly reported in its issue of 24th August.

This was not to be, as the current site at Writtle was being developed as an agricultural college, where Rosemary was to go ten years later. The Ministry of Agriculture farmed the land, with their manager, Ken Rampling, at East Hall, while Mrs Meeson continued to live at Church Hall. East Hall and 150 acres near it were used from the 1950s by the Agricultural Research Council, whose headquarters were at Wellesbourne, in Warwickshire, as the National Vegetable Research Station. Their farm manager was David McVittie from 1955. It was used for experimental work on seed breeding and multiplication. The main vegetables trialled were brassicas,

AD 'Rawty' Martin at East Hall barn, 1940s.

plants of the cabbage family, which were grown in small netted areas. Mrs Meeson died in the 1950s and Brian Rice, then farm manager, went to live at Church Hall.

Church Hall, '*A fine medium sized Georgian Farmhouse, 8 cottages ... extensive outbuildings and 736 acres*' was sold on Friday 6 September 1963. It was bought and then farmed by Mr D H (Biff) Rayner whose father farmed at Oldbury Farm, Great Wakering, not far across the River Roach. The Daily Telegraph reported that '*In a Parliamentary written reply, ... the proceeds* [from the sale] *to the 'King's Fund'.*' This Fund was described as existing '*to help those disabled in the service of their country.*'
East Hall was eventually sold in November 1977, when NRVC consolidated its activities at Wellesbourne. The buyer was again Biff Rayner, who reunited the two farms.

PEACE

Tuesday 8 May 1945. '[Zillah] *went to S'end ... to the Gaumont to see 'A Song to Remember' about Chopin's Life. We had Churchill's speech announcing PEACE at 3 pm. ... Shops closed & Southend en fete for VE Day.*'
Rosemary and her parents joined the thousands in London to celebrate the end of the war.
    '*We stood in the Strand & watched the Royal Procession go by on its way to St Paul's. Later we stood outside Buck Palace to see the Royal Family come out on the balcony – the King & Queen, Princess Elizabeth & Princess Margaret.*'

Rosemary and her mother went up to London again.

Friday 11 May. 'My mother & I went into St Paul's and met the American artist Frank E Beresford who was painting the bombed area of the cathedral. He autographed a copy of his painting of Middle Temple Hall called 'Armistice Day 1940', and added St Pauls 'VE'+3.'

Paglesham held a Thanksgiving service at 4.30 pm on the Thursday and another in the morning on Sunday, which included '*a special form of prayer*' for the occasion.

A different surprise came in July. From Zillah's diary,
Thursday 26 July. 'ELECTION RESULTS ANNOUNCED. A great surprise – a real landslide in favour of Labour & a massive majority of 205. For 416, Opposition 211.'
Churchill, who had led the country through the war, was out and Clement Attlee became Prime Minister.

With no prior mention of the war in the Far East, nor of the dropping of atomic bombs,
Wednesday 15 August. 'Good news before breakfast that JAPAN's SURRENDER came through at midnight. Scouts [from Chislehurst] *busy this day building a bonfire in front of Plough. Mrs B came to ask us to attend the lighting & would A play for Community singing. Mrs Fleming came in to hear King's Speech…'*

Southend was rather livelier. Mrs Redfarn wrote in her diary,
Wednesday 15 August. 'Official VJ Day. The ships were letting off coloured Very lights. Everyone seemed half mad. Bonfires everywhere. Fireworks being thrown around haphazardly among the crowds. Bandstand: Dancing was in progress. Long lines were snaking around doing the Conga. The Palace Hotel was floodlit. Sailors were climbing up the lamp-posts. We were glad to get home to peace & quiet.'[10]

THOSE WHO SERVED IN UNIFORM IN WORLD WAR II

Benjamin Atkinson
Donald Atkinson
John Boreham
Gladys Brown
Alfred Keeble
Kenneth William Keeble
Oliver Keeble
Jack Thorogood

---

[10] See '*Under the Flight Path*' for more details of Paglesham and the Rochford area during WWII.

14 POST-WAR

There were great shortages after the war and rationing continued for many years. Bread coupons were introduced for the first time in July 1946, for two years. Sweets were only '*taken off the rations*' in 1953, with rationing of the last two items, meat and bacon, ending in 1954. People were still encouraged to grow food for themselves.

Mrs Mercer, the WVS organiser, talked to Zillah about the newly-formed national Village Produce Association (VPA), and suggested that Athelstan might like to start one in Paglesham. Athelstan discussed this with Alan Boardman, and sixty people attended a meeting on 27 March 1946. The VPA not only encouraged vegetable and flower growing but also the keeping of chickens and pigs. A speaker from the Essex Garden Produce Committee spoke about the benefits of having an organisation, and the Head Gardener of the Essex Institute of Agriculture (which Alan had attended) was also there to answer questions.

At the next meeting, on 6 April 1946, 35 people were present. Alan was elected chairman, with Athelstan as secretary and Ken Kydd as treasurer, and the Paglesham VPA started. As many members kept chickens, a Poultry Club was formed, which bought chicken-food in bulk. Monthly talks, films and discussions were held, and the first of the annual '*Produce and Flower Shows*' was held in the Mission Room on Saturday 24 August 1946. There were

37 classes in five sections covering vegetables, flowers, fruit, preserves and eggs, and cookery. The recipes included '*dried egg,*' although '*Ordinary Egg may be substituted for Powdered Egg.*' The judges had lunch at Cupola House and Rosemary was dying to know if she had won a prize. She had entered in '*Class 25. Bunch Wild Flowers in jam jar, for children under fifteen (Entry Free).*' Zillah was another keen exhibitor, entering her handicrafts and some flowers.

PVPA Show, 1953. Zillah, far left.

The PVPA grew both in scope and membership. The size increased with more classes, including handicrafts, and more participants. The Shows moved to marquees at various places – Cupola House Meadow, South Hall, Paglesham House, East Hall and Church Hall, where one was also held in the barn. Sideshows were soon added with a coconut shy in 1948, expanding to a wide variety of stalls in later years. Vegetable and flower classes still provided serious competition, with floral art coming in the 1960s. Cookery and handicrafts joined the other classes. The ladies developed reputations for baking excellent cakes (sampled at many other events) and both sexes competed in the home-made wine section. Spring Shows were started in the Mission Room.

PVPA Spring Show in the Mission Room, 1985.

A friendly tug-of-war between Church End and East End started in the 1960s, and country crafts in the 1970s, when Barn Dances in the marquee in the evenings were popular. Fancy dress was a feature at the East Hall field one year, with the parade led by two attractive 'Spanish dancers' on horseback.

The AGM on Saturday 31 July 1948 was visited by a Ministry of Food *'Mobile Canteen Kitchen ... Free Cookery Demonstration.'* Annual suppers were inaugurated in 1949, held in the Plough and Sail, with Mr and Mrs Tom Loader providing a steak and kidney and oyster feast. Whist drives became regular events, eventually being run monthly by Dick Thorogood. Other notable events arranged over the years included walks, a treasure hunt round the village, dances and angling competitions. Derrick Wood, by then living at The Chase, was Chairman for 14 years. During his time there were flights to the Dutch bulbfields in 1960 and to Paris the next year.

The PVPA had expanded into being a major focus of much of the village's social life. It was said that the WI looked after the ladies' interests and the PVPA after the men's, although the ladies were very much in that as well, forming half the committee by 1956.

CHANGE AT EAST END

In 1946 the Nicholls sold The Chase to Mr Ingram, who turned it into a *'Residential Hotel or Country Club.'* The advertising handout, a simple Roneo'd sheet, described it as

'PAGLESHAM CHASE ...is associated with the romantic history of the Essex rivers. Its old country house atmosphere has been retained and improved with the introduction of modern conveniences and furnishings.

The Chase Hotel sign.

'Standing in the centre of 55 acres of its own farmland [farmed by Alan Boardman] and immediately encompassed by 6 acres of gardens and orchards ... frontage on to the tidal, sea-water River Roach; thus every sort of recreation is possible – bathing, boating, fishing, riding, tennis, croquet, rambles etc out of doors; and billiards, table tennis, bridge etc indoors...
'Here is no modern seaside resort ... but a delightful old Essex yachting centre and rustic fishing village,

world famous for its superb Paglesham Oysters.'
Despite this promotion the hotel was not a success and was back on the market in 1948.

The *'modern conveniences'* were slight by today's standards. There were 11 bedrooms shown in the 1948 sale catalogue, of which seven were fitted with *'lavatory basins, hot & cold supplies',* but there was only one bathroom and one *'WC with low level Suite'*. There was both a dining room and a large restaurant, and a *'Cellar Bar'*. The water was pumped up to storage tanks, and this may have been by electric pumps. There was certainly electric power and light – electricity had been laid on to Paglesham early in the war. But there was no mains drainage, made-up drive or proper car parking!

The hotel venture was good for employment as several village people got jobs there, but it didn't last long. When the sale took place on 12 June 1948, the main difference from that of 1903 was that there was no oyster business. Zillah bought their mother's house, 2 The Chaseway, and also number 1, described as *'The Pair of Picturesque Freehold Cottages.'* Alan Boardman bought 50 acres of land and the farm buildings, stables and coachman's cottage. Alan needed the cottage for his farm workers and Zillah's Aunt Minnie moved to a cottage in Waterside Lane – now called Rats Hall – before finally living in number 1, next door to her sister.

Boarded Row had rentals between 3s 6d and 5s per week, except No 6 which was let furnished at £5 per month – a surprising 25s per week. Barn Row was then four dwellings each let at amounts between 2s 6d and 5s per week. Both Rows had four rooms in each cottage, two up, two down. Shop Row and Brick Row were slightly larger, with a third room upstairs, but Brick Row rents were between 3s 5d and 4s weekly, while those for 2 to 6 Shop Row were 3s 9d, 5s, 6s, 5s, and 3s 6d. Number 1, with the additional shop, was 8s per week. In terms of sanitation, they still had only a wash-house and outside bucket toilet.

Snow and elm trees, with Mission Room, one of several hard winters.

To add to post-war hardship, the winter of 1947 was another very hard one. Snow started in mid-January and continued off and on for the next two months. The village was cut off at times and farm workers dug through the snowdrifts. There was also a shortage of coal.

Clearing snow by hand, January 1947.

CHURCH CHANGES

Another change in 1946 came with the retirement of Rev Jennings. He had been very Victorian and Zillah could be mildly critical. She wrote '*a long sermon today*' and on another occasion, '*The Jennings disapprove of raising money by entertainment & expect it to fall from the skies!*'

The new man was Rev A L Harriss who became the first holder of the joint benefice of Canewdon and Paglesham. He lived at Canewdon vicarage, and the Paglesham rectory was sold to Mr Jack Burrows, owner of the Southend Standard. The new rector was popular and soon formed a choir, which wore blue surplices and blue 'mortarboard' caps. Rosemary was one of the dozen or so who joined. He was followed in 1954 by Rev G C Ludlow.

There had long been a Congregational church in the village. This was held in a partly brick building built in 1838, beside Claverham Cottage, but the Rochford minister felt that this building was, according to a report in the *Southend Standard* on 29 July 1954, '*very old and dilapidated. ... It was cold, damp and badly lit*' and was discouraging the congregation. With the preacher, Mr D Seefelt of Leigh, he arranged to bring a small timber church from Sutton, the other side of Rochford, to a new site opposite the school. The building was split in two and the 10-ton larger section was brought by road, without mishap, in the early hours of Friday morning, 23 July. The sixteen feet wide building squeezed through the middle of Rochford with two inches to spare getting into East Street! The second part arrived on the next Wednesday morning, and the new church opened on 2 October 1954. The chapel still has services, taken as always by the minister from Rochford.

Congregational Chapel negotiating Rochford, 23 July 1954.

Rev Norman Kelly succeeded Rev Ludlow in 1957. He was a bachelor, who did not drive, and cycled round both his parishes. Paglesham church roof was in a poor state, so fund-raising was started with a large fete at Winton Haw in 1961 which raised £170. In total, £2500 was spent in treating the roof for death-watch beetle and re-roofing. At the same time, sixteen gravestones, mainly from the eighteenth century, were brought in and laid in the chancel area to preserve them. Increased erosion of those still outside has shown the wisdom of this decision.

Rev Kelly kept strong links with Westminster Abbey, being friends with the Dean, Canon Carpenter, and in later years he acted as a helper there once a week. In 1969 he secured the great west doors of the Abbey to hang in the tower arch in Paglesham Church. Surprisingly, the tall arch at Paglesham dwarfs the new doors, but with long curtains as well, a considerable amount of draught was stopped. They were erected in memory of Rev Jennings with the aid of a donation by his daughters.

FLOODING

The start of February 1952 was busy for Zillah, with a meeting of the PVPA in the evening of Monday 4th with a talk by the '*Parks Supt.*' Tuesday saw her at Rochford Hospital, still helping to cut gauze for bandages, and having tea with Mrs Perry to discuss the next day's WI agenda. The speaker from the Essex Records Office could always inspire an interest in history, one of Zillah's particular interests.

Wednesday 6 February 1952. '[Zillah went to the Mission Room to] *get ready and meet Mr A C Edwards off bus. Introduced him to M and took him to WI where he gave a talk on Essex, some documents relating to Paglesham … Then he came back to tea with M & left on 5.30 bus.*' Her diary entry ended, '*Great shock today to hear King George VI died suddenly in early hours.*'

The country started 1953 looking forward eagerly to the new Queen's coronation in June. But tragedy struck much sooner, on the night of Saturday 31 January 1953.

Alan and Phyllis Boardman had gone to a dance at Delph House in Rochford Square. Rosemary had not been well and stayed at home. She wrote in her diary, '*Very windy & terrible. M & D went to Delph House in evening. Mrs Lapwood came in* [to keep Rosemary company]. *When they came home rang up* [the Police], *water all over the marshes. High tide at 1.30.*' Rosemary always remembered that there was a brilliant moon and that the very strong wind was causing Cupola House to sway.

'*My father rushed down to see if his pigs at Chase Farm were flooded, but the slightly higher ground on their side of a ditch had saved them. Mother & I watched from an upstairs window as the flood came nearer and nearer. It stopped 1½ fields away.*'

The regular high tide had been increased by low pressure and strong winds to create a surge which swept down the east coast from Lincolnshire, wreaking its greatest havoc in Holland, where over 2,000 died. All who saw it agreed that one tide had not gone out and the next had added to it. The death toll in Britain was 307, of which 58 were on Canvey Island, which was completely under water, and 55 in the rest of Essex.

The marshes round the village were sheets of water, but all the houses in Paglesham were a few feet above the flood level except for the pair nearest the boatshed. It had been in one of these that Minnie had lived. Frank Shuttlewood at the boatyard suffered as his wood had to be rescued from surrounding fields and he had to wait until his boatshed could be cleaned out. He was used to

Flooding between The Chase (in trees) and seawall, February 1953.

water coming in, but not to that level. At Church End, walls had broken and the water had just reached a pig shed near the bend in the road near the Punch Bowl Inn. Those pigs swam out! They also found out the following day that, as Rosemary's diary said,

'*All Wallasea and Potton under 8 ft of water. Went to see it – terrible number of breaches. Our lower fields by the seawall under water. All Mr Perry's* [marshes] *at Barling, Wakering, Stambridge, all terrible. Canvey Island many dead.*'

The wood at Davy and Armitage's timber yard on Wallasea Island floated everywhere.

Foulness Island was completely cut off, with no telephones working, and there were worried relatives in Paglesham. Boats soon went off from the village and from Burnham-on-Crouch and anchored in the Roach, before taking dinghies over the wall. While everywhere at Foulness except the Church was awash, most of the inhabitants were safe; only two died, but there was a great loss of cattle and sheep.

Over 50 years later it is hard to appreciate how limited communications were at the time, and the difficulties in providing warnings from the first inundations up the coast. Rosemary's father's phone calls were not believed at first, but it would have been too late for much to have been done by then. Other warnings received were treated as routine, as high tides were to be expected. At Jaywick, where there was much loss of life, messages had to be sent on foot or bicycle, as the telephones were put out of order.

On 4 February 1953, Southend Corporation was given the task of filling the 11 breaches in the seawall of Potton Island and the three on Rushley Island. Work started the next day. A base for these operations was made in Paglesham boathouse. Hilda Grieve, in the definitive book on the Essex floods, *The Great Tide*, said that work was 70% secure on Potton by the 7th, but Rushley was a different proposition as it was only accessible at high tide. On Friday 8th February Rosemary wrote, '*8 bus-loads of men came to mend seawall at Potton.*' They and their equipment were ferried across to the island opposite the boatshed. Radio links, run by Marconi Wireless Telegraph Company operators, made communications easier.

Pumping water away by boatshed, 1953.

Thousands of men – troops and volunteers – were employed on similar tasks around the many breaches on the Essex coast, in wind, icy cold, snow and rain. A pump near the boatshed started pumping water off the Paglesham marshes.

As tides were getting higher, Frank Shuttlewood built a new gate three feet high compared with the previous one's modest 18 inches. The seawalls were raised as well by digging out bigger 'delphs' or ditches on the landward side. They have since been raised another 20 inches, with extra support for the base of the wall.

Once the walls had been repaired and the water pumped or drained off, the land had to be treated with gypsum to counteract the effects of the salt. It was soon back in cultivation but it was some time before it fully recovered.

The River Roach had once been a hive of activity, with several oyster merchants having layings almost continuously on the foreshores on the Paglesham length of the river and in the side channels. At one time there might have been a dozen or more smacks working the numerous layings of these merchants. This had dwindled to a mere token of those days, with just the Keebles' *Vanguard* still in the oyster business by the 1950s.

In the 1950s, there was one sailing barge, the *Lord Roberts,* making regular passages up-river to Rankin's Stambridge Mills with loads of grain for the mills, but she had a motor fitted in 1951 and had her sails taken off in 1956. She ceased to work in 1963. Motor-powered coastal cargo boats took over, and one of Hubert Keeble's jobs was to pilot these vessels up to Rankin's mills when summoned by a blast on a siren. There were several farm wharves which had been used to take grain away and bring back manure from London. These wharves disappeared when the seawalls were raised after the floods, but the one in Paglesham Pool at the end of a track from Church Hall can still be seen.

Rankins' Thames barge, *Lord Roberts.*

The Thames barges made a grand sight while they lasted, their sails towering above the seawall. The last barge-load of grain was taken up to Stambridge in 1970 in *Cambria,* skippered by the famous Bob Roberts.

Frank Shuttlewood was still building boats, although none as large as his father James's working boats – the barge *Ethel Ada* in 1903 or the oyster smack *Doreen,* built in 1898. James had died in 1936, but one of his boats was the *Grace Darling,* lost in the evacuation of Dunkirk. Frank's were still

Tiny Mite, built 1956; *Doreen,* built 1898, beside boatshed.

traditional timber vessels and he continued the tradition by building occasional barge-yachts, Dione in 1936 and Nancy Grey in 1939. The 35 foot barge-yacht, *Tiny Mite,* was launched in

1956 and was a familiar sight at Paglesham for many years. But pleasure yachts and sailing dinghies were more common. *Halloween* was built for Len Chopin, and is still sailed in the Roach by his son, Rodney.

Many barges and oyster smacks had roughly two foot long half-models made, from which the full-sized boats were scaled up. Some of these survive to provide a happy reminder of the Shuttlewoods' skills.

Messrs WH and LG Norris bought the boatyard in 1960, and soon the boatyard was mainly used to fit out Glass Reinforced Plastic (GRP) hulls brought in. These were large and sleek, but hardly traditional. Today the yard is owned by Essex Boatyards Ltd and is full of large pleasure cruisers, with a floating jetty beside the hard and extensive moorings in the river.

QUEEN'S CORONATION

Paglesham naturally had a celebration for Queen Elizabeth's Coronation. Plans were started in April, with Mrs Barbara Rampling, the wife of Ken, the manager of East Hall Farm, in charge, assisted by Mrs Davies, the school headmistress. They lived in the repaired farmhouse. A Pageant re-enacting scenes from local and Paglesham history was the theme.

This was the first time that the celebrations were timed round the television coverage at Westminster Abbey, and a set was hired to go in the school for people to watch. A few bought their first television set for the occasion. It was then in black and white; everyone later went to the cinema to see it in colour on Pathé News.

Queen Elizabeth's Coronation Pageant, 2 June 1953.

The day, 2 June 1953, started with the exciting news that Hilary and Tensing had reached the summit of Everest, the first time this had been achieved. Television started at 11 am, with tea following at 4 pm. The Pageant itself involved a cast of 72, and much rehearsal. Scenes started with Ingulf, the Saxon thane who gave Paglesham Church to Westminster Abbey in 1066, then came the invasion of Danes, and Tudor times. Lord Rich had owned land in Paglesham; '*Lady Rich* [played by Phyllis Boardman] *and her Ladies sang Greensleeves, Cherry Ripe and Now is the Month of May',* while Rosemary was one of the Ladies. Rosemary proudly wrote in her diary that she had won First Prize for Fancy Dress! 'William Blyth', the famous Paglesham smuggler, and his mates sang sea shanties. 'Mr & Mrs Laver,' – she was a Victorian Wiseman – of East Hall, were followed by 'Miss Laver' in a crinoline. The hoops were almost certainly supplied by Zillah Harris – she lent the crinoline frame to Rosemary 14 years later for her wedding. Finally 'Children of the Empire' came on in the costume of the various parts of the British Empire, and recited their parts. Then everyone joined in 'Land of Hope and Glory' and 'God Save the Queen.'

The Pageant was held in a field opposite the school and lasted from 5.30 to 6.45 pm and was followed by a short 'Coronation Service' conducted by Rev Harriss, a 'Fancy Dress Parade,' a 'Comic Football Match,' and, from 9 to 10 pm, dancing and a bonfire. The weather had had a lot of rain but fortunately this had stopped before the Pageant, although it was unseasonably cold. It had been a memorable day for Paglesham.

TIME AWAY

Another reason for remembering 1953 for Rosemary was that she passed her driving test.

'I had been driving our grey 'Fergie' tractor on the fields since I was 11! If I had a trailer which jerked behind the tractor when starting, my father would say 'The flies are biting badly today,' a reminder that it was not long since the days of horses. In fact there were still a number about. On my 17th birthday in April, my father took me out on the roads for my first lesson.

'I passed my test in Southend in July. My main memory was stopping and starting on the hill in Palmeira Avenue. How different driving was then, with relatively few cars about.'

Rosemary left Westcliff High School that year and did a year's practical, which was required to go to college, on their own farm. Lunts Farm was small, but in the early 1950s there were still four men working for her father, with three or more women working when needed at planting or harvest time. With pigs, cattle, chickens, market gardening and arable, it was good training. A year at Writtle Agricultural College (the successor to her father's college), taking a Certificate in Agriculture in 1954/55, followed, before another year at home.

'I got a job at the National Institute of Agricultural Botany (NIAB) in Cambridge in October 1956, working on seed production. I had only been there a week when, watching the University 'Rag Day' parade, I saw a young man hanging from a crane collecting for Poppy Day. Later that day I was introduced to him by a mutual acquaintance. Mark Roberts had just started at Pembroke College reading Engineering.

'At the end of his course in 1959 we were married, and moved around for seven years with his job of designing and building roads and bridges.'

MECHANISATION and FARMING CHANGE

Rosemary's father, Alan, was always interested in the politics of farming. At this time farms of 100 acres were still viable and he felt that mechanisation was the way forward. He was a member of the Farmers' Club in London and gave a talk there on 'High Production on a small Farm' in 1952. He was Chairman in 1959. He was also Chairman of the National Power Farming Conference in 1962, giving a lecture, 'British Methods and Machines to Meet the Challenge.'

He was on committees of the local National Farmers' Union, the governing body of National Vegetable Research Station at Wellesbourne, which ran the trials at East Hall, and put up for election to the Potato Marketing Board.

On the farm he was always looking for ways to save time and energy. Time and Motion

Alan Boardman on Massey Harris combine, late 1950s.

studies enabled him to do things more efficiently. Rosemary still remembers the threshing machine coming to the wheat stacks behind the farm buildings, with mice running out of the stacks as they lost their cover. There was usually a man or a dog ready to despatch them. Alan bought his first combine in 1947, an Allis Chambers with an eight foot cut and pulled by a tractor. In the 1950s he had a 10ft cut Massey-Harris which still required a man on the back to deal with the sacks of grain and tailings, which were dropped on a chute to the ground. Each sack weighed about two and a half hundredweight (125kg) He devised a platform to stack them so that they could be later slid sideways on to a trailer, saving effort. In 1966 he bought a new Massey-Fergusson 400 with 'Hydraulic Unloading Auger' (£2800!) and devised his own blown-air system for ventilating his bulk storage. He went back to some market garden crops and had planters for cabbages and potatoes, though they were still picked up by hand. They were delivered by lorry to the wholesalers, Essex and Kent, or H West, in Southend.

However, the size of machinery increased faster than he could have guessed. Small general farms have been squeezed out of existence, generally being bought up by larger neighbours. At the same time the number of men employed has come down, and the traditional tied cottage has become a thing of the past.

A different change came in 1964 when George Perry retired to his native Cornwall. His wife had died in 1952 and was buried in Paglesham churchyard. When George died in Plymouth in 1968, he was buried with her. South Hall Farm was sold to C H Cole and Son, large-scale farmers from Orsett and West Tilbury. The Devon cattle were also sold, and in the 1960s all the grazing marshes, as elsewhere in Paglesham, were drained and turned over to cereal crops. Sugar beet and oilseed rape were later.

Digby Fairweather and George Perry near Stannetts, 1960s.

George Perry befriended a young Digby Fairweather, who was learning to be a jazz trumpeter. The family had moved into Stannetts in 1959, and in the 1960s the sounds of Digby practising drifted across the fields to Redcroft. He lived in an ideal location to practise – a long way from the next houses! He was a gifted player and performed in the church to raise funds. Other jazz enthusiasts gathered for gigs played in the cellar of The Chase, with Derrick Wood's support.

Although Digby started work as a librarian, he turned professional in 1977 and had his first solo album in 1979 with *Havin Fun* which Zillah had mentioned in her diary. He became well known in top jazz circles and on the radio. He has given a number of performances in Paglesham since.

WOMEN'S INSTITUTE

The Mission Room was home to the WI, which flourished during the war years and continued with a wide variety of subjects at its meetings, including a summer one held in a garden. The 21st birthday party in 1954 was held in the garden at Ingulfs, the home of the President, Mrs Burrows. The photograph shows that all but two present wore hats (even Rosemary, the youngest there). Those seated were Mrs Lucking (Past President), Mrs Farquharson (Chairman of the Essex Federation of WI), Mrs Nancy Burrows (President), Miss Zillah Harris (Secretary), Mrs Anfilogoff and Miss A M Wiseman (both Past Presidents). This must have been one of the last photographs of Minnie.

WI 21st Birthday, 1954
Seated, centre, Mrs Burrows, Zillah, Mrs Anfilogoff, Minnie.

The WI formed a drama group the next year. Zillah was involved, but retired as Secretary in 1957. There are no further entries in her diary about getting to the Mission Room and getting it ready. While membership was strong, it was not always easy to find members willing to fill the main posts – a recurring problem with many organisations. But while there were threats of closure, the WI found volunteers and survived.

A GENERATION PASSES

Minnie had moved into 1 The Chaseway, next to her sister. Zillah had spent considerable time keeping an eye on her, as she was 87 in September 1954, while Pet was only two years younger.

Zillah's diary is blank at the beginning of 1955, possibly because she was too busy looking after Minnie, who died on the 9 January, aged 87. Minnie was buried on Thursday 14 January in front of the church, rather than with most of the family to the north. The gravestone reads simply, '*In Loving Memory of Alice Maud, daughter of Fred and Rose Wiseman. 1867 – 1955.*'

A newspaper obituary on 13 January 1955 read,

'Two years ago Miss Wiseman fell, when in Southend, breaking her leg. She made a remarkable recovery and was able to get about quite well with the aid of a stick . Described locally as "a bit of a character," Miss Wiseman ... took an active interest in all activities. For 20 years she was a member of Paglesham WI, being its President for two years. ... She was a keen gardener and the family have asked friends not to send flowers because she hated to see blooms die on a grave.'

After an interview with Pet in 1951, the Southend Standard included an article, under a heading of *'Her Gentleness of character is a lesson worth learning."*
Thursday April 5 1951. '... She is so good to animals that if she sees a worm in the road while walking to church ... she picks it up and puts it on the verge so it won't get run over, [said] *Mr Jim Thorogood. Later over a glass of home-made wine, sprightly white-haired Mrs Harris told of her life-long devotion to animals, birds, flowers and the countryside in general. I cannot bear to see them suffer and my daughter Zillah is the same. ... Here we are practically teetotal, yet I made wine every year until one day Zillah told me there were 90 bottles strained off in the attic! ... The trouble with the World today? Not enough kindness, says Mrs Harris.'*

Memorial to Dr Bernard and Mary *'Pet'* Harris, 1965.

Pet lived another four years, and died on 14 May 1959, aged 89. She had been a widow for just over 42 years. She was cremated and her ashes were interred with those of her husband, Bernard. The Rev A L Harriss, previously Rector and then Rural Dean, officiated. She left a remarkable £27,748 net, but she and Zillah were always careful.

With her passing, another generation had gone. Pet had outlived both her older and her younger brothers to see a post-war world greatly different to the one they had known.

A NEW START

Zillah had been kept busy during the last few years, and if she kept a diary only some have survived. She started another in 1960, this time in a large foolscap 'Boots Scribbling Diary' which gave her more space to write, and her writing was no longer the tiny script of previously. She starts with a poem she had written for a *'WI competition for January for which I got 2nd prize.'* It sounds as if she was mentally stepping away from the previous generation.

> *'Greetings for 1960*
> *'The pages turn – and at the gates*
> *A little figure stands and waits,*
> *The Old Year dies – the new is here*
> *To wish you all a Glad New Year.'*

Now she only had Athelstan to keep an eye on, but she refers to him only occasionally. She cooked meals for him and mended clothes, *'did A's room,'* and notes him mending a radio, or going to Rochford or Southend, usually without further reason. He seemed quite well most of the time but had various times when he '*felt a bit sick*' or had other minor problems. He did do outside jobs like '*cleaned the gutters*' and occasionally brought food home from Rochford. Most of the time they lived separate lives. Athelstan enjoyed gardening and kept bees, making copies of notes on bee keeping, in typical Harris fashion, on random pieces of paper. Several of these were on the back of large paper Union Jacks, advertising '*Forces Day*' from the wartime.

Zillah was now into her 60s, and decided that she would like some help and for a year or so, 'Mrs J' came in on Monday mornings and on other days to do various jobs. '*Mrs J did crocks, and sitting room*', or '*... kitchen*', is typical. Zillah took on overall responsibility for the house, doing her '*usual chores, '*arranging for repairs to her bedroom floor or the mending of a broken window. She loved her cats, particularly Tuppy in 1960, fed them well and worried about their health and if they stayed out longer than she expected. Letting them out in the morning and feeding them are frequently mentioned, as well as getting flea powder and seeing the vet. She must have had a rabbit and fish as she bought food for them as well as cat food. Feeding the birds was another job which she would have enjoyed because of her love of all creatures, shared by both her mother and aunt.

Zillah also adopted unwanted cats in Paglesham, taking on one or two when their owners had died. She sympathised with others' problems with their pets and tried to help whenever she could. She continued to visit the PDSA in Southend, talking to them about the strays they had to deal with.
Saturday 23 April 1960. '...getting in PDSA coach for trip to Ilford Sanatorium.
   KJ [Kathleen Jennings, the earlier Rector's daughter] *was waiting for me & we saw abt 8 horses in boxes, dogs, one with 5 pups, ... The Cemetery was full of pathetic inscriptions, many on marble crosses...*'

Sorting out her mother's affairs was still going on throughout 1960, with Zillah making several visits to the bank, transferring documents from her mother's name and visiting Tate's about the gravestone. Athelstan looked over the estimate for their mother's inscription on their father's stone, the brief '*Also the ashes of his wife, Mary Buckland Harris, 1869 – 1959.*'

They were also going through cupboards and drawers, throwing away Minnie's letters (which probably went for salvage), and reorganising the cottage. Her wartime thrift continued – she also returned skewers to the butcher. In the evenings she often just read the newspaper, listened to the radio, or watched television by invitation at someone else's house, often Miss Munn's. She also enjoyed embroidery and writing letters and her diary. Athel had a gramophone and his own radio, which Zillah could find trying.

Zillah had one or two people she went to see and was very good about comforting other people. It must have pleased her when,
Friday 5 February 1960. 'Miss M [Munns] *called fairly early & we discussed holidays & she said she would like to have me as a companion. She brought a bundle of brochures for me to decide.*'
Monday 8 February. 'Returned Miss M's travel brochures & she will look out those coach

trips which appeal to her & then I can decide. I watched Panorama & This is Your Life. Came home at 8.45. Chores, mended coms & had a bath.'

Having watched *'Princess Margaret's wedding to Mr A Armstrong Jones on TV'* at Miss Munn's on Friday 6 May, she *'spent rest of day working hard to get jobs done,'* before they went off on holiday the next day. Her diary is blank while she was away, except for notes of expenses. They had coffee at Abbeville that day, sent *'PCs from Fontainebleau',* on Sunday and were in Barcelona a week later. There was a *'Steamer to Palamos 5s 5d'* on the Monday before the diary resumes at home on Saturday 20th. They had set their sights wide. She later went to the Ideal Home Exhibition with Miss Munns and on several other trips with her around the country.

THE PLOUGH AND SAIL and THE PUNCH BOWL

The public houses were generally only frequented by men until after the war. Even after the PVPA started the Harvest Suppers in the Plough (as it gets abbreviated to), which ladies attended, the older ladies were reluctant to go into any pub. Neither Zillah nor her mother went into the pub for a drink, although they saw great changes during their lives.

In Victorian and Edwardian times, when Mrs Kemp was in charge, The Plough was a favourite of the oyster dredgers and was itself famous for its oysters, costing 3s 6d (17½p) a dozen. Brakes had come out on tours from Southend, but it is not known whether they were allowed to stop for a drink! The Territorials joined the locals at the bar and two or three hundred oysters would be opened in a night. But it was still the 'local'. The Loaders took over in 1929, and their son Tom and his wife Ilene were the landlords during World War II. After the war, a red public telephone box stood on the corner of the car park. By the 1950s and 60s, many were coming out by car for drinks in the evening and at weekends. Sailors would come up from the river, and others walked or cycled. Other food was also being served, and Paglesham was a regular place to go to for a drive.

Ilene Loader's business card, 1960s.

Vic Cardy, Walter Wood, Bill Robinson, *'Wopper'* Staines in the Public Bar, 1960s.

Ilene Loader was also a keen member of the WI, becoming President from 1957 to 1963, when Zillah was on the committee.

The Plough is a building dating from about 1600, with a central door and a tiny lobby. This led into the saloon bar on the left, with, to its right, the Loaders' private sitting room. There was a tiny serving hatch in the bar, with to its right, a door into a second, public, bar with sawdust on the floor and a dartboard on the wall. Dominoes and shove ha'penny would have been played at the small tables.

J F T Wiseman's exhortation in his poem written in 1888 to
'.....Go then without fail ... to the pub – Plough and Sail,
At East End you'll find it – when there don't forget,
Order oysters, bread, butter, with stout (heavy wet).
... tis Courage's brewing, and marked with XXXs.
was still being followed 75 years later, even if the beer had changed to Mann's, when Ken and Hazel Oliver took over the pub in 1963.

With fewer traditional workers in the fields and on the river, the Olivers applied themselves to attracting a new clientele. They reorganised the existing arrangements, making the saloon the bar for the locals, and smartened the public bar with plush seating, eventually opening up their sitting room to be part of the bar and extending behind and increasing the range of food served. Attractive pub signs, with both plough and sail depicted, replaced the Mann's plain board.[11]

The No 10 bus still brought customers out, as well as serving the villagers, turning round and waiting in The Endway, immediately outside the Plough. The service had changed from the red buses of Westcliff Bus Company to the green of Eastern National when an article in 1971 in the Southend Standard considered the future of the country bus in relation to Paglesham. They calculated that 'there were around 60 cars owned by the 90 or so households.' This meant that a third of the families (including Zillah's) had no car and many of the other cars would have been used to take one of the family to work in Rochford or beyond. At the time the bus ran every two hours, which provided a useful shopping service, although Zillah often walked around Southend waiting for a return bus. A year later the blue Southend Corporation buses took over, but the route was still No 10.

In the 1970s, Paglesham and Stambridge WIs joined forces with a choir, singing a variety of songs. Many were written by Betty Davies and sung to well-known tunes. The first verse of one, appropriate to the buses, was,
'Oh where? Oh where has the country bus gone?
Oh where, oh where can it be?
It was due at the stop at a quarter to one
And now it's a quarter past three!'
A highlight was performing for the Duke of Grafton at an event in London!

The list of licensees at the Punch Bowl goes back to the eighteenth century and then the pub was on the path south from the church to where the school was built. It moved to the present tall building, which had been tenements and once had a sail-maker's loft, in Victorian times. In the 20th century, it also had its own customers, but it remained a 'local' under the Layzell

---

[11] Ken and Hazel's second son, Mark, runs the Plough and Sail in 2009. Their eldest son, Trevor, has a pub in north Essex, and his son, Jamie, has made a name for himself on television and in other catering roles!

family, before also extending its catering side and smartening up for a more choosy public. Although the Harrises had walked to the shop fifty yards away, they would not have thought of visiting the pub.

In due course, with restrictions on drink-driving, both the Plough and the Punch Bowl became well-known for their meals, and continue to attract many customers.

ATHELSTAN

When Pet had not been well in 1955, Athelstan and Zillah took turns to keep an eye on her. Athelstan's diary (his only diary to survive) details their keeping watch on Pet, and shows a side of him not seen in Zillah's. It also records his beekeeping events such as moving the nucleus of a colony to a new site, feeding them or extracting honey. He is also concerned about his own health, which had given him problems since before the war, possibly contracted during the Great War, but these are not detailed. Whatever they were, he was unfit for service in the Second World War.

Athelstan Harris at the organ, Paglesham Church, c1960.

In 1966, a young Rex Berrecloth from Rayleigh was learning to play the organ, and the Rector suggested he might be of use at Paglesham. He came and played for a 4 pm evensong and met Athelstan, who was the regular organist. This meeting was to be of considerable significance for Zillah. Rex went on to play at times and occasionally was invited to 2 The Chaseway, having expressed a wish to improve his technique. Although Rex had met Zillah at church, he rarely met her at home. She kept out of their way while he talked to Athelstan.

At the end of January 1968, East End was at last getting a mains sewerage system, with a works near the boatyard. The flat ground meant that it could only just get as far as Cupola House, and houses had to pay to be connected. This caused considerable disruption in the village and by the Plough and Sail. The WI Committee, on 31 January at the Mission Hall, decided that future meetings would be held at Redcroft because of the noise. The bus had to turn round and go back to the Mission Room to wait when the works reached Buckland House on 1 February, and Zillah noted difficulty in meeting a friend!

Both Zillah and Athelstan were both ill with a chesty flu on Friday 2nd, doing little for some days. Zillah was not fit enough to go to the WI on Wednesday 7th, while Miss Munns phoned the doctor to come and see Athelstan the next day. Zillah could not understand what Athelstan was saying, which she attributed to his teeth, but he had breakfast and dinner and came downstairs for a time.

Thursday 8 February 1968. '*I cldn't hear A coughing when I awoke at 7.45 & on going to his room found him lying across the bed dead. I dressed & went to MM* [Miss Munns, who had been a nurse] *who came after b'fst. She had phoned Dr S'well who came early. After inspection he called the police, 2 came out & I had to sign a lengthy statement. They contacted Tate's & he came out & took A to hosp.*'

Miss Munns '*gave me scrambled eggs for tea … I refused MM offer to stay there for the night.*' She tried to keep warmer by sleeping downstairs, although '*v distressed.*'

Miss Munns came every day to see that she was coping, and Dr Southwell visited her on the Monday. She kept on with her '*chores*' and seemed better by the Wednesday. The funeral was on the Friday.

Friday 16 February. '*…Crematorium where Ralph and D had just arrived. … into waiting room before service which Mr Kelly took. As there was one too many of us to go in Joan's car, Vivi went with Mr Tate & Mr Kelly. The girls got tea while R & I interviewed foreman re sewage for this house.*'

Zillah's cousins had rallied round and even found time to deal with more mundane matters!

ORGANISTS

Mrs Chamberlain had been the organist for over 30 years at St Peter's, Paglesham, before she retired in 1958 and Athelstan took over. On his death, Jim Thorogood played for a couple of years. Unfortunately he became ill and died in 1970, when Rex Berrecloth took over. Following Athelstan's death in February 1968, Rex recalls,

'*I did not meet Zillah again for another 20 months, except on the odd occasion when I attended Paglesham church, at which she attended nearly every service. It was not until October 1969 that our paths were to cross.*

'*At that time I was engaged to Lynda* [Acketts]. *We had no plans to marry in the immediate future. … Rev Kelly knew* [this but] *said that there was chance of a house for us to rent in Paglesham, and that someone with church connections was wanted. Somehow he persuaded us to go and look … at No 1, The Chaseway,* [where Minnie had lived] *where we met Miss Harris, as we came to know her. She showed us No 1 and we fell in love with it straight away. The house was on a limited time offer, so we had to accept. Six months later we moved in on the 27 June 1970, the day we got married!*

'*On the day we moved in Miss Harris had placed a white vase with beautifully perfumed deep red roses in the kitchen, with a lovely note welcoming us to our new home and wishing us many happy years there.*

'*There was a selection of furniture* [in the house], *including a settle, a Regency sideboard and a beautiful Victorian chest,* [which] *we lived with for some months – until Zillah donated it to the Southend Museums. Of particular interest was a large, intriguing, oil painting in a shed.*'

This may have been the painting of the Harris family group which later hung in Prittlewell Priory.'[12]

Shortly after moving into their new home, Rex started playing the organ in St Peter's.

---

[12] See Appendix 1, page 134

CHURCH END

When Church Hall was sold in 1963, the Punchbowl Cottages were sold separately. They had been allowed to fall into a ruinous state and only two of the six were occupied, as they were no longer required for farm workers. Four years later, an application to demolish them was fiercely opposed, as they formed an important part of the street scene of Church End, then clearly visible on the approach to the village as well as at close range.

A row of cottages opposite, called Bedford Row, had already been lost without trace except for a group of trees. An ancient block of three or four dwellings called the Causeway or Winton Haw beyond the church had also been knocked down in order to build a modern Winton Haw in 1959.

In the end Punchbowl Cottages were too far gone, but the planners insisted that they should be rebuilt in a similar style, with dormer windows to the front bedrooms, so at least the attractive view has been saved.

The adjacent row of weatherboarded cottages was next in the firing line, with Biff Rayner fighting the proposed Preservation Order to be made in 1967 by the Rochford Rural District Council, the Chairman of which was Derrick Wood, who lived at The Chase! The row constitutes an interesting collection of houses of different dates with different roof lines and

Bedford Row, opposite the Punch Bowl, Church End, c1910. (Demolished)

floor levels. The last one, with two and a half stories, is probably the oldest, with a substantial timber frame. At the time it was the Church End shop and Post Office, run (following the Atkinsons) by Jim Cousins. It was proposed to follow the example of Punchbowl Cottages and replace them with buildings of a similar style. Described as *'five 18th Century and earlier cottages'* by the Council for the Protection of Rural England, their spokesman said that for them to be replaced *'by modern buildings would be to construct bogus scenery.'* He also stressed the need to preserve old villages on the edge of large urban areas such as Southend. Fortunately this view prevailed, and in more recent times they have all been successfully modernised without demolition.

Jim Cousins kept the shop going while he pursued his building and other skills, but it was no longer

Punch Bowl, Punch Bowl Cottages, Post Office Row, Church End, 1960s.

viable as a shop. It was bought by Ian and Angela Puzey, who set about restoring it. Angela was a doctor in the group surgery in Rochford and was living in the modern house next to Zillah with Ian and their daughter, Mandy. Ian and Angela had become involved in village affairs, organising many events. Angela was also greatly appreciated as a doctor and received an MBE for her work and effort in the community. She had become another Dr Southwell, whose devotion to his patients had been shown in his care of Rosemary.

The ancient Finches farmhouse survived the Sixties by having a second weatherboarded extension on the rear, known jointly as '*Finches and Maules.*' The small field in front was well mown and became an attractive cricket field, where the '*Poor Cricketers of Paglesham*' frequently challenged other local teams, in the true

'*Poor Cricketers of Paglesham*' tie.

tradition of village cricket. Special rules applied for shots into the overhanging willow tree, while '*The Poor Cricketers*' flaunted their own tie.

EAST END

A group of cottages, Cobblers Row on Waterside Lane, had been demolished, probably before the war, and East Hall was another dwelling to go, despite a fight by the Rochford Rural District Council. The Southend Standard had a headline '*Damp and Rotting*'. It continued, '*The fate of centuries old East Hall Farmhouse is now out of the hands of Rochford Council and with a higher authority.*' Zillah took up the fight for the house, which had been home to her great-great-aunt, Lucy Laver, from 1820 when she married William Laver until she died in 1876. Zillah wrote to the National Trust, of which she was a member, and at their suggestion to the Society of Ancient Buildings

The house was set in a dry moat, which is still there, but the damage caused by the high explosive bomb in 1941 was a factor in the decision to permit demolition. It was replaced by a typical 1960s modern house in front of the old one, which was then pulled down.

Redcroft was a large house, and large houses were not popular in the 1960s. Mrs Anfilogoff had been unable to sell it, but and it was saved when eventually Rosemary's father bought it in 1959. He let it to the Smiths for an Old Persons' Home until that closed and the authors bought it

The shop, East End, 1970s.

from him. Rosemary recalled,

> 'In 1966, we moved back to Paglesham with our three young daughters, living at
> Redcroft, the house built by Arthur Wiseman in 1899, and lived in more than twenty years
> earlier by Mrs Anfilogoff. I soon started a Playgroup for local children in the house,
> which ran for seven years, and then had other playgroups to see the wide variety of
> mainly farm animals that we had.'

The house had taken on a new lease of life. Thirty years later it was modernised and
continued to be the family home we had enjoyed.

The shop at East End, a lean-to attached to 1 Shop Row, had previously been run by Mr and
Mrs Walter Cripps for over 25 years, followed briefly by another Mrs Cripps, who was no
relation. The shop was narrow with a long wooden counter running down the left as one
entered, with tins of biscuits in front of it. At the back of the shop one door led into their house
and another to the cellar, where perishable goods were still kept.

Mr and Mrs Stan Cheverall took over the shop in 1956. Stan was an ex-army major and a keen
sailor. He became an Auxiliary coastguard and helped search for missing boats, usually at
night, from Stambridge to the mouth of the River Roach. He became Chairman of the
Rochford branch of the British Legion in 1960, until they left the village in 1974. Paglesham
people were pleased when he added a sub-post office, as that at Church End had closed. In an
interview when he retired in May 1974 he said,

> 'From then on I became the mother and father of the village, for not only did people shop
> at the stores, but they came to me for advice on pensions, finance, savings, licences,
> Premium Bonds and even investments.'

Zillah was a regular customer and collected her paper daily. She abbreviated him to 'Mr
Chev' in her diary.

The Cheveralls were followed by Mr and Mrs Phillips, who added some antiques and bric-a-
brac to the attractions, having those in the front room. Garden urns were displayed outside the
shop, with signs to the 'Trading Post.' When Mrs Phillips retired in 1986, it closed, and a
village meeting place went. Derrick and Daphne Woods converted the shop into a
comfortable home and moved from The Chase.

Bread was delivered to houses by Clement's and Arthy's, and Fance and Horner's had meat
rounds. All came from Rochford. Milk was delivered for many years by Walls Dairies of
Rochford, and today by Dairy Crest from Southend-on-Sea. Mr Younie from the shop in
Canewdon delivered groceries (and still does), so the Paglesham shop had competition.

A few other new houses were built at East End in the 1960s and 70s. The Griews built a house
beside Buckland Cottages and a bungalow at the far end of The Chaseway, just beyond Roche
House next to Zillah. Swatchways, between the Plough and Barn Row, 'Cobblers' on the site
of Cobblers Row, and two more properties in the garden of Milton Villa in Waterside Lane are
the extent of development. Most of the individual houses in the terraces have been
modernised and extended or joined with a neighbour, and all six of the Victorian New
Cottages have had major additions.

Zillah helped with research even before we moved to Redcroft. We gave our first talk, on '*Old Paglesham,*' at the AGM of the PVPA in the Plough and Sail in 1964. This was also the time we began to know Zillah Harris better (although she was always called Miss Harris). She went to the inaugural meeting on 20 January 1967 of the Rochford Hundred Historical Society (RHHS), as we did, and went with the authors to many of its meetings.

We gave a talk in 1969 on the history of Paglesham to the RHHS in the Mission Room. Hubert Keeble, living in Buckland Cottages, almost next door, and who was carrying on the oyster business, brought in a tray of oysters at all stages of their growth. Rosemary remembered,

> '*At the same time we put on an exhibition at Redcroft. Zillah had recited her family tree to Mark, which became one of the exhibits. She then lent some of her photographs and heirlooms. Some of the eighteenth century pottery and glass is now in the Southend Museum. Even then we had no idea of the extent of her treasures! This was the impetus to write my first book, 'Paglesham, Life in an Essex Marshland Village,' and Zillah helped me with information. I remembered going to her library, but did not realise of course that she was also recording my visits! Being born in the village, I have always been accepted by, and able to talk to, any of the old people in the village, which has been very useful.*
>
> *Zillah enjoyed babysitting for us occasionally, and coming to Sunday lunch. We didn't realise how often she had come over to Redcroft 50 years earlier and she was too reserved to mention her memories of Arthur and Tottie Wiseman and her cousins.*
>
> *I had just started getting the book together in November 1971 when my father suddenly died of a heart attack. There was no time for grieving as his pigs had to be fed and other arrangements made on the farm.*
>
> *My mother had not been involved in the farm, but she took it on with the help of good farming neighbours, Wallasea Farms and then the Stacey family at Scotts Hall, Canewdon. The pigs were sold. Keeping them fed and watered with the children and playgroup running was too big a job. In due course, Mark got involved in the paperwork which was building up with new regulations.*'

Zillah's library closed after 37 years on 21 November 1970, being taken over by a 'Mobile Book Van.' The van carried 2,500 books compared with the 200 which Zillah could change every five months, but another small piece of history ended.

Meanwhile, Rosemary continued with the Redcroft Playgroup and also with the book, eventually getting it ready for Mr Edelin at Unicorn Press in Southend. He helpfully advised on technical details, type-set it and printed it in 1972. Preparation had been difficult. Alan Boardman had been a keen supporter of the project, and would have been able to help answer

Zillah borrowing books from the new *Mobile Book Van, 1973.*

Mark and Rosemary with Zillah, dressed for
the book launch party, 4 July 1972.

many of the questions which arose about the village. It was decided to launch the book to coincide with the celebrations for the school centenary in 1972. There was a party at Redcroft a few days earlier. Zillah was a guest, and noted,

Tuesday 4 July 1972. 'Spent a good part of the day turning out dresses suitable for wearing at R&M's party on Saturday & tried them on last thing couldn't find belt to go with the '37 turquoise blue dress. Sat up ever so late looking in boxes in lowest drawer where it used to be kept to no avail.'

THREATS DEFEATED

In the 1950s atomic power stations were being planned and in July 1955 it was announced that one of the first would be sited at Paglesham on the East Hall land given by Rawty Martin ten years earlier. A big fight was put up, and although a site investigation had shown that it was suitable for the heavy foundations, it was eventually rejected because of insufficient water in the river for cooling.

Derrick Wood, 1977

A much bigger protest went up when the Maplin Sands, off Foulness, was listed as one of the four short-listed for London's third airport. An 'Action Committee Against Foulness Airport' was formed in March 1969. Derrick Wood, who was on the Rochford District Council as well as being Chairman of Paglesham Parish Council, was elected Chairman.

The threat was not just from the noise of aircraft on the runways to be built on reclaimed land, but also from the location of the anticipated associated city and the routes of road and rail links to London and the rest of Britain. The line of these links was shown on maps produced for the Roskill Commission and reproduced with extensive reports by both local and national papers. The route crossed the River Roach near Paglesham Pool, skirting East End, East Hall and then Church End before crossing the River Crouch. Paglesham's rural peace would have gone.

Posters at the boatshed, 1973 (Photo Neil Gulliver)

Derrick Wood and Peter Smith of Barling Hall – also in the development area – and owner of the land at Finches and Maules, Church End, presented the case against Foulness at the local and later hearings in 1970 to considerable effect. The Roskill Commission did not prefer Foulness, but Paglesham was horrified when the Government decided on Foulness as the preferred site in April 1971.

A new, larger body was formed, known as 'The Defenders of Essex,' incorporating parish councils and conservation bodies, again with Derrick as Chairman. It was felt that the wildlife significance of the rare undeveloped coastal area deserved preservation and that the site's isolation made it of least value to the traveller and that of all the potential sites, it would require most supporting development. This would need to absorb large areas between Southend, Basildon New Town to the west and the river Crouch.

Foulness Airport and route from reclaimed Maplin Sands, January 1973.

Fundraising, protests and responses to Consultation Documents continued for another two years, with extensive national coverage. A new newspaper, 'The Maplin Times' was launched in July 1973 with six of its 24 tabloid pages devoted to 'Maplin.' The Prime Minister, Ted Heath, who was a noted sailor and visited Paglesham, where he was received politely but left with no illusions. An effigy of him was thrown in the river!

Eventually, in 1974, the proposal was dropped. Paglesham celebrated with a cricket match in September 1974 between past members of the disbanded research team of the Roskill Commission and 'The Poor Cricketers of Paglesham' on the suitably rustic pitch in front of Finches and Maules. The Southend Standard reported that '*The Defenders of Essex clouted over a century but the Roskill Commission side trounced them in time for celebrations at the local pubs.*' If this match was a friendly one, the campaign had been determined and thorough.

OYSTERS

One threat which did not pass affected the oysters. The flood of 1938, the ice in 1940 and 1947 with an electric storm, followed by more flooding in 1953 with its mud slides, had set back numbers drastically. The winter of 1962/63 was one of the most severe. Ice floes on the river washed out the oyster beds and killed the oysters. It was almost the final nail in the coffin of the industry.

The Keeble family ran their oyster business from Fred and Arthur Wiseman's sheds just upstream of the boatshed. Their layings were in the Crouch and in creeks opposite Paglesham, some of which had also been the Wisemans'. The Ministry of Agriculture had taken some layings

Remains of Ministry oyster workings, June 2009.

downstream, renovated and fenced in some of the pits, and carried out research into the native oyster's problems, including a devastating disease, Bonamia.

Increasing pollution also badly affected both the oyster and fish stocks. Antifouling paint used by the growing numbers of leisure sailors was one cause, a second was the effect of sewage from the growing population of the Rochford area. A new treatment works at Stambridge, with a new lagoon in what had been Stannetts creek made in the 1960s, came too late to save the oysters.

Hubert Keeble had managed on his own during the Second World War. Afterwards his brothers George, who had been a police constable, and Alf, who had been in the merchant navy, returned to hep run the business. They were joined by Hubert's son Ralph. They bought the *Vanguard,* which had been at Dunkirk, to help them. Stocks of oysters were too small to have a 'spat-fall' to regenerate naturally, and oysters were brought in from, mainly the Solent. They also used *Vanguard* for fishing in the river or on Maplin Sands.

Hubert, born in 1900, and George, born in 1903, wanted to retire. Doug Whiting, a close family relative, came in about 1971 to keep the oyster business going with Alf, who was ten years younger than Hubert, and Ralph. But the problems were too great for the business to survive long and, in 1977, Ron Pipe bought the *Vanguard* and the layings together with what oyster stock remained. When Hubert died in 1974, George in 1976 and Ralph in 1977, the industry had virtually ceased. Alf died in 1980.

Oyster cultivation in Paglesham Pool, (left) June 2009. (Wallasea Island and Burnham-on-Crouch in background.)

Old railway carriage, washed up in 1953 floods.

In the early 1980's Doug Whiting purchased the Vanguard, which was semi-derelict, with the idea of restarting the business in association with the then owners of the layings. The Rochford District Council unsuccessfully tried to stimulate interest with Oyster Fayres and several pubs were encouraged to serve oysters, raw and cooked, but the Paglesham oyster industry had died.

Today oysters are again being cultivated in Paglesham Pool, where they were grown 500 years ago. These are not the native oysters which made Paglesham's name, *oestrea edulis,* but a different variety which are grown in mesh sacks on tables, rather than on the ground, so they no longer need costly and time-consuming work to keep them free of mud and parasites. They still attract attention, being featured on television in 2006 as *Paglesham Natives* was published. The oyster pits are slowly silting up and the railway carriage, washed up on the 1953 floods, which the Keebles used for storage, has gone.

ELM TREES

The road to East End had been a tunnel through mature, two to three hundred year old elm trees. Dutch Elm Disease started attacking elms at the end of the 1960s, with some losses and other trees hanging on. By 1970 it was becoming obvious that the disease was spreading. The disease was caused by a fungus carried by a beetle under the bark. Leaves would appear, only to wither. Some trees had limbs cut off to reduce the spread, but others were cut down. It was a disaster for the look of Paglesham as well as elsewhere in the country.

In an effort to prevent trees being felled which might survive, in 1975 a group of 30 villagers led by Daphne Wood, Derrick's wife, climbed into some of the elms due to be felled with banners *Save Our Trees* and *Go Home Axeman.* Paglesham again featured in the national papers and on television and the report was heard on radio around the world! The group stayed until a Tree Preservation Order was put on 20 of the trees by the Rochford District Council. However, over the next few years, more trees succumbed and had to be felled. Many of the trees were in hedgerows, so not only the roadside scenery changed, but the whole countryside.

Elm avenue, with Rose Cottage (later rebuilt as Hove To) looking from Redcroft gateway towards Cupola House, c1910.

Elm trees being felled opposite Plough and Sail, 1970s.

Other mature trees were lost in the storm of 16 October 1987, which swept across much of south east England. In Paglesham, trees came down across the roads bringing down electricity and telephone wires. Redcroft alone lost 20 trees, both specimen trees planted by Arthur Wiseman ninety years earlier, and hedgerow hawthorns. Boats on the river also suffered and the village was without power for several days.

With the loss of the big trees and the demand for bigger fields for larger machinery, farmers were encouraged to take out more hedgerows. One of the most obvious views was that coming into Paglesham, where there is now effectively a single expanse. This had been a number of fields, divided between both parishes and farmers. Boundaries are now visible only as a change of crop on straight lines, efficient but a very different scene from the previous thousand years, both visually and ecologically.

SCHOOL CENTENARY

A large plaque showing 1872 on the central part of the school indicated the enlargement of the school and remains there as part of its modern role as a house. This was the reason for celebration. A Pageant was organised – in the Church Hall barn again – and a lot of hard work was put in by both the children and adults. All 40 children took part on 15 July 1972, some taking more than one role. The headmistress, Mrs Dorothy Sime, wrote in the log book,

> *'Today everything went perfectly. ... The audience was unbelievable. We had expected 400 – 450 but there were nearer 600 in the afternoon. The children put everything into their performance... The hula-hula chorus for the Lazy Coconut item was favourite and received an encore...'*

All the children took part. Other popular items were 'Ten little speckled frogs,' 'Waves and Dancing Girls,' and an Empire Day Parade, with eight national costumes, ending with 'Brittania.'

School Centenary Pageants, Programme, 15 July 1972.

The children's part was followed by an equally appreciated performance by a cast of 16 adults, under the direction of Geoffrey Dye. A Centenary Song covering the 100 years had been written and was enthusiastically sung to the tune of the *'Battle Hymn of the Republic'* better known as *'John Brown's Body.'* Everyone joined in the chorus,

> *'Glory! Glory! To the village!*
> *Raise your glasses without spillage:*
> *Toast the ancients, middle-aged and young,*
> *As we all go marching on.'*

Scripts were disguised as Victorian slate-boards.

The 'Hula Hula Chorus', 1972.

Each of the children received a commemorative mug made by Mrs Linda Wood, a potter who lived at OBS Cottages. A dance was held in the evening to round off another typical Paglesham event.

The Pageant came as a finale for Mrs Sime, who retired a week later, having *'enjoyed every moment of my 14 years as head of the school.'* She had been a very popular head. She had been assisted in the later years by Mrs Rosemary Amis as Infant Teacher, Mrs Maisie Francis as School Secretary with Mrs Mary Keeble as an assistant. Mrs Grace Young acted as caretaker, living in the schoolhouse. When Mrs Sime left in 1972, the rooms were used for craft work and as a Staff Room. There had been only the two classrooms, a cloakroom and a tiny office.

John Glynn, who followed, organised a street market outside the Chaseway to raise funds to equip the new rooms. He arranged swimming lessons at Doggetts School in Rochford and sailing lessons on the river after school. Several parents bought Mirror dinghies, which were used by anyone learning. As late as 1983 he was able to buy a portable colour television with money from the Centenary Fund!

By then there were only 14 pupils, and closure became inevitable. In the last year children were given many outings, from Redcroft to see the animals to Greenwich Maritime Museum. The school finally closed on 20 July 1984. A farewell party brought back many ex-teachers and old pupils, with old school photographs inspiring many to reminisce. Another era closed with the school.

No1 and No 2, The Chaseway, rear view, 1970s.

WATERSIDE FARM

Rosemary's parents were tenants at Cupola House and, after Alan's death, his wife Phyllis had to leave at Michaelmas 1973, after 36 years. It was a sad time for the whole family. Alan had converted the stables at The Chase, which he had bought with the land and farm buildings in 1948. The stables were modernised and Phyllis moved in, surrounded by her own land which she called Waterside Farm. She continued to farm the land with the help of others, both round East End, which had been JFTW's, and the rented land at Finches at Church End, which had been the Quy's – another branch of the Wiseman family – so we still felt a close connection with the past.

Cupola House was sold by the Hutleys in 1974, having been with the same family for over 170 years. A large swimming pool was built in the middle of Phyllis's immaculate lawn, and the farm buildings were deliberately burnt down. In the middle of 1975, a fire started in the kitchen stairs and the rooms above were destroyed. Fortunately the main part of the house was saved, as was the original corner cupboard in the kitchen.

The house stood forlorn until Jeremy and Alison Zabell lovingly restored it to its old self, keeping the built-in shutters, putting back the Georgian window panes and modernising the facilities. They also created a beautiful garden for themselves and their two young children, Benjamin and Olivia. The remainder of the land had been sold to Biff Rayner, who amalgamated it with his own fields.

Phyllis was fortunate that the price of wheat began to rise in the 1970s and '80s. The land was able to grow wheat for bread-making which sold at a premium. Another crop appeared at that time, peas grown for freezing. This was again done by contractors, this time Rankins at Hampton Barns, Stambridge, (once farmed by J F T Wiseman!), who had the necessary cleaning and chilling equipment. The fields were prepared and the peas sown and finally harvested by them. The timing of this was crucial to the hour, and the village was sometimes surprised when big harvesters arrived in the middle of the night. The drivers were on the same level as bedroom windows!

NEIGHBOURS

Rex and Lynda Berrecloth soon found that Zillah was a very pleasant landlord and neighbour. Rex wrote in 2009,

> *'Miss Harris always loved cats. She would adopt or care for stray cats, or take on those that needed a home. When her great friend Miss Hodgetts died, she adopted her cat. Miss Hodgetts' ashes were also interred in the Harris family plot at St Peter's. She was given a kitten ... and asked us to think of a name for it. As a temporary name, he was called Baby Boy, which stuck. When Miss Harris died, we adopted Baby Boy ourselves.*
>
> *'Miss Harris always had a love of any living thing, whether it was cats, or garden creatures or tiny insects. She had a great respect for life and living things. It was understandable that when she died she left her entire estate to the PDSA.*
>
> *'Over the years we became very close to 'Auntie' Zillah, as we came to call her. However, we always called her Miss Harris out of respect.'*

On Easter Sunday 1975, Rex and Lynda's first child was born. In her diary Zillah wrote,

Sunday 30 March 1970. 'Up in good time & saw R's car outside which was not there at 2.30am. Found his note in [letter] box 'It's a girl. Emma Jane. Mother & baby doing well'.'

'Auntie Zillah' wrote a letter the next day, congratulating them.

> *'Dear Lynda,*
>
> *Rejoice with them that rejoice! And this I do most sincerely as I send congratulations to you and Rex.*
>
> *Clever girl Lynda, - or was Emma Jane the clever girl to postpone her appearance and thus become an Easter chick in the cosy warmth of the hospital while it snowed outside, and last but not least to have dad on vacation, and the bonus of bank holiday visiting. ...*

> *To be able to share so early on in such good news made me feel very honoured and more like an aunt, or great aunt, instead of one of those wicked landlords/ladies of whom we read so much. ...*
>
> *God bless you all.*
>
> *With love from your affectionate Auntie Zillah.'*

Thursday 3 April. 'Rex called for me to visit Lynda ... Found Lynda v well & bright & EJ is a nice little baby, v good until near the end. ... I took Lyn a box of notelets & 'pyjamas' for the baby.'

Emma's christening group, August 1970.
(l to r) Maisie Thorogood, Lynda & Rex Berrecloth, Zillah, Winnie Keeble, Rose Keeble, Dick Thorogood.

Zillah went to Emma's baptism in August, giving her a set of silver spoons with Emma's initials engraved in place of her own. She also attended the baptism of their second baby, David, giving him a Christening mug. They gave Zillah Christmas presents but she would not accept ones for her birthday.

Zillah frequently went to meetings and on outings or holidays with the National Trust and the Rochford Hundred Historical Society. In 1970, for example, with the NT she went to Dedham in April, and to Westonbirt Arboretum in Gloucestershire, Lavenham, and Warwick Castle in the following months. She also went to Fishbourne, Hampshire, with the RHHS in May and for a weekend in Lincolnshire in July. Rex noted,

> *'She would always send us a postcard. She sent one from the Lake District describing the lovely scenery. Zillah was an economical writer! She would write very small and include much detail on half a postcard.'*

She probably inherited some of this from the cards her father had sent her 60 years earlier.

Every year she invited Rex and Lynda to the WI Harvest Supper in the Mission Room, where they enjoyed the occasion. They recalled,

> [Zillah] *'never would eat all her supper. She would carry a 'doggy bag' with her, into which she would put scraps of food to take home to give her cats a treat!*
> *'Her favourite place was her garden. It was a bit of a wilderness, but if a plant wanted to grow in a particular place, she would let it grow. ... Honesty seeded itself everywhere. In the autumn Zillah would collect the silvery plants, separate the 'pennies', remove seeds for sowing, then sell the dried plants for fundraising in the village, decorating the church or for a local charity.'*

FUNDRAISING

The church repairs in the 1960s had not tackled the tower. When bits of stonework in the tower started falling off it had to be roped off and fundraising started in earnest. We (the authors!) devised a series of events over the next 16 years. First, Country Fayres were held initially at Redcroft in 1978 with the idea of showing crafts being practised. The sheep were shorn and our daughter Allison's horse was shod. There was spinning and weaving going on and a historical display indoors. There were other stalls and refreshments. Zillah put in her diary, the day before,

Friday 23 June 1978. 'It was a terrible day, thunder going and returning all the time and raining heavily. We all thought it was not promising for tomorrow ... cleaning and polishing things for display at Country Fayre tomorrow.'

Saturday 24 June. 'Ready to be at Redcroft before 11am ... took up my position in charge of 'Paglesham Past & Present,' in lounge. Interesting to talk to people.'

Zillah continued to be a help and encouragement to our historical researches.

A similar Fayre took place in 1979, and by then sufficient funds had been accumulated to apply, successfully, for grants which enabled work to start on the tower in 1980. As

Work on Church tower, 1980.

a churchwarden, Zillah signed a thank you letter with Rex for the offer of a grant of £22,000 from English Heritage after church on Sunday 21 October 1979. In 1980, the whole of the top of the tower was taken down by Bakers of Danbury, a new string course was put in and the battlements rebuilt. This was a major undertaking costing over £30,000, but there was insufficient money to finish all four sides below the top. The east face was done to protect the nave roof, but the remainder was less urgent.

Zillah would have been delighted to see her much-loved church repaired for future generations, but she did not live to see it.

ZILLAH HARRIS

All through 1979, Zillah continued to do her daily chores, bus into Rochford and Southend, talk to and help neighbours, look after her cats and tend the garden. She regularly went to the shop to collect the *Daily Telegraph* which she read and passed on to Rex and Lynda in the evening. They took her to church with them on most Sundays.

She still read about family connections from the collection of papers she had. In May she read '*The Life of Frank Buckland,*' the Victorian naturalist and a close friend of her grandfather who had named his house, a son and Zillah's mother after him. At other times it was the writings of J F T Wiseman, or books on Australia, where there were other Wisemans.

In June she noted,
Wednesday 6 June 1979. 'Standard [had] *a piece abt Roberts family & the Good Life as they were demonstrating* [spinning and weaving] *at the Essex Show. Also Digby Fairweather, who is launching his album of records. A hurried rush off to WI. ...'*
Saturday 8 June. 'I put [Rex and Lynda's son] *David's present in the box with the paper & in the evening they came to thank me & bring 2 pieces of b'day cake. ... Went to bed abt 11pm to save fuel.'*!

At the beginning of July she went on a National Trust coach holiday to Llandudno, going off daily on the usual tours of the local sights – Conway Castle, Plas Newydd House, Bodnant Gardens and the Llanberis Pass among them. She returned a week later, catching the last bus back to Paglesham from Southend about 10 pm. Zillah retained her stamina and her interests!

In August, an example of her love of animals was shown, and in October, of her consideration. They are small details but typical of her nature.
Tuesday 14 August. '[Lynda] *brought me a young sparrow wch the cat had caught, I think. I kept it in my hand till its breathing was normal, then it struggled free & flew off & out of the open window.'*
Monday 1 October. 'There were some medlars on the counter [at the shop] *& when I commented on them Mrs P* [Phillips] *said she hoped to get a recipe for them & I said I cld provide one.'*

Zillah always kept active. On 8 September 1979, she walked half-way to East Hall for the PVPA Show in September 1939 before being given a lift. There she bought jams and cakes from the WI stall, tomatoes and a cucumber. She also bought plants and had long talks with various people.

Saturday 3 November 1979. 'Went for paper after feeding cats & getting ready to go on 8.56 to York Rd [Southend]. *Took book rest & small shelf to PDSA, ... L's suede shoe to cleaners... Walked to a NT bazaar in Electric Ave bought ... an amaryllis for wch charged 10p, but I gave 20p & cheap at that, gave* [Mrs Walker] *a china ornament for the NSPCC, ... Got several signatures for* [a petition against] *battery hens.'*

On the Sunday she went with Rex to a service at Canewdon church, then *'adjourned to the vicarage to meet Bishop Knapp Fisher, Archdeacon of Westminster, who had preached the sermon.'* On the Tuesday she continued *'took a vegetable dill & 2 small pudding basins to PDSA'* in the afternoon and, as a church warden, signed forms in connection with the church tower for Rex in the evening.

Sadly, Zillah died two or three days later. Rex discovered her.
'This was a dramatic and traumatic event. Zillah always had the Daily Telegraph and a delivery of milk. After finishing with the paper, Zillah would deliver it to us in the early evening. The paper was undelivered and when the milk was not taken in on the Saturday, I tried knocking on the doors and looking inside but the blinds were drawn. I eventually broke in and found Zillah lying dead on the dining room floor. I called Dr Angela Puzey who lived next door, and she confirmed that she had died, of heart failure it transpired.'

Zillah was cremated and her ashes interred in the same plot with her parents' and Athelstan's. At 83, Zillah had had a full and eventful life. She was not the centre of the community, she was too private for that, but she had played a significant part in many aspects of the life of the village and of many of its people, most obviously in the war years. A major part of Paglesham's history died with her.

15 POSTSCRIPT

THE CHASE

Fundraising for the tower resumed with Paglesham Open Gardens in September 1980, when over twenty gardens prepared to be visited. On the Friday evening, however, there was a very bad storm with rain which crushed a large tent at Redcroft and threatened calamity for the show. Rosemary remembered,

'At Redcroft we heard noises of heavy vehicles going past late in the evening, and guessed something was wrong. The rain had stopped and we all rushed up to the Plough to find that The Chase was ablaze and fire engines were at work. The house was lived in partly by Derrick Wood, with Bill & Nan Peel in another part and John & Connie Osbourne in the old kitchen area. We learnt that lightning

The Chase after fire damage, 1980.

had struck the electricity supply starting the fire in the middle of the house. We were able to help by bringing tea for the firemen, guide them to more water supplies in Frances Griew's swimming pool and carry some of John's art materials and belongings to safety. We didn't get to bed for a long time.'

Despite the loss of their gardens and an exhibition, the rest of the village had a successful Open Gardens day! The whole of The Chase was gutted and it was many months before the Woods and Peels could move back in to The Chase. John and Connie moved away.

After Derrick Wood moved to the old shop, the house was bought by Robin Slater, who started to bring much of J F T Wiseman's ownership together again. This included the Peels' part of the house and, when Phyllis Boardman sold up in 1997, the farm buildings and some of the land round it.

REDCROFT

Postcard of Redcroft farm animals, 1982.

Redcroft had had a varied life since the war, as an old people's home and then our activities! After the Playgroup, for 17 years Rosemary hosted busloads of schoolchildren in the summer term to see 14 varieties of animal and bird. Redcroft Farm became better known than those of the big farmers as there were sometimes over 500 children who visited in a week! These visits were set up in conjunction with the Essex Education Committee, which arranged courses for the teachers. For the last ten years Redcroft provided farmhouse bed and breakfast. In addition, the Hostellers' Sailing Club had its headquarters at Redcroft for many years!

Redcroft has since been modernised and given the substantial garage and stables which it had lacked. The garden has been extended into the animal paddocks.

CUPOLA HOUSE

Cupola House has also seen a major changes since the Zabell's modernised it after the fire and created a garden fit for a 'gentleman's residence', as it was once called. Zillah would be intrigued by the appearance of the cupola on its roof in 2008, built by the present owner. This was cleverly designed from the minute illustration of an estate map of 1803 and the continued presence of the stairs leading into it. Not even Zillah's mother would have seen the original!

Cupola House with new cupola, 2008.

130

Larger 'Country Fayres' were held at East Hall barns for three years, when one attraction was a 'Sheep to Shawl' display. Wool was shorn, spun, plied and knitted into a jumper during the event. Crowds were attracted to these shows, with over £2,000 being raised for the church each time. But cost of work on the tower had escalated and the final repairs seemed less urgent.

Meanwhile, a series of 'History with Flowers' exhibitions was staged annually over 9 days. In 1989 the theme was World War II, being the fiftieth anniversary of its commencement, and three evacuees returned to see where they had been. One of these was Barry Barber, who had stayed with Zillah half a century earlier. The other two, Vera and Thirza Britton, had been at Church Hall. In 1990 the conversion of the school into two houses inspired a 'Children' theme to the exhibition and to Rosemary's second book *The Children of Paglesham.*

'History with Flowers' Exhibition in the church, 1989.

The little 'Tin Tabernacle' will be ignored by most people driving past, but the centenary of the Mission Room provided more than enough stories for *A Century of Paglesham Life.* Ian and Dr Angela Puzey had moved from living next door to Zillah to the Old Post Office at Church End, and had become even more involved in village affairs. Angela collaborated with Rosemary for the new book.

The Mission Room had been given by Zachary Pettitt in 1893 for church services in winter and as a village hall, and it was the obvious choice for an exhibition to launch the book. This was on the same day as the PVPA Show – Saturday 4 September 1993. The Show was held in the Garden Field, opposite the Plough, and many helpers and visitors dressed up in Victorian costume for the occasion. As always the exhibition included artefacts, documents and photographs; the Show included the numerous flower, vegetable and handicraft classes in a large marquee, with sideshows outside.

Appropriately, the next day – Sunday 5 September 1993 – a service was held in the Mission Room at 9.30 am. A celebration tea was then served in the marquee and Zachary Pettitt's granddaughter, Sue Moore, was welcomed as guest of honour, with her daughter-in-law, Paulette Nicholls (Col Nicholls' daughter-in-law) and her two daughters. Sue brought along a large silver tray presented by the village to Zachary 100 years previously, which highlighted the historic event.

Sue Moore and Paulette Nicholls, with the Pettitt silver salver, 5 September 1993.

This was the last exhibition which we organised while in Paglesham, as we moved to St Osyth in 1994 to live nearer our three daughters, although we wrote *Under the Flight Path* in 1995, in which Zillah's diary entries provide the background to other wartime activities in the area.

FARMING

Diversification became the means of keeping smaller farms towards the end of the century, but Paglesham's big farms absorbed Waterside Farm when Rosemary's mother moved to St Osyth and then sold her land. But the larger farms were also changing. South Hall was already owned by C H Cole and Son, and when the two Paglesham foremen, Brian Fletcher and Ken McVittie retired in 2008, the farming operations were to be run entirely from out of the village. South Hall staged the County Ploughing Match in 2008, with horse-drawn ploughs and rarely-seen steam engine ploughing – an interesting end to an era.

At Church Hall, Biff Rayner died in 2008 and his widow, Margaret, and their three daughters continue to run the farm. Biff had hosted the Ploughing Match in 2005.

West Hall had been farmed by the Cottis family of Lambourne Hall, Canewdon, since 1934. They bought Waterside Farm in 1997. Philip and Marie-Ann Cottis live at West Hall. His father, Roy, is still at Lambourne Hall Farm. West Hall is run as part of a 1,600 acre enterprise spread over several farms in the area.

With the end of Waterside Farm and the animals at Redcroft, there were no farm animals left in the village. There were still riding horses at Ingulfs and Church Hall.

HMS BEAGLE

This famous ship served as a Coastguard Watch Vessel at Paglesham for 25 years after her better known role carrying Darwin round the world. She had been broken up in 1870, with a single reference in the Wiseman records when they bought,
31 August 1870. 'Half a ton of pig iron (Beagle) £1. 10s.'

In recent years, the remains of the hull are believed to have been located under the mud where she was berthed for most of her time. A BBC *Ancestry* television programme in 2007 featured the search, and Ann Boulter, who helped with costume displays in the 'History with Flowers' exhibitions, wrote a book about her part in the continuing saga[13]. 2009 is the bicentenary of Darwin's birth and the 150th anniversary of the publication of his The *Origin of Species*.

ORGANISATIONS

In 1993, the Paglesham Women's Institute celebrated its sixtieth Birthday with a party at Lambourne Hall, and its seventieth in 2003. About the same time, it was decided to open an evening section to help the many who now went out to work and could not get to afternoon meetings. This reflected the changing society in the village. The Institute is still going strong.

The PVPA has expanded its activities from the Summer and Spring Shows to include talks, suppers, sailing days and Open Gardens. The last started to raise money for children's play

---

[13] *'Watch Vessel No 7'* by Ann Boulter, pub 2008.

equipment for the field opposite East Hall. The field had been bought and named 'Frances Field', after Frances Griew, who had pressed for the open space for many years. So the PVPA still flourishes, running the annual summer in the Frances Field. A booklet, *Memories,* was produced by Ian and Angela Puzey to celebrate the sixtieth anniversary, in 2006, of a vital part of Paglesham life.

Zillah had been a founder member of both these village organisations, faithfully attending meetings, serving on the WI committee and entering the PVPA show. She would be quietly pleased that she had helped guide the two organisations which had been at the forefront of social change in the village, and that both were still flourishing thirty years after her death.

Founder Member, Mrs Ethel Ducker, cutting the WI 60th Birthday cake, 1993.

ST PETER'S CHURCH

Rev Norman Kelly always said he '*would leave the Church in a box'*, and he continued in post until his death at the age of 92 in 2003. He still cycled in the course of his duties until the last twenty years, when he was given lifts. He had held weekly services and supported all the fundraising events and the exhibitions in the Church. Canewdon church was full for his funeral, and he was buried just west of the tower.

Zillah had written her will in the 1940s, leaving everything to the PDSA. A more recent one had not been signed. Zillah and her mother had given several of their older items of china, glass and costumes to the Southend Museum and Colchester Museum. The contents of the house, which must still have been a treasure trove of family memorabilia, were bought by a Rochford antique dealer. Fortunately, Margaret Pinkerton, the granddaughter of Frank Buckland Wiseman, Zillah's uncle, was able to have all the Wiseman archives, and other letters and diaries were also later returned. The Gallipoli letters are now with the Imperial War Museum.

Paglesham Natives, published in 2006, was based on the earlier Wiseman ledgers, diaries and letters. The proceeds helped to restart fundraising for repairs to finish the church tower. In the years since 1980 when the battlements were restored, the stonework deteriorated further, particularly on the window tracery. It again became sufficiently dangerous for it to be cordoned off. The main west window is dedicated to the Pettitt children, whose story was included in that book.

The incumbency is now held with Canewdon, South Fambridge and Ashingdon, where the Priest-in-Charge, Rev Timothy Clay lives. The congregation at Paglesham is still active and it is hoped that, again with the grants received from English Heritage and others, work will start on another round of restoration in 2009. We feel that Zillah would be pleased that her stewardship of the family's history had helped to keep the fabric of the church intact, and that the history continues to inspire the life of the village.

APPENDIX 1 : BERNARD HARRIS's FAMILY

DEVON

The Harris family came from Barnstaple, Devon. Papers handed down suggest a lineage from a John and Priscilla Harris, born in 1656. Zillah may be the source of this information as there are records taken down by her in 1931 from tombstones and monuments probably in Barnstaple. A large Victorian painting, painted in about the 1830s, of the family 'at home' in Barnstaple hangs in the Priory Museum, Southend. It shows George and Grace Gibbs Harris (who were buried in Paglesham churchyard, and have a memorial in the chancel) and their eight children with their servant, 'Old Mary', seated round a table or playing musical instruments. A key, by Bernard, gives a 'who's who', including his father, George Henry, who is holding a flute.

The Harris family, 1830s (Key by Dr Bernard Harris.)
(l to r) Old Mary, Henrietta, Gdfather, Aunt Carrie, Gdmother, Aunt Grace, Aunt Lizzie, Uncle James, Uncle John, Aunt Louise, Father [George Henry]

The eldest was John, who married and had eight children. Then came George Henry, whose three children included Edward Bernard, who married Mary Buckland Wiseman (Pet) in 1894, followed by James, who took Holy Orders and became Rector of Paglesham and had 3 children. Next was Elizabeth who became the Paglesham schoolmistress, but did not marry. Then came Louisa, Grace and Caroline, who each married – Caroline twice, first to Charles Lock, and then (in Paglesham) to Rev Barton Lodge – and finally Henrietta, who remained unmarried. When George Henry Harris was baptised in the Parish Church, Barnstaple, on 25 September 1816, the family lived in the High Street. His father was described in the register as a draper.

George Henry Harris as a young man kept a scrapbook in which he copied out items that he found interesting. Subjects include a copy of *Bounaparte's letter to the Prince Regent 1815, Female Society,* and *Employment* by Dr Johnson, among numerous others. Most are dated in the 1840s, well before he married. In 1848, when he was 32, he started a journal, and gave his business address as 76 King William Street, in the City of London. He also had an apartment.

The diaries are full of social information, noting his working hours (often till after 6 pm, and six days a week), his social engagements and people he saw. On Sundays he usually attended 'Divine Service', going to a wide variety of churches from St Mary Woolnoth, close to home in the City, to those in Westminster or south of the Thames. When his father visited him from

Barnstaple he often beat him at chess, or played whist with others. He frequently walked great distances to all parts of London, several times writing, '*walked to the West End and back*'. He refers to dining with his friends or eating in different establishments, often at the famous 'Cheshire Cheese' in Fleet Street.

BROAD GAUGE

George Henry was Secretary to the Taw Vale Railway and Dock Company, and dealt with their affairs in London. The River Taw flows into its estuary at Barnstaple and it may be that he worked for them in Devon. The Taw Vale Railway was a new line first mooted in 1838, extending from the Brunel's Great Western broad gauge main line at Exeter to Barnstaple. George was involved at the time of the debate over whether that seven foot gauge or the 'National' gauge should be used. He listened to parliamentary discussions from the Speaker's Gallery, met people involved, read reports, noted Board Meetings and conducted other business. On 2 February 1848, for example, he wrote '*the Rly. Commrs. ...decided that the extension line be laid down on the broad gauge. Saw Joseph Locke Esq. on the subject*'. Locke was an associate of Robert Stephenson and, with Stephenson and Brunel, was one of the great early pioneers of railways. He also had correspondence with Thomas Brassey, probably the biggest contractor in the industry at the time.

LONDON LIFE

When his 23-year-old sister Caroline came up to London on 5 June 1848, staying in lodgings in Eaton Square, he saw her often. He took her walking through Hyde Park, to an exhibition at the Polytechnic Institution, to Westminster Abbey and St Paul's, to the Guildhall, the London Docks and down the river '*to Greenwich to see the Park, Hospital &, saw the pensioners take their tea*'. On 22 June, having '*Attended the Office till 6 o'clock*', he '*met Caroline at Westminster, showed her the new House of Lords, Robing Room, Dining Room, Library, Committee Room &...*'. The Palace of Westminster had been burnt down in 1834, and the new House of Commons was not finally reopened by Queen Victoria until 1852. Caroline did not leave until 29 June.

He referred to the Crystal Palace several times, but without much detail. On Christmas Day, 1850 after attending '*Divine Service at St Peter's, De Beauvoir Square*' in the morning. '*Walked to Hyde Park and back. Saw the great progress which has been made in the creation of the Crystal Palace.*' The construction was a big attraction. On '*Sunday 23 February 1851 .... to Hyde Park and saw the exterior of the Crystal Palace – about 100,000 persons in the Park.*' At last, when it was finished, on '*Thursday 1 May 1851. Weather dry and cold. ....called on Mrs Tanqueray but in consequence of her being up late last evening she did not feel well enough to go to see Her Majesty's procession. I accompanied Henrietta* [his sister] *and also R Carver* [a relative of his future wife, Christiana]. *Never before saw the Park so crowded.*' He visited the '*Exhibition*', several times and noted that '*it closed at 5pm*' on 11 October. On the 15th he wrote '*The Exhibition of Industry of all Nations was attended by the Commissioners & the Exhibitors, & the prizes awarded – when this World's Fair finally closed.*' Unfortunately he never mentioned the contents of the Exhibition!

ATTRACTION

In 1851 he also had a meeting which sounds almost like Bernard's 38 years later! He had met the Primets fairly often, but on 1 August 1851 he '*called on & saw Mrs Primet & her sister*

Christie'. The next day *'Mr & Mrs Primet & Christie Carver called & I returned with them as far as their house.'* He noted the next day, *'Christie Carver's birthday Aetat* [aged] *23'*. He saw her again on the 8th and on the 10th, he *'drank tea at the Primets' & accompanied Christie Carver to Westminster Abbey in the evening & returned to supper.'* From then on he saw Christie almost daily, escorting her to many of the sights he had shown his sister Caroline. On the 23rd, the Primets had another person to stay in their house, so *'Christie Carver ... returned with me to stay a few days with Henrietta.'* On 1 September, *'Christie Carver dined at home with Henrietta. I presented the former with a Gold Chain'*. Christie did not return to the Primets' for a fortnight and finally had to return to Somerset on the 16th. Before then George had met Mrs Carver, and when her father came up to London, George wrote on 9 October, *'Mr Carver, Mr Primet & John* [his elder brother] *dined with me, by invitation' at Simpsons in the Strand & there were upward of 140 persons in the room'*. The next day, George went *'to Canonbury Terrace and spoke to Mr Carver on the subject of his* [blank] *& returned to the City.'* He continued in his journal, *'Wrote to Christie & informed her of the result of my interview'*. He does not tell his diary the result, but a week later he told his father about Christie! He spent Christmas with the Carvers in Taunton, going for long walks *'with Christie and Mary'*, Mary obviously acting as chaperone. He returned to London and the office on New Year's Day 1852. From that day his salary was increased to £300 per annum. At the end of the month he started looking *'at furnished apartments'*.

On 2 February 1852 he noted that, *'1st sod of the N D Railway turned.'* This was at last the start of construction of the railway after 13 years of planning.

On 2 April he *'engaged apartment @ 34 Duncan Terrace, Islington of Mrs Richardson @ 40/- per week from the 15th April instant, consisting of 2 parlours with folding doors – top front bedroom on the 2nd floor including bed linen, plate & attendance & boot cleaning. Coals 6d per scuttle.'* He then *'attended at the Guardian Life Office & was examined by the Physician Dr Geo Darling & the Surgeon.'*

SOMERSET WEDDING

On 14 April, he *'Attended the Office till 3 o'clock. Left by the 4.50 express train for Taunton.'* George Henry Harris married Christiana Carver on 15 April 1852 in Wincanton.

George and Christie had four children – Isabella Mary, born 10 March 1853; Frances Louisa,

born 26 October 1854; Harry McClintock, born 7 June 1857; and finally, after a long gap, Edward Bernard, on 25 January 1864. Having started married life just north of the Angel, Islington, by the time of Bernard's birth they were living at 141, Queens Road, (now Queensbridge Road) Dalston. George's occupation was still given on the birth certificate as *'Secretary to a railway'*.

St Dunstans, *foot of Muswell Hill.*

Bernard's family moved to '*St Dunstan's, foot of Muswell Hill*', soon after Bernard had established his medical practice. Sometimes called St Dunstan's Cottage, this was actually a substantial house near Alexandra Palace and less than a mile from Holy Innocents' Road, so Pet was able to get to know Bernard's family. His parents were George Henry and Christiana Harris, and his older sister Frances.

St Dunstan's had five bedrooms, and when it was sold in 1919 had a '*Bathroom with hot and cold supplies*' as well as a '*Hall, Drawing Room, Dining Room and Morning Room and China Pantry, Kitchen, Scullery and good Store Larder, and outside W.C.*'

Bernard inherited his father's sense of duty, both in business and in religious matters, an interest in a variety of subjects, and an enjoyment of his spare time.

BERNARD HARRIS's VOYAGES : APPENDIX 2

OFF TO SEA

His first appointment at sea was from on 11 May 1911, was as surgeon on the Royal Mail Steam Company's steamship *SS Aragon*, sailing to South America. He was staying then at St Dunstan's, and in the next fortnight he made final arrangements, returning to Paglesham. He went to Southampton and returned to London from there. '*Had to come up to Waterloo to examine emigrants but too short a time to come over*' to see Zillah, who had gone to St Dunstan's, on the day before he sailed from Southampton.

The *Aragon* was a twin-screw ship on the South American run, having made her maiden voyage in 1905. At 9,588 gross tons (gt) she was capable of 16 knots. Having left England on the 26 May, she left Madeira on the 31st and reached Rio de Janeiro on 11 June. Postcards were sent from each landfall. '*The Aragon waiting to get alongside the wharf 22/6. I had quite a nice lot of men at my table last night & met many masons & if I come again I shall not lack invitations...*' Some comments raise obvious but unsolved questions! '*I found Mr Harris' brother & his wife are coming to dinner aboard tonight (22nd) and taking me to the theatre afterwards.*' Who were these Harrises?

After reaching Buenos Aires on 22 June, she started back at 10 am the next day, calling at Santos, close to Rio, and Salvador ('*Bahia*') before heading for Vigo in Spain and Southampton, from where a postcard to Athelstan at Ongar Grammar School says, '*Shall see you soon, old boy*'.

His next voyage started on the P&O's *SS China* just before Christmas. Postmarked '*Sandown*' a card reads: '*English Channel. 9pm 22nd Dec 1911. Left Tilbury 1.45pm off Southend 3.30pm & I thought of you all at Paglesham... This will go off by pilot at St Catherines.*' Postcards follow from Gibraltar and Marseilles (28 Dec) en route to Port Said.

Postcard of P&O SS *China* to Zillah, '*for your collection.*'

Here he transfers to *SS Osiris*, a small 1,728 gt P&O '*Express steamer*'. A month later he is in Brindisi, Italy, arriving back at Port Said on 31 January. More short trips back to Brindisi follow, with all cards posted at Port Said. Bernard clearly is fascinated by Egypt, judging by the number of cards he bought during the months he was based there and the details of the sights he sends to his two children. In March he goes down the Suez Canal: '*We ... reach Suez 7pm & return after handing over mails and £100,000 to Salsette...I see Sunda does not leave London until 12 April*', and '*Held up in Bitter Lake despite 'P'flag = Privilege or Patience.*'

POSTCARDS

Bernard was a good correspondent while on his travels, trying to maintain his close relationships despite the separation. He sends separate postcards to his wife, son (usually when at Ongar Grammar School) and daughter Zillah, to his mother or his sister Frances at St Dunstan's (foot of Muswell Hill) and to Gerrish, his Solicitor, and probably to others which have not returned to the archive. As a ship's doctor, he probably had plenty of time on his hands, hinted at in some comments.

Scores of postcards are still in the family records. He posted some and sent some in batches, presumably in another cover, and occasionally via other people returning to England ahead of him. There are also large numbers unused.

He seemed to have used them as a geography lesson for his children, asking Athelstan, then at Ongar Grammar School, to look up places he mentions. His interests were widespread, and his annotations on some cards comprehensive. For example, he gave details of the size, age and history of the sphinx, and details of the Suez Canal. Cards of Ceylon (Sri Lanka) show general views, cocoa processing, jugglers,

Postcard from Bernard about '*Betel Nuts*' from Kandy, Ceylon (Sri Lanka).

working elephants, antiquities and Kandyan Chiefs, among many others. Elsewhere he pointed out on the pictures buildings of interest, lighthouses and harbours he visited. He even brought back some silvery eucalyptus leaves from Cape Town and bougainvillea from Heliopolis.

He made good use of his time ashore, visiting the sights and sometimes people he met. He spent considerable time in Egypt, so visited Cairo and the pyramids, although he did not venture far into the pyramid of 'Kheops' and did not attempt to climb higher! In Ceylon he visited Kandy from Colombo, and possibly other places for which there are cards.

Occasionally he illustrated them himself; two delightful postcards as they passed Crete homeward bound in February 1912 have beautiful watercolour views of the snow-capped mountains. These were painted on the backs of menu-cards of the P&O *SS Osiris*, which also showed how well he fared! From the dinner menu for 5 February 1912 he ticked '*Consomme d'Esclignac*', *Filets de Breme Grillé*, *Cotelettes de Mouton Soubise*, *Celeri au Jus*, *Glace Marie Louise, Desert* and *Café*'. If he indeed ate all these, his constitution seems to have been remarkable, particularly if he was sailing 'for his health'!

TITANIC

While in Port Said he made arrangements to transfer to the *Sunda* when it arrived at the end of April 1912. On the 18th he wrote to his wife,

'*Dear old Molly, … heard from Mr B it is all right about the Sunda… The next news was the awful disaster & I fully expected it was another P&O ship Mr B would tell me of, but he soon mentioned the Titanic. I do not and have not thought these leviathans are the right things – too many eggs in the shape of human lives in one frail basket. We shall hear further news shortly, at present we hear of 1600 drowned & Captain dead. I trust Dr Simpson was not on her. A Dr A W Comber comes out as Surgeon of the Sunda & we exchange at Port Said. … Lovely to hear from Frances, she tells me Arthur Smith is going to India on Arabia (we connect with her at P.Said on 24th, so I may see him) or the Orsova but she is an Orient & Australian ship, & he wd have to tranship at Colombo by her … I will drop a line from* [Port Said] *before sailing for India…*'

The 'unsinkable 'Titanic had struck an iceberg on her maiden voyage on 15 April and sunk.

On 24 April from Port Said, he added a more personal note to his sister at St Dunstan's. In a similar card to Athelstan on the same day, he said,

'*What a terrible disaster the Titanic & I greatly fear poor old Dr Simpson is drowned for his place wd be in the last boat with the Commander & Chief Engr. And there were not sufficient boats!! Poor old chap but a noble death. "women & children first." And that brave Marconi youth, & that string band who in the face of death could play "Nearer my God to Thee". The Mates wd be in charge of a boat each & so get the best chance. I have very little time for 'mates' speaking generally. I hope the Lodge will look after Simpson's boy & the Doctors of Hornsey & friends should place a brass tablet to his memory. Wish I were home to see about it. I am very distressed over it.*'

Dr John Edward Simpson, aged 37, was Assistant Surgeon on *Titanic* and did not survive. He had lived close to the Harris family in Tottenham Lane, Hornsey, and was also at sea for his health. No memorial plaque was erected but there was an obituary in the Hornsey paper.

FURTHER VOYAGES

Bernard wrote these messages while '*in the floating dry dock, a most wonderful arrangement, but very unpleasant with all the noise, shouting, scraping off the paint, hammering, taking off one propeller, etc & I hear they will work all night & our engineers will have 48 hours on end & NO extra pay. I am not surprised sometimes at 'Strikes'... The Osiris looks a monster when out of water! What the 'Titanic' looked like out of water I cannot imagine.*'

Bernard did transfer to *Sunda* and found '*a Major Hingley on board (a writer on Bridge) of the 7th Middx. (Hornsey is the 7th Territorial) knew poor old Simpson.*' The tragedy continued to find links home.

Sunda sailed on 27 April 1912 and reached Kandy in Ceylon (now Sri Lanka) on 12 May, when large numbers of postcards were bought and posted. They were in Calcutta before the end of May, leaving the Kiddepore Dock on 2 June, calling at Colombo, Aden (19th), Suez (24th), and Malta (29th) on the way home. (A number of cards had their stamps steamed off. Some cards are annotated by Bernard, '*For Zillah's Collection*'. He spent Christmas at Paglesham.

There is only one card after that until February 1913, suggesting that Bernard was at home during the gaps in the postcards. The single card is from Bernard at St Dunstan's to '*Master Athel Harris*' at Ongar Grammar School. '*Have you received my letter with cheque & foreign stamps? Mother also writes that you haven't written to her to acknowledge parcel etc. This won't do!*' Bernard stamped his name rather than signing off. He sounds genuinely cross with Athelstan!

Birthday card for Zillah, signed by the officers of Union Castle RMS *Guelph*, 14 February 1913.

Winter weather cannot have been good for his illness, so it is not surprising that he changes to the 4,917 ton Union-Castle liner *Guelph* for a cruise round South Africa, leaving on 7 February 1913. This time Bernard was in Teneriffe (14 February, wishing Zillah '*A very happy birthday, Valentine's Day 1913*', the card signed by the eight '*Officers*'), Durban (8 and 9 March), '*Off the Zulu Coast*'(10th), Laurenco Marques (11th), and back to Durban (15th) and Port Elizabeth on the 20th. He was due in Cape Town, but for some reason no postcards survive. He returned home via St Helena, '*I was charmed by my few hours at Jamestown, St Helena*) (28th), Ascension Island and Las Palmas, arriving back in early April.

One wonders if Bernard deliberately chose new routes to visit. He was assiduous in exploring and sending back 'geography lessons' to his two children. A few weeks later, he was aboard another Union-Castle *RMS Gascon*, sending cards from Gibraltar and telling us that in May 1913, '*15th left London; 16th left Southampton; 17th Passed Ushant 9 am; 18th Crossing Bay, C Finisterre 5 pm; 19th Abeam Berling Rocks 11.30 am and 20th Gibraltar.*' They called for six hours at Marseilles on 23rd, then Naples on 25th, '*Having my nap at Nap-les ... I am very fit*', Malta on 27th, '*Just seen a submarine gliding along and 5 Torpedo Destroyers put out to sea with us*', and so to Port Said and the Canal, leaving Suez on 2 June.

They were '*nearing port Soudan*' on 3 June, and were in Aden, '*an important trade and coaling station*' on the 6th. Again Bernard goes exploring – to the Tawela Tanks '*ancient reservoirs in remarkable preservation*' and '*to the Lighthouse and the wireless station. The coast road ... leads to the camp of the Aden Troop & Camel Corps.*' He also takes time to draw in pen and wash the view of Aden from the sea by moonlight, '*Lofty massive rocks rising from the sea with a majesty of gloom worthy of the Inferno.*'

By 17 June he was at Mombasa, then in British East Africa, and on 4 July at Laurenco Marques, '*Portuguese township, capital of Province of Moçambique*', returning north to Porto Amelia (11th) also '*Africa oriental portugueza*' and to Zanzibar on the 13th. He was back in Naples on 2 August, commenting to Athelstan, '*I shall be glad to be back home. Fed up, as all are.*'

Along the way he had advised Athelstan to keep up his playing of the organ – a valuable skill as it turned out. Three weeks later, Athel received another card, from school. '*Dear Harris, I am leaving Ongar in three weeks' time , so that I shall not have the pleasure of teaching you next term. I hope next time I hear you play, you may surprise me, in the right way. F Holloway.*' Perhaps this too encouraged him to keep it up.

Bernard's travels were not over for the year as on 11 November he sends cards home from *SS Pretorian* at Quebec, '*I had a walk round the plains of Abraham ...*', and Montreal (14th) where he was taken by the Chateau de Ramezay. He left at 6 am on the 15th, was off Montreal at 4 pm, and expected to be in Glasgow about the 24th. He had seen another part of the world, and had not finished.

January 1914 saw him sending cards from *SS Patuca* from Limon in Costa Rica and Colon in Panama, with details about the Panama Canal which was due to open that August. He is in Limon again on 23 April on the '*Bayano*', after '*an uneventful run of 4475 miles in 16 days 14 hours. We leave here tomorrow for Colon (Panama) and on Saturday start homeward bound reaching Avonmouth on Sunday (May 10th).*'

His next ship, the Union-Castle SS *Galeka*, would take him into different conditions in 1915[14].

---

[14] See page 32.

BIBLIOGRAPHY

Century of Paglesham Life, A.   ISBN 0 9516370 1 0
by Angela Puzey & Rosemary Roberts. Pub. 1993 by MA & R Roberts
The story of the Mission Room and village life through its use.

Children of Paglesham, The.   ISBN 0 9516370 0 2
By Rosemary Roberts. Pub. 1990 by MA & R Roberts
Detailed look at children's lives and the story of the school.

Essex Gold.   ISBN 0 9 900360 92 5
by Hervey Benham.   Pub. 1993 by Essex County Council (ERO)
Covers oyster culture and the Essex oyster businesses.

Essex Weather Book.   ISBN 1 872337 66 X
by Currie, Davidson & Ogley. Pub. 1992 Froglets Publications and Frosted Earth
Useful coverage of historical weather events.

Fortunate Life, A.   ISBN 0 14 006225 4
by A B Facey. Pub. 1981 by Freemantle Arts Centre Press WA
Pages 254 to 280 give a first-hand account of his experiences at Gallipoli as an Australian soldier
to compare with those of Bernard Harris.

Great Tide, The.
by Hilda Grieve. Pub. 1959 by Essex County Council
Detailed description of the 1953 floods, with excellent introductory history of the sea defences.

Memories, Paglesham Village Produce Association, 1946 – 2006.
Compiled by Angela Puzey. Pub. 2006, privately.

Paglesham – Life in an Essex Marshland Village.
by Rosemary Roberts. Pub. 1972 by MA & R Roberts
Covering the whole range of Paglesham history.

Paglesham Natives – 400 Years of Lives, Loves and Labours in an Essex Marshland
Parish. ISBN 0 9516370 3 7
by Mark & Rosemary Roberts. Pub. 1995 by MA & R Roberts
Gives a full story of the Browning/Pettitt and Wiseman families and the oyster business from the family
papers.

Toasted Tea and Cinders ISBN 0 86 3321135
by Sybil Brand Pub. 1986 by The Book Guild
Includes a delightful description of life in Paglesham.

Watch Vessel No 7 – HMS Beagle at Paglesham.
by Ann Boulter. Pub. 2008 by Rats Hall Publication
A personal account of the discovery of HMS Beagle at Paglesham

Zeppelins over Southend. ISBN 978-0-900690-58-7
by Ken Crowe. Pub. 2008 by Southend-on-Sea Museum Service.
The story of SE Essex in the First World War.

NAMES INDEX

Key *ft* = family tree
   i = illustration

Acketts 115
Allen 76
Amis 124
Anderson 47,87,88
Anfilogoff 62,62*i*,68,72,78,90,91,96,
109,118
Arbin 63
Archer 52
Arthy 118
Askey 79
Atkinson 25,25*i*,46,85*i*,93,98,116
Attlee 98

Baden-Powell 31
Baker 117,128
Baldwin 71,72
Barber 76-78,77*i*,82,89,91,131
Barbour 59
Barker 83
Barnes 26
Bees 59
Bell 76-78,77*i*,80,82
Bentall 63,83
Beresford 98
Berrecloth 114,126-129,126*i*
Bettyman 50
Bilham 65
Bird *ft*,40
Blake 14
Blyth 106
Boardman 58,65,65*i*,66,69-75,71*i*,
80-89,81*i*,91,92,94,95,95*i*,97,
99-101,103-109,119,125,130
Boreham 95,98
Boulter 132
Bowen 95,95*i*
Bradley 69*i*,83*i*
Brand 24,26,51,57*i*
Brassey 135
Bright 76,90,93
Britton 79,131
Brown 26,28,56,82
Browning *ft*,3,24,52,72
Brunel 135
Buckland 128
Burns 7
Burr 41
Burrows 31,60,102,109
Burt 32
Bush 39,39*i*,54

Caernarvon 39
Callan 33i
Cant 59
Cardy 63,75,82,83*i*,112*i*
Carpenter 102
Carter 59
Carver *ft*,135,136
Casement 52
Catterell 47

Chamberlain 20,74,76,90,115
Chant 71
Chapman 40
Cheverall 118
Chopin 106
Christian 41
Churchill 39,79,83,86,92
Clarke 53
Clay 133
Clements 118
Cole 108,132
Comber 139
Constable 4
Coine 46
Cook 41-45,45*i*,47,48,52,55,60,67,93
Corke 36
Cottis 81,132
Cousins 26,126
Cox 80
Crippen 27
Cripps 118
Curtis 41,46

Dannatt ft,27
Dargue 58
Darling 136
Darwin 2,132
Davies 44,93,106,113
Davis 62
Davy & Armitage 104
Dixon 71
Doak 10,51
Down 14
Ducker 133
D'Wit 45
Dye 124

Edelin 119
Edwards 103
Ellis 91
English 63

Fairweather 108,109,128
Falket 21
Fance 83*i*,118
Farquharson 109
Farthing 30
Fisher 129
Fleming 98
Fletcher 29,53,63,69*i*,83*i*,90,132
Flynn 75,76,82,93
Forsdick 25,30
Francis 124
Fraser 23,48,60

Gabriel 32
Galpin 69
Garon 41,48,73,77,85
Gay 14
Gerrish 38,90,138
Gibbons 43
Gilmour 27,29
Glynn 125
Grafton 113
Grainger 33*i*

Grieve 118,
Griew 130,133

Hall 5
Harris *ft,(*vi)*i*,1,2,6-10,7*i*,9*i*,
14-18,16*i*,18*i*,20,21,27-61,28*i*,
29*i*,33*i*,37*i*,39*i*,56*i*,66-72,71*i*,74-79,
82-85,88-96,99-103,99*i*,106,
108-120,119*i*,120*i*,125-141
Harriss 60,102,107
Hatch 20
Hatton 42,47
Heath 121
Hempstead 24
Hess 90
Heywood 47
Hillary 106
Himmler 95
Hines 83*i*
Hingley 140
Hitler 74,90,95
Hodgetts 126
Hogarth 4
Holloway 141
Holmes 26
Hooker 33*i*
Horner 118
Hornsby 43
Hunnaford 17
Hutley *ft*,19,19*i*,20,26,26*i*,52*i*,59,
65,72,75
Hutton 41
Hymas 65

Ingram 100
Ingulf 106
Izod *ft*,7,7*i*

Jackson 20
Jennings 60,83,87,93,102,103,111
Johnson 134
Jones 14,112
Judge 60

Kaiser 41
Keeble 62,62*i*,63,76,80,83*i*,90,91,
105,119,122-124,126*i*
Kelly 43,102,115,133
Kemp 25,53,70,71,76,79,83*i*,112
Killick 83*i*
King 27,41
King Edward VII 24,27
King Edward VIII 72
King George V 24,27,70,71
King George VI 73,92,103
Kitchener 51
Kydd 99

Lane 84
Lant 59
Lapwood 25,76,91,103
Laver 106,117
Layzell
Lea 25,10,13,19,23,
Leech 5,12,16

143

Legge 26,40
Lely 4
Loader 89,100,112,113
Lock *ft*,134
Locke 135
Lodge *ft*,28*i*,134
Lucking 109
Ludlow 102

Mann 112
Marconi 30,104,139
Marlowe 7
Martin 64,65,70
Marven 63
Mason 45
May & Baker 86
McLean 54
McVittie 132
Meeson 30,35,64,70,79
Mercer 93,94,99
Mills 69*i*
Moore *ft*,131
Morrison 87,88
Moss 25
Mumford 19
Munns 111,112,114,115
Murdock 64,79
Mussolini 95
Myring 96

Nelson 39
Nicholls *ft*,4,21,43,66,78,100,131
Nightingale 27
Norris 106
Nuffield 86
Nunn 33*i*

Offin 35
Oldbury Jones 70
Oliver 113
Osbourne 129,130
Owen 49

Parry 8
Pavelin 86
Peacock 60
Peel 129
Perry 62-64,95,103,104,108
Pettitt *ft*,1,3,4,6,10,12,13,19,21,24,
25,35,52,52*i*,53,58,131
Phelps 59,60
Phillips 17,53,118,128
Pinkerton *ft*,53,133

Pizzey 4
Playle 28
Popplewell 27,50,53
Potton 26
Powell 26
Prendegast 44
Primet 135,136
Princess Margaret 112
Pritchard 39
Puzey 117,131,133

Queen Victoria 3,19,135
Quy 65,79,89,125

Raison 50
Rampling 106
Rankin 105,125
Ravenscroft 46
Rawlings 62*i*
Rayner 116,125,132
Redfarn 94
Rice 24*i*,25,28,40,46
Rich 106
Richardson 136
Riley 28,40,70
Roberts 2,21,39,105,107,117,118,120*i*,
127,129-132
Robinson 28,28*i*,112*i*
Robson 62
Rollin 84
Roskill 120
Rowntree 59
Rutherstein 59
Ryan 44,47,48
Ryman 58

Samson 47
Saunders 41
Scratton 20
Seefelt 102
Sennett 55
Shakespeare 7
Sharp 83*i*
Shelley 41
Shuttlewood 5,47,71,80,92,103-106
Sidney 36
Sime 80,124
Simpson 29,30,30*i*,72,139,140
Slater 130
Smeaton 56
Smith 20,26,65,92,120,139
Smoothy 43
Southwell 86,90,115,117

Sparrow 89
Squier 87
Stacey 119
Staines 112*i*
Stebbing 41,46,48
Stephenson 14,135
Stone 54
Strutt & Parker
Suttle 83
Swire 93

Tabor 49
Tanqueray
Tarbet 43
Tate 115
Tensing 106
Thorogood 83*i*,100,110,115,126*i*
Tolhurst 35

Underwood 22

Van Dyck 4
Vellacot 44

Walker 129
Warner 79
Watkins 69,77,91
Webber 33i
Wellesley 39
Wellington 39
West 108
Weston *ft*,(vi)*i*
Whiting 122
Whittingham 63
Willans 46,78,91
Wilson 90
Wiseman *ft*,(vi)*i*,1,2,4-15,9*i*,11*i*,
15,9*i*,11*i*,15*i*,20-23,22*i*,25,27,34,40,
41,43-45,47,48,50,51,53,61,61*i*,
62,65-68,76,77,90,91,101,103,109,
110,113,119,121,125,132-134
Wolsey39
Wood 26,45,69*i*,83*i*,
100,109,112*i*,116,118,120,121,123,
124,129,130
Woodthorpe 21
Woodward 59
Woolton 85
Woolworth 77

Young 33*i*,
Younie 118

Zabell 125,130

GENERAL INDEX

Key   *A* = Australia
      Ex = Essex
      F = France
      I = illustration
      Is. = Island
      P = Paglesham

Abbeville *F* 112
Abson *F* 56
Aden 140,141
Aegean Sea 32
Africa 29,30,32,71,87,91,141
Albania 75
Albert *F* 56
Aldham *Ex* 3
Alexandria 36,38,39,47
America 29,46,49,57,81,137
Angers *F* 16
Anzac Cove 36-40
Ascension Is 140
Ashingdon *Ex* 49,84,93,133
Australia 2,10,12,36,37*i*,38,51,67,71,90,
96,128
Austria 40,74
Avonmouth 32,33,141

Bahia 29*i*,137
Ballards Gore 1,32,35,41,53,71,83
Beagle 2,132
Barcelona 112
Barling *Ex* 85,96,120
Barn Row *P* 24*i*,25,102,118
Barnstable 6,14,18,134,135
Barry 33
Basildon *Ex* 121
Bedford Row *P* 116
Belgium 16,56,79
Benfleet *Ex* 49,91,93
Bideford 15,17
Birmingham 40
Boarded Row *P* 20,21,69-72,71*i*,
75,88,88*i*,101
Boatshed, *P* 5,20,22,24,70,71,80,89,
103-106,104*i*,121
Boulogne *F* 57
Bradwell 16
Bream 80
Brentford 55
Brentwood *Ex* 45
Brick Row *P* 20,101
Brightlingsea *Ex* 18,46
Brighton 67,69
Brindisi 138
Broomfield *Ex* 53,54
Bruges 16
Brussels 116
Buckland House/BH *P* 4,5*i*,12,23,27,28,
32,34,35,40,41,43,44,46-51,61,70,75,
92,114,118,119
Buena Aires 137
Burnham-on-Crouch *Ex* 11,17,35,42,
89,104
Bury St Edmunds 62

Cairo 55,60,139
Calais 57
Calcutta 140
Cambridge 84,107
Canada 65
Canberra *A* 67
Canewdon *Ex* 3,25,35,52,53,58-60,62,
69,71,74,78,83,84,87,89,95,102,114,118,
119,129,132,133
Canvey *Ex* 11,62,84,103,104
Cape Town 139,140
Castleton 69
Ceylon 30,51,138-140,138*i*
Chase, The *P* 4,4*i*,20,21,35,51,54,58,
61,61*i*,66,71,74,76,78,91,100,103,108,
109,116,118,125,129,129*i*,130
Chaseway, The *P* 20,58,101,109,114,
115,118,124,124*i*,147*i*
Chelmsford *Ex* 4,5,12,53,65,84,90
China 83
Chingford *Ex* 76,78,89
Church *P* (iv)1,3,6,7,10,11,13,19,21,23,
28,44,47,50,51,53,54,56,57*i*,59-61,71,
73,74,84,85*i*,90,91,101,102,106,108,
109,102,110,114,115,127,127*i*,129,131,
131*i*,133,134
Churches, other 12,45,46,49,53,70,84,
128,134 See also Holy Innocents' and
Congregational
Church Hall *P* 11,19,21,27,30,35,62,
64,65,73,79,79*i*,82,97,99,100*i*,105,115,
124,131,132
Christ's Hospital 22
Clacton *Ex* 40
Claverham Cot 102
Clements *P* 21,64-66,81,92,95*i*
Clements Hall 35,50
Clovelly 15,18
Cobblers Row *P* 107,108
Colchester *Ex* 45,46,59,133
Cologne 82
Colombo 51,67,139,140
Colon 141
Congregational *P* 102,102*i*
Constantinople 36
Coogee *A* 67
Cornwall 11,63,108
Costa Rica 141
Cowes 34
Creeksea *Ex* 35,42
Crete 90
Crouch *Ex* 42,121
Crystal Palace 135
Cupola House *P* 3,3*i*,13,20,26,48,58,59,
65,70,72,73,75,81,82,82*i*,86,89,91,92,
94,95,99,104,114,123*i*,125,130,130*i*
Czechoslovakia 74

Danbury *Ex* 128
Dandenong *A* 96
Darcy *Ex* 16
Dardenelles 32,36
Dawlish 55
Dedham *Ex* 127
Dengie *Ex* 42

Devon 2,6,14,17,18,20,55,108,
134,135
Downham *Ex* 20
Dunkirk 80,93,121
Durban 140

Earl's Cottage 15,15*i*
East Hall *P* 24,46,62,64,64*i*,65,70,
82,86,88,89,97,99,100,106,107,117,
131,133,147*i*
Edinburgh 51
Egham 32,55
Egypt 29,36,38-40,52,55,60,
138-141
Englefield Gn 31
Epping 79
Exeter 17,18,55

Fambridge *Ex* 133
Farnborough 55
Felixstowe 18
Finches (& Maules) *P* 65,66,117,
120,121,125
Finisterre *F* 8,141
Fingringhoe *Ex* 46
Finsbury 8,44
Fishbourne 127
Fishguard 49
Fontainebleau *F* 112
Forest of Dean 80
Foulness *Ex* 11,37,104,120,121*i*
France 27,53,55,56,72,80,83,91
Frances Field *P* 133,147*i*
Frinton *Ex* 18

Gaba Tepe 37,37*i*,38*i*
Gallipoli 35-39,40,43,133
Germany 27,33,36,55,59,71,
74-76,79-81,85-92,95
Gibraltar 8,32,32*i*,37,40,54,137,141
Glasgow 141
Glenthorpe *P* 71
Gloucestershire 127
Gold Coast 50
Goldhanger *Ex* 16
Gore, The. See Ballard's Gore *Ex*
Goulburn *A* 67
Gozo 8
Grantham 90
Grapnells *Ex* 3
Great Waltham 27
Greenock 54
Greenwich 125
Guy's Hosp 6

Hadleigh *Ex* 20
Hampshire 127
Harfleur *F* 56
Haverfordwest 44
Hawaii 90
Hawkwell *Ex* 35
Hendon 67
Herne Bay 11
Heybridge *Ex* 16,63
Hobart *A* 67

Hockley *Ex* 20,49,65
Holland 70,79,103
Holy Innocents' 8-10,14,17,17*i*,28,
32,37,137
Hornchurch *Ex* 86
Hornsey 2,8-10,14,16,28-32,37,41,
54,55,61,90,136,138-140
Hove To *P* 123*i*
Hungary 75

Ilford 54,111
Imbros 38,39
India 71
Ingulfs 60,106,109,132 See also Rectory
Ireland 27,52
Isle of Man 69
Isle of Wight 11,27,34,41
Islington 136
Istanbul 36
Italy 71,75,138

Japan 8,71,90
Jaywick *Ex* 104
Jersey 45
Jutland 51

Kalorama *A* 95,96
Kandy 138*i*-140
Kelvedon *Ex* 45
Kenilworth 69
Knaresborough 69

Lake District 127
Lambourne Hall *Ex* 132
Langenhoe *Ex* 46
Las Palmas 140
Laurenco Marques 140,141
Lavenham 127
Le Havre *F* 54
Leigh *Ex* 11
Lemnos 36,39,40
Leningrad 91
Limon 141
Lincolnshire 103,127
Lithuania 75
Liverpool 59
Liverpool St.Stn. 32
Llandudno 128
Loftmans *Ex* 3,19,35,52,58,59
London 2,8,11,14,15,22,23,27,31-33,
41,43-45,47,50,52,54,55,58-63,65,67,
69-71,75,78,80,82,84,86,89-92,95,
97,105,107,113,120,134-138,141
Lunts *P* 3,65,66,72,107
Luxembourg 79
Lydney 80

Madeira 137
Maplin Sands *Ex* 121,121*i*,122
Malta 8,32,33,35,55,67,137,140
Maldon *Ex* 15,16,41,42,88
Manningtree *Ex* 22
Marchiennes *F* 56
Marine Cottage *P* 4,20
Marseilles *F* 32,39,40,137,141

Mediterranean 29,32
Melbourne *A* 96
Messel 75
Metropole Ho. 35,35*i*
Nexico 61
Milton Villa *P* 21,49,53,118
Mission Room *P* 1,4,4*i*,23,30,68,70,
95,96,99-101*i*,103,109,114,119,127,
132,133
Mistley *Ex* 4
Moçambique 141
Mombasa 141
Moreton *Ex* 45
Moruya *A* 67
Mudros Bay 36,39
Munich 74
Muswell Hill 9,14,136

Naples 141
Newcastle 58
Newport 33
New Cottages 71
New Row *P* 20
New Zealand 70
Norfolk 59
Northampton 59
North House *P* 64
Nottingham 21
Nuneaton 44

OBS Cottages *P* 124
Ongar *Ex* 16,29,45,46,137,138,140,141
Orsett *Ex* 108
Ostend 16
Oysters 1-4,10-13,19-22,24,25,30,34,
43,47,52,61,62,71,72,80,91,101,105,106,
112,118,121-123

Paddington 44
Paglesham House *P* 26,28,46,49,53,
56,63*i*,99
Paglesham Pool *P* 24
Palace Hotel *Ex* 35,35*i*
Palamos 112
Panama 20,141
Paris *F* 9
Peldon *Ex* 16,45,46
Perth 67
Plough & Sail *P* 21,21*i*,24,25,47,69,83,
84,100,112,112*i*-114,118,123*i*
Plumtree 21
Plymouth 67,108
Port Amelia 141
Port Elizabeth 140
Port Said 8,30,38,67,137-139,141
Potton Is. *Ex* 104
Prittlewell 20,115
Punch Bowl *P* 26,62,62*i*,104,112-116,
113,115,116,116*i*
Purleigh *Ex* 11

Quebec 30,141

RAF/RFC 55-57,86,89
Rawreth *Ex* 49
Raynes Park 59

Reading 86
Rectors 1,2,5-7,13,19,21,23,60,
101,102,110,115,133,134
Rectory *P* 6,6*i*,7*i*,23,54,102
Redcroft *P* 13,13*i*,15,17,26-28,32,
46,48,51,61,61*i*,62,62*i*,68,76,78,90,
94,96,108,117-120,122*i*,123,
129,132
Reigate 55
Richmond 58
Rievaulx 69
Rio de Janeiro 137
Roach R. *P* 24,47,78,84,85,100,
104,105,118,121,121*i*
Roche House *P* 118
Rochford *Ex* 19-21,41-50,53,59,63,
69,75,78,80,81,83,86,90-94,103,
110,113,117,118,120,121,125-128
Rokesly Ave. 8
Royal Ter. *Ex*
Rushley Is. *Ex* 104
Russia 27,36,83
Ryde 41

Salvador 137
Sandringham 71
Scarborough 69
School *P* 1,3,26,30,40,41,60,75,
76,92,92*i*,107,124,124*i*,125
Scotland 11
Serbia 55
Shadwell 23
Shenfield *Ex* 53
Ships, steam 8,24,29,30*i*,32-34,
36-40,137-141
  other vessels 18,22,80,105,
106,123
Shoebury(ness) *Ex* 19,20,37,46-48,
59,72
Shop (Ch End) *P* 25,25*i*,93,116-118
Shop (East End) *P* 24*i*,25,27,47,117
Shop Row *P* 20,25,28,28*i*,58
Shropshire 80
Slovakia 75
Somerset 136
South Africa 21
South America 29
Southampton 137,141
Southend-on-Sea *Ex* 1,5,9,11,22,
23,25,26,35,35*i*,41,53,59,60,64,65,
65*i*,69,74-76,79,81-86,90,91,94,
104,107,108,110-113,115,117-121,
129,133,134,137
Southchurch *Ex* 20
South Hall/Farm *P* 62-64,63*i*,64*i*,
89,92,99,108,132
Southminster *Ex* 42,43,48,82
Spain 75
Sri Lanka see Ceylon
Stafford 44
St Albans 59
Stambridge *Ex* 4,20,49,60,65,71,
83,89,90,93,96,105,113,125
Stannetts *P* 62,81,85,95,108,122
Stapleton 80

St Dunstans 9,14,15,29,32,33, 43,45,48,136i,137
St Helena 140
St Osyth 132
Stoke Newington 94
Stratford 65
Sutton *Ex* 48,65
Suez 8,67,138,140,141
Swatchways *P* 118
Sydney *A* 67

Tampico 61
Tasmania 67
Taunton 136
Taw Valley 135
Teneriffe 140
Territorials 31,31i,32,38,40-48,45i,52-55
Tilbury *Ex* 67,108,137
Tillingham *Ex* 42
Tintagel 17
Titanic 24,29,30i,139,140
Tottenham (Lane) 9,25

Turkey 36,37,75

Valenciennes *F* 56
Valetta 32
Vigo 137

Wakering *Ex* 88,94
Wales 14,33,44
Wallasea Is. *Ex* 3,11,22
Walsingham 59
Warners Br. *Ex* 84,88
Warwick 97,127
Waterside, The *P* 43,45,45i
Waterside (Cottage) *P* 27,58
Waterside Farm *P* 125,132
Waterside Lane *P* 22,24,28,28i,34,58, 70,70i,117,118
Wellesbourne 97,107
Well House *P* 24,24i,50,51,92
Wellington 67,70
Welshpool 45
Westcliff *Ex* 60,87,107,113

West Hall *P* 62,64i,65,81,88,92,132
West Mersea *Ex* 16,18,24,35,45,46,66
Westonbirt 127
Westminster 102,106,128,134-136
West Wycombe 52
Wickford *Ex* 41,48,49,54,84
Wickham Bishops *Ex* 41
Wigborough *Ex* 16,45
Windsor 71
Winton Haw *P* 102,116
Witham *Ex* 20
Wivenhoe *Ex* 46
Women's Institute 68,90,96,100, 103,110,113,114,127,132
Woodham Walter *Ex* 15,16,18,27
Writtle *Ex* 65,107

Yokohama 8,61

Zanzibar 141
Zeppelin 35,40,40i,41,45

PVPA Summer Show, 2009
Frances Field, East Hall.

No 2, The Chaseway, 2009.

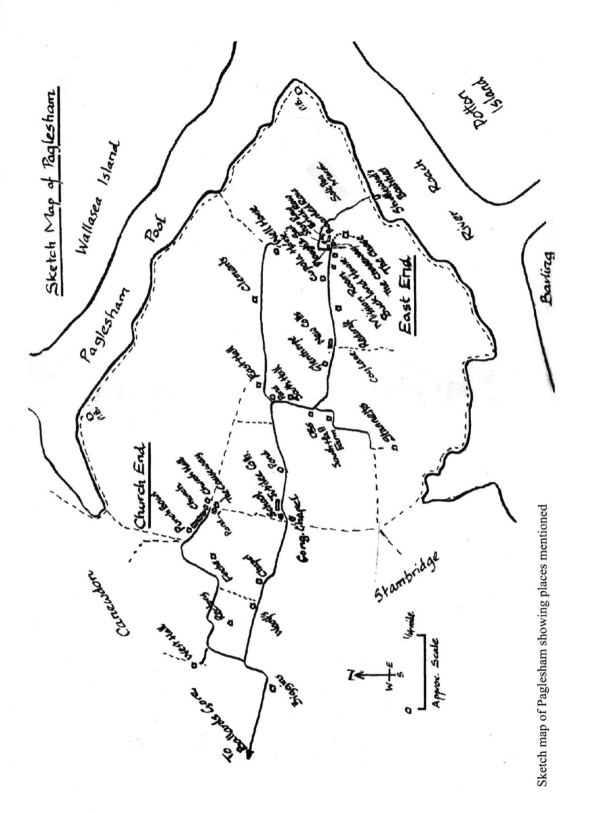

Sketch map of Paglesham showing places mentioned